Walking Places in
Washington, DC

OTHER TITLES AVAILABLE FROM OUT THERE PRESS

Guides to Backcountry Travel & Adventure

Arkansas
Georgia
North Carolina
Pennsylvania
South Carolina
Virginia
West Virginia

Sea Kayaking Florida & the Georgia Sea Islands
Sea Kayaking the Carolinas

Walking Places in Florida

Walking Places in
Washington, DC

by Don & Marjorie Young

out there press
asheville, north carolina
www.outtherepress.com

Walking Places in Washington, DC

Out There Press
PO Box 1173
Asheville, NC 28802
www.outtherepress.com

Maps by Simply Maps

Library of Congress Catalog Card Number: 00-110028
ISBN: 1-893695-03-4

The author and publisher have made every effort to ensure the accuracy of the information contained in this book. Nevertheless, they can not be held liable for any loss, damage, injury, or inconvenience sustained by any person using this book. Readers should keep in mind that walks in wilderness areas of county, state, and national parks have some risk. Please be careful.

Cover photographs & Design: James Bannon

Manufactured in the United States

10 9 8 7 6 5 4 3 2 1

For our girls—Kelly, Jo, Andrea, and Manger;
and our boys—Kent, Vinny, Dan, and Jimmy

Table of Contents

Acknowledgments

Our profound thanks to the many Chambers of Commerce, Convention & Visitors Bureaus, and other agencies and offices that provided us with information, suggestions, and encouragement during our exploration of the Washington, DC area.

Especially helpful were Mindy Schneeberger Bianca, Public Relations Coordinator in the Maryland Department of Business & Economic Development; John Fieseler, Executive Director, and Beth Finneyfrock Rhoades, Tour Marketing Manager, for the Tourism Council of Frederick County, Maryland; and Susan Motley, Director of Tourism, and Doretha Vaughan, Public Relations Assistant, at the Richmond, Virginia Convention & Visitors Bureau.

You're a great bunch of people...and you do a magnificent job!

Preface

Without diminishing the historical and cultural importance of Philadelphia, Boston, and a number of other American communities, both east and west, it can be argued that Washington, DC is America's most symbolic city. It symbolizes America's history. It houses our most important government offices—the White House, the Capitol, and the Supreme Court. It showcases many of our most cherished monuments, memorials, and museums.

At the same time, Washington is a city of average, work-a-day people striving to earn a living, raise their children, and make the most of their leisure time. People who enjoy dining out, going to the theater or to a concert, watching a baseball game, or playing a game of golf. In the city as in the suburbs, Washington is truly a place where Nature and History live side-by-side.

Strolling through this part of the country, one is reminded that, like our children, America has grown rapidly over the years. We are reminded that our nation's forefathers lived on this continent as citizens of Great Britain for over 150 years, and during that time established 13 highly-independent colonies that stretched along the Atlantic Ocean from Massachusetts to Georgia. After a century and a half of British rule, a small group of public-minded individuals agreed that such an arrangement was no longer tolerable and spearheaded a movement to create a new type of government—one that eventually would come to be called the United States of America.

The nation's capital is surrounded by the states of Virginia and Maryland, two of the nation's original 13 colonies. The others included New Hampshire, Massachusetts, Rhode Island, Connecticut, New York, New Jersey, Pennsylvania, Delaware, Georgia, and the Carolinas.

Maine, originally a part of Massachusetts, did not become a separate state until 1820. Florida, which belonged to Spain at the time of the American Revolution, did not become a part of the United States until 1845.

Modern Virginia reflects the numerous and varied contributions of such pioneers as Henry Clay, William Henry Harrison, Patrick Henry, Thomas Jefferson, Robert E Lee, Lewis and Clark, James Madison, John Marshall, George Mason, James Monroe, Zachary Taylor, John Tyler, Booker T Washington, George Washington, and Woodrow Wilson. It is the Virginia of the Potomac and Rappahannock Rivers, of the Blue Ridge Mountains, and of Chesapeake Bay.

Just to the north and east is the Maryland we so often identify with Francis Scott Key, H L Mencken, Edgar Allen Poe, Upton Sinclair, and Tom Clancy. Through it pass the historic waters of the Susquehanna, Patuxent, Choptank, and Nanticoke Rivers. Its eastern boundary is the Atlantic Ocean.

And resting in the midst of this historical region is our nation's capital, Washington, DC.

Indeed, this *is* a land where History and Nature live side-by-side. It is a place to be explored...treasured...and enjoyed.

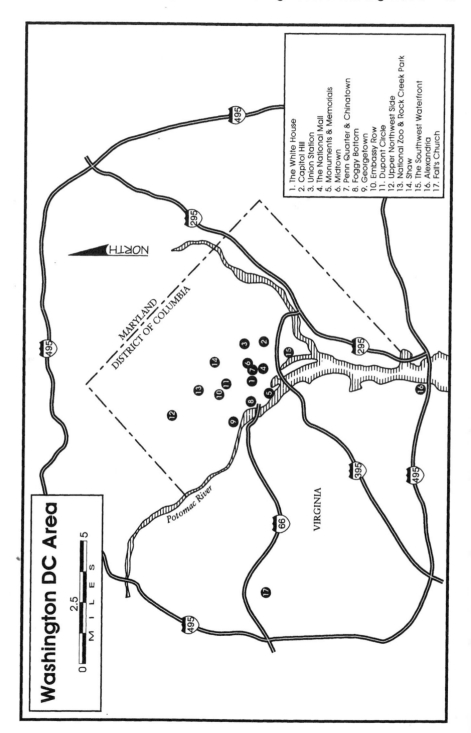

Washington DC Area

MILES
0   2.5   5

1. The White House
2. Capitol Hill
3. Union Station
4. The National Mall
5. Monuments & Memorials
6. Midtown
7. Penn Quarter & Chinatown
8. Foggy Bottom
9. Georgetown
10. Dupont Circle
11. Embassy Row
12. Upper Northwest Side
13. National Zoo & Rock Creek Park
14. Shaw
15. The Southwest Waterfront
16. Alexandria
17. Fall's Church

NORTH

MARYLAND
DISTRICT OF COLUMBIA

Potomac River

VIRGINIA

Introduction

History

To many of us, Washington DC has been the nation's capital *forever*. Of course, that isn't true, but the city does embody much of the history and tradition with which we have lived throughout our lives.

When the Revolutionary War ended in 1776, the new nation faced a number of key problems, most of them far more critical than deciding on where the new nation's capital should be located. Between 1776 and 1783, Congress met in a variety of locations—New York, Baltimore, Philadelphia, Lancaster, Princeton, Annapolis, York, and Trenton. When a statue of George Washington was authorized in 1783, when the State House in Philadelphia was serving as the nation's temporary capitol, somebody suggested that the permanent capitol ought to be mounted on wheels so that it could follow the government around.

When it came time to select a place to build a capital, other problems arose. The North didn't want the capital to be located in the South, and the South didn't want it to be located in the North. Finally, Alexander Hamilton, a northerner, and Thomas Jefferson, a southerner, worked out a compromise. If the South would help the North to pay off the debts incurred during the Revolutionary War, the North would agree to let the new "federal city" be built in the South. The deal was struck.

Once a site had been selected, a city had to be planned and buildings had to be constructed before Congress eventually would be able to move in. It was agreed that the temporary capital of the United States should remain in Philadelphia throughout the remainder of the eighteenth century while this work was being done.

George Washington, a former surveyor, was empowered to choose the site for the new capital and get things rolling. He was instructed to find a site "not exceeding 10 miles square" (100 square miles) somewhere along the Potomac River—a body of water that the Native Americans had called "The River of Swans." As a resident of Mount Vernon, Virginia, Washington knew the area well, and selected a spot at the juncture of the Potomac and Anacostia Rivers—a curious choice because, at that time, the area was little more than a muddy, mosquito-infested bog.

Maryland contributed 69.25 square miles to the project, and Virginia an additional 30.75 square miles. (Virginia later complained that the project was moving too slowly and its land was deemed unnecessary, so its land was returned to the state in 1846, explaining why the present city of Washington covers just 68.2 square miles, rather than the originally-authorized 100 square miles.)

To lay out the new city, Washington engaged a French military engineer named Pierre Charles L'Enfant. L'Enfant had distinguished himself during the Revolutionary War and had later remodeled the New York City Hall to serve as the first seat of the federal government. L'Enfant's creation would become the world's first planned capital.

Starting to work in 1791, L'Enfant announced that Jenkins Hill (now Capitol Hill) was "a pedestal waiting for a monument." The focal points of the capital city, as he envisioned it, would be the Capitol, the "presidential palace," and an equestrian statue, which was to stand where the Washington Monument stands today. Benjamin Bannecker, an African-American surveyor, inventor and mathematician, assisted in the planning.

L'Enfant planned avenues 160 feet wide that would radiate from a series of squares and circles, each of which was to be adorned with a sculpture or a fountain. The ceremonial center of the city would be The Mall, which was to be surrounded by embassies and other important government buildings.

Unfortunately, L'Enfant was a genius as a designer but a disaster as a project manager. He alienated nearly everyone with whom he came in contact. He refused to cooperate with building commissioners, and he refused to cooperate with Washington's appointed surveyor, Andrew Ellicott. When he refused to submit a preliminary set of blueprints so that they could be used in helping to raise funds to build the new city, President Washington had no other choice but to fire him. L'Enfant had been on the job for just one year.

In 1792, the cornerstone for the Executive Mansion was laid. A year later, construction began on the Capitol. Congress—which then consisted of just 106 representatives and 32 senators moved into its new home, and President John Adams took up residence in the nation's new Executive Mansion in the fall of 1800. Traveling from Baltimore to Washington by horse and buggy, President and Mrs Adams became so lost that they "wandered for two hours without finding a guide or path." Not a single room in the mansion was fully completed, and the main stairway had yet to be constructed. Newspapers referred to it as "the palace in the wilderness."

At the time the Adams family moved in, the city held fewer than 400 houses. Pennsylvania Avenue was hardly more than a muddy, mosquito-plagued path through the swamp—an area that one newspaper referred to as "the great Serbonian bog." Washington was called "a city of streets without houses" and Georgetown was called "a city without streets." A French diplomat is known to have inquired: "My God! What have I done to be condemned to reside in such a city?"

While the country worked to iron out its internal problems after the Revolutionary War, a great deal of resentment remained regarding our former relationship with Great Britain. Britain aggravated the issue even more by arguing over territorial rights and by incarcerating a number of American seamen.

On June 18, 1812, the United States declared war against Great Britain. Two years later, on August 24, 1814, 5,000 British troops under the command of Adm George Cockburn and Gen Robert Ross sailed up the Potomac River, defeated 7,000 American soldiers led by Gen William H Winder, and then sacked and burned the Executive Mansion, the Capitol, the Library of Congress, a number of newly-built ships, and some naval supplies. Fortunately, it rained heavily that night, minimizing the damage caused by the fire. A tornado the next day further tended to discourage the British invaders.

By 1817, the executive mansion had been rebuilt. Where the British assault had blackened the walls, the smoke-stains were covered over with white paint, and since that time America's presidential palace...the executive mansion...the home of our president...has been known simply as The White House.

After the devastation caused by the War of 1812, Congress came within nine votes of moving the capital somewhere else, but it eventually elected to keep it where it was and continue the task of developing the city of Washington. Unfortunately, America had yet to become one nation "of the people, by the people and for the people." Strong regional interests resulted in a great deal of turmoil, and ultimately the nation became embroiled in a bitter Civil War.

Washington was the Union's principle supply center and an important medical center. The rotunda of the Capitol Building became first a barracks and then a military hospital. The city's churches also were used as hospitals, and the parks became campgrounds. The city was soon ringed by a series of forts. Washington's population doubled during those troubled years, principally due to an influx of former slaves, who came seeking asylum.

The Civil War came to an end when Lee surrendered to Grant on April 8, 1865, but once again, various groups attempted to move the nation's capital somewhere else. St Louis bid several million dollars for the privilege of becoming the capital in 1870, for example, but their offer was eventually rejected.

In 1871, former Governor Alexander R Shepherd was named to head a territorial government established in the District of Columbia. He accepted his new responsibilities with enthusiasm, and over the next three years he supervised the improvement of 300 miles of half-laid streets, built 128 miles of sidewalks, erected 3,000 gas lamps to illuminate the city's streets, and had a sewer system installed. New parks were created and decorated with fountains. Some 6,000 trees were planted. But as dramatic as those civic improvements may have been, they virtually bankrupted the city. Congress abolished the territorial government, replaced it with a three-man commission to conduct the city's business, and literally ran Shepherd out of town. Disgraced, the former Governor took his family to Mexico and remained there until 1887.

In 1900, Michigan Senator James McMillan took a personal interest in improving the city. He fought to create a committee comprised of landscape architect Frederick Law Olmstead, sculptor Augustus Saint-Gaudens, and architects Daniel Burnham and Charles McKim to create "the city beautiful." At his own expense, McMillan sent the committee to Europe for seven weeks to study the landscaping and architecture of the European capitals, and when the committee returned he encouraged them to develop a system of city parks, select sites for government buildings, and beautify The Mall. The committee also created the Lincoln and Jefferson Memorials, Arlington Memorial Bridge, Union Station, and a reflecting pool modeled after the one at Versailles.

At long last, Washington was on its way to becoming a nation's capital of unexcelled grandeur. And it has grown considerablyover the intervening years. From "a howling, malarious wilderness" at the confluence of the Potomac and Anacostia Rivers, it has become one of the world's most beautiful and exciting cities.

After the automobile came along, and congestion inevitably began to choke the city's wide boulevards, it became evident that much of the traffic could be diverted by constructing a "ring" around the city on I-95, the interstate highway that links Baltimore, Maryland on the northeast with Richmond, Virginia on the southwest. Today, I-495 diverts traffic along the north and west sides of the city, while I-695 runs along the south and east sides, and together have come to be known as the Capital Beltway.

Many of the sights that you will want to visit during your stay inside the Beltway will cover a time-span of 200 years or more. To do them justice, they deserve all of the time that you can reasonably afford to give them, but *resign yourself to the fact that you will not be able to see and do everything on a single trip.*

For the most satisfying visit, plan your trip as far in advance as possible.

- Determine what it is that you most want to see and do. Reserve the rest for another visit.
- Write ahead to obtain tickets to the most popular sights.
- Whenever possible, make your reservations well in advance.

How to Use This Book

This book is divided into 17 main tours and a handful of sidetrips. The majority of these are located withing Washington, D.C.; a few others are nearby in Virginia and Maryland.

Washington is a large city, full of exciting things to see and do. Many visitors find themselves overwhelmed by it all. So that you can get the most benefit out of your visit to the nation's capital, we have "subdivided" the city into a number of separate and distinct regions. In that way, you can select the regions of greatest interest to you, place them in your order of preference, and (hopefully) avoid wasting a great deal of time running from one end of town to the other...then back again.

The walks recommended in this book will expose you to a variety of experiences—the cultural experiences of a region immersed in the nation's history and the experiences associated with going out into nature and enjoying the beauty of the region beyond the city limits.

It is our intention to see that you know *where to go* when you visit Washington and the communities inside the Capital Beltway; that you know *why it's an interesting place to see*; and that you *know how to get there*.

Cultural Heritage Walks

With so much history to draw upon, the nation's capital offers plenty of culture for visitors to explore. This is not to say that *modern* culture must be overlooked.

Theater is available nearly year-around, both indoors and outdoors, dramatic and musical, for adults and for kids. Much of it is provided free of charge.

There are world-class museums of every description. They cover life in ancient civilizations...and modern art. They deal with aerospace...and with science. It is hard to find a subject, in fact, for which a museum has yet to be created.

This book will direct you to them, as well as to Washington's several college campuses and impressive array of churches, monuments and memorials.

Natural Area Walks

Although Washington and its environs encompass a bustling metropolitan area, outdoor experiences have not been ignored. An extensive park follows the entire length of Rock Creek. Walks along the Potomac River...and much of the Anacostia River...are often pastoral and serene. The National Arboretum is here...as well as the National Zoo.

In addition, there are local, state and national parks either within the Beltway or nearby.

Flora and Fauna

People living inside the Beltway love their gardens, many of which are frequently open to the public. Especially attractive are those that can be found on some of the historic old plantations for which this part of the country is famous.

Arguably the Number One floral attraction in the capital is its riverside collection of Japanese cherry trees. Thousands of visitors travel to Washington each year to see the cherry trees in blossom.

Getting oriented

Those who are accustomed to cities that are laid out in neat little squares may find Washington a difficult place to get around in at first. To understand the street plan more easily, remember that the US Capitol is the heart of the city and that the streets are numbered north-to-south and east-to-west, using The Mall, North Capitol St, East Capitol St, and South Capitol St as the arteries from which the streets are numbered, thus dividing the city into quadrants—Northeast, Northwest, Southeast, and Southwest.

The streets running north and south were assigned numbers (5th St), while the streets running east and west were assigned letters (M St). The letters J, X and Z were excluded. As the city grew, the number of streets started to exceed the number of letters in the alphabet so they began to use two-syllable names (Randolph) for the new streets. After that came a series of three-syllable names (Tewkesbury). And finally, an alphabetical listing of trees (Apple Rd) was used.

Knowing this, it should not be difficult to locate the address you seek. 1200 H St NW, for example, would be at the intersection of 12th St and H St in the northwest part of town. So far, so good.

At this point, there is only one other mystery to be resolved. Washington's early planners superimposed a network of diagonal streets over the city. The shortest distance between two points being a straight line, these diagonal arteries, named for various states (Massachusetts Ave) enable traffic to get across town more rapidly. Where the streets intersect, numerous small parks have been created in the circles and triangles that were created.

Still lost? You needn't be. It all makes sense once you get used to it. Carry a city map with you while you're out. They're generally free and they're available almost everywhere, including the desk at most hotels and motels.

President Clinton ordered Pennsylvania Ave closed to vehicular traffic in May 1995. Since then, H St has become one-way eastbound between 13th St and 19th St NW and I St has become one-way westbound between 11th St and 19th St NW.

Practical Information

Perhaps the best source of information about the city and its immediate environs is the **Washington, DC Convention & Visitors Assn.** (800 /422-8644, www.washington.org), 1212 New York Ave NW. The **DC Committee to Promote Washington** (202/724-5644, www.washington.org), PO Box 27489, is located in Suite 200 of the same building and can be equally helpful.

A **Visitor Information Center** (202/328-4748) is located at 1300 Pennsylvania Ave NW, and information kiosks can be found at The Ellipse, Jefferson Memorial, Lafayette Park, National Gallery of Art, Washington Monument, Air & Space Museum, Museum of American History, and Museum of Natural History.

The **International Visitors Information Service** (202/939-5566) at 1630 Crescent Pl NW is a non-profit volunteer organization that provides special services to visitors from abroad. There is a "language bank" of volunteers who can speak in dozens of different languages, and foreign-language publications and brochures are available. The staff can provide assistance with accommodations, sightseeing, dining, and other tourist needs, and the center is open weekdays from 9 am to 5 pm. Telephone service is available seven days a week from 6 am to 11 pm.

Passes for the White House, the House and Senate galleries, the Capitol, the Supreme Court, the FBI Building, the Bureau of Engraving and Printing, the State Department, the Kennedy Center, and the National Archives can be obtained by writing to your Representative (c/o US House of Representatives, Washington, DC 20515) or Senator (c/o US Senate, Washington, DC 20510). Tickets can be reserved no more than three months in advance, and normally no more than five tickets per family will be issued to visit any one facility.

Half-price "day-of-show" tickets and full-price advance tickets to events taking place in 60 different Washington institutions can be obtained through **TICKETplace** (202/842-5387) at two locations in the city: The Old Post Office Pavilion at 1100 Pennsylvania Ave and at the Lisner Auditorium at George Washington University, 21st St and H St NW. The ticket windows are open from noon to 6 pm Tuesday through Friday and from 11 am to 5 pm on Saturday. Discount tickets for Sunday and Monday performances are sold on Saturday.

Both Maryland and Virginia also offer free information services. These are listed later in the book in the sections devoted to those parts of the Washington area that are located inside the Beltway.

Other excellent sources of information outside Washington, DC are the individual *city* and *county* Chambers of Commerce and Convention & Visitors Bureaus that can be found in most communities of any size. Many of these resources are readily available on-line via the Internet.

And speaking of the Internet, here are a few more links that you can reach through your computer:

www.city.net/countries/united_states/district_of_columbia/washington
www.washweb.net
www.infi.net/washmag

National Park Service & US Forest Service

For information regarding the national parks and forests, contact the **National Park Service**, Department of the Interior, Office of Public Inquiries, PO Box 37127, Room 1013, Washington, DC 20013, 202/208-4747, www.nps.gov; the **US Forest Service**, US Department of Agriculture, Washington, DC 20250, 800/245-6340 or 202/720-1127; and/or the **US Fish & Wildlife Service**, Department of the Interior, 300 Westgate Center Dr, Hadley, MA 01035-9589, 413/253-8322.

Other Outdoor Organizations

Other outdoor organizations that provide free information include the National Audubon Society, 700 Broadway, New York, NY 10003-9562 (212/979-3000, www.audubon.org), which has chapters in Washington, DC, in Bowie, MD, and in Annandale, VA, as well as a subsidiary, the Audubon Naturalist Society, www.capaccess.org/snr/ans.html.

Another excellent source is **The Nature Conservancy**, 4245 N Fairfax Dr, Suite 100, Arlington, VA 22203-1606.

When to Go

When you are deciding on when to make a trip to Washington, DC, there are two "seasons" to consider: the climatic season and the governmental season.

As far as climate is concerned, the spring and fall months are, as you might expect, very pleasant in that area. Summer, however, can be quite hot and steamy, and winter can be very cold, snowy, and slippery.

Ignoring weather considerations, many people go to Washington to visit the various offices of government. Often, the president is traveling...or entertaining important individuals from other countries...in which case, the White House may not be open to the public. Similarly, Congress and the Supreme Court do not sit year-around, and a number of extraordinary factors frequently influence their activity. To be sure you won't be disappointed, call the office of your local congressman or senator (in most cases, found listed in the front of your local telephone directory) and ask if the offices that you wish to visit will be doing business at the time you would like to go.

What to Wear

Catering as it does to elected officials, foreign chiefs of state, executives of major corporations, and other such dignitaries, Washington is a somewhat formal city. To be sure, there are numerous places to visit in which tourist garb is quite acceptable, morning and evening, but there also are a great many places where traditional business attire is more appropriate, if not mandatory. To save yourself some embarrassment, ask the concierge at your hotel how to dress or, barring that, take the time to telephone ahead and inquire.

What to Bring

A good map will help a great deal, but these are readily available all over the city. And be sure to take your camera, of course.

When visiting areas away from the hustle and bustle of the city, wearing comfortable shoes, shorts, and normal "tourist" attire is quite acceptable. Don't forget your sunglasses, a hat, some sunscreen, and if you are accustomed to one, a hiking stick. Water is always a good idea...and a pair of binoculars might be useful.

Pests & Dangers
Animals
The most likely source of trouble here would be an angry dog. A few varieties of poisonous snakes do inhabit this region, but your chances of encountering one, even in the woods, are extremely remote.

Insects
Mosquitoes and flies are the major pests inside the Beltway, although bees, wasps, hornets, ticks, and chiggers are always a possibility, especially if you travel into the hinterlands. A little insect repellant should take care of things nicely.

Be aware of the fact that black widow spiders inhabit this part of the country, too. Simply keep that in mind when reaching into cobweb-bedecked corners.

Crime
Metropolitan Washington has an uncommonly high crime rate. The figures decline considerably during the daylight hours and when one moves into the suburban communities. Exercise the same level and type of caution that you would expect to exercise in any major city. If you are planning to go out at night, ask if the place you are planning to go is in a good neighborhood.

Transportation
By automobile—Chesapeake Bay poses a formidable barrier to motorists heading into Washington from the east, although the Chesapeake Bay Bridge does provide easy access to the capital from the Delmarva Peninsula via US 50/301.

Those driving to Washington from the northeast (Baltimore, Philadelphia, New York City, and beyond) generally find I-95 their fastest and most direct link, while I-83 provides an alternate route from the north through York, Pennsylvania and its environs. Various combinations of I-70, I-80 and I-90 will convey midwesterners to Frederick, Maryland, where they can pick up I-270 for their final leg into Washington; and numerous Interstates link with I-81, which follows the Appalachian Mountains from the southwest to the northeast on its way toward the capital.

I-95, which follows the Atlantic coast all the way from Miami, Florida to Washington and beyond, is a route well-traveled by Southerners.

By air—The Washington area is well-served by three separate airports, the nearest of which is **Ronald Reagan National Airport** (703/419-8000), located four miles south of the city along the Potomac River in Alexandria, Virginia. The ultra-modern facility reopened in July 1997 after a 10-year, $1 billion renovation. It provides beautiful wall-size windows that overlook the river and features a wide variety of shops and restaurants, plus numerous works of art that are scattered throughout the complex. Metro's yellow and blue lines take you to within easy walking distance of the baggage claim area and will take you downtown for only $1.10 to $1.40, depending on the time of day. Taxi fare to town is $12 to $15, which includes a $1.25 airport surcharge.

Dulles International Airport (703/661-2700) is located in Chantilly, Virginia, 26 miles west of the city. A new terminal that doubled the size of the airport was designed by IM Pei and opened in 1996, and then a second midfield terminal was opened in 1998. Yet another terminal is in the planning stages. From downtown Washington, take Constitution Avenue to the Theodore Roosevelt Bridge and head West on Route 66. Bear left and follow the signs into the airport. From Key Bridge, take Route 29 to Route 66 and then follow the signs to the airport. Free tours of the facility are offered on Mondays and from Wednesday through Friday at 10 am, but reservations are required. Taxi fare to town is about $40.

Located about mid-way between Washington and Baltimore, **Baltimore-Washington International Airport** (301/261-1000 or 800/435-9294), PO Box 8766, BWI, MD 21240, is a handy alternate for those who do not mind the added travel-time in and out of the city. Also recently remodeled, the terminal has a bilevel observation gallery with computerized interactive displays. The Smithsonian Museum Shop is a great place to browse while waiting for the next flight. AMTRAK trains to BWI leave Union Station (800/872-7245) near downtown Washington every hour between 7:20 am and 10:10 pm, while Maryland Rail Commuter Service trains (800/325-7245) operate between the airport and

Union Station from 6 am to midnight on weekdays only. The AMTRAK fare is $10; the MARC fare, $4.50. Highway access to the airport is excellent.

Airlines serving the Washington-area airports include **Air Canada** (800/776-3000), **AirTran** (800825-8538), **America West** (800/235-9292), **American** (800/433-7300), **Continental** (800/525-0280), **Delta** (800 /221-1212), **Midway** (800/446-4392), **Northwest** (800/225-2525), **Southwest** (800/435-9792), **TransWorld/TWA** (800/221-2000), **US Airways** (800/428-4322), **US Airways Shuttle** (800/428-4322), **United** (800/241-6522), and **Western Pacific** (800/930-3030).

Do-it-yourself fliers have two local airports from which to choose. **Montgomery County Airpark** (301/963-7100) is located at 7940 Airpark Rd in Gaithersburg, Maryland. From the city, take the Metro to Shady Grove and then taxi to the airport, or if you have a car, take I-270 to the Shady Grove exit, turn right onto Shady Grove, and drive about five miles to the airport.

College Park Airport (301/864-5844), 1909 Cpl Frank Scott Dr, College Park, Maryland, opened in 1909 and is the world's oldest continuously-operating airport. It was here that the Wright Brothers taught the first two Army officers how to fly (1910), the first bomb was dropped from an airplane (1911), and the first US Air Mail service was dispatched (1918). There is a recently-upgraded museum (301/864-3029), and visitors can get a bite to eat in the 24th Aerosquadron restaurant (301/699-9400), which is colorfully decorated with WW I air force memorabilia and offers diners a nice view of the runway. A weekend Air Fair is held here every September. To or from the city, take the Metro at College Park.

Airport shuttles—To whisk you in and out of the city from the airport, **Airport Express** (202/829-6210) and **Washington Flyer** (703/685-1400 or 888/927-4359) serve passengers at National and Dulles, while **Airport Connection** (301/441-2345 or 800/824-6066) and **Super Shuttle** (800/258-3826) serve BWI. In addition, the **Montgomery Airport Shuttle** (301/990-6000) travels between National Airport and Montgomery County, Maryland from 5 am to 11 pm, serving those who are headed for Bethesda or Gaithersburg. Some hotels also provide shuttles to and from the airports. But if you like to travel in style, **Diplomat Limousine** (703/461-6800) will have a limousine waiting for you at National or Dulles to take you wherever you want to go, and **Private Car** (800 /685-0888) will do the same for those who arrive at BWI.

By train—Washington is serviced by **AMTRAK** (202/906-3000 or 800/872-7245, www.amtrak.com). Trains arrive at and depart from Union Station (202/906-3000), 60 Massachusetts Ave NE. By Metroliner, New York is just 3-1/2 hours away. AMTRAK provides discounts for senior citizens and disabled passengers, and also offers a Great American Vacations package (800/321-8684) that enables travelers to take the train to Washington and then fly home on United Airlines.

If everything has gone according to schedule, America's answer to the European TGV high-speed "bullet trains" should be servicing the nation's capital from Boston and a number of other eastern cities. Powered by overhead electrical lines, the 150-mph train called **Acela** (from "acceleration" and "excellence") hopefully will ease some of Washington's auto traffic, air traffic, and air pollution problems once it is placed in servicde. The anticipated train fare from New York to Boston is pegged at $130 as opposed to $202 for air fare.

By bus—Both the **Greyhound Lines** (800/231-2222) and **Peter Pan Trailways** (800/343-9999) provide service to Washington. The Greyhound terminal is located at 1st and L Sts NE, four blocks from the Union Station, but it is in a bad neighborhood so it is advisable to come and go in a taxi.

By taxi—Washington cabs work on a zone system, which means that you can go anywhere within your current zone for a flat rate of $3.20 ($2.80 if it's within a subzone of Zone 1). If you go from one zone to a second zone, the fee increases to $4.40; to a third zone, $5.50; to a fourth zone, $6.60; and so on. Refer to the accompanying zone map to calculate your cost, and tack on an extra $1.25 for each additional passenger. The maximum basic fare for one person traveling within the District is $12.25, but baggage-handling and the time of day could increase the fare.

Washington's major taxi companies are **Capitol** (202/546-2400), **Diamond** (202/387-6200), **Liberty** (202/636-1600), and **Yellow** (202/544-1212).

Car rentals—For those who prefer the freedom of transporting themselves around town, cars may be rented from **Alamo** (800/327-9633), **Avis** (800/331-1212), **Budget** (800/527-0700), **Hertz** (800/654-3131), or **Thrifty** (800/367-2277).

By city bus or subway—Two of the finest metropolitan transportation systems in the world— Metrorail and Metrobus—are operated by the

Washington Metropolitan Area Transit Authority (202/962-2766, www.wmata.com), 600 5th St NW, fax 202/962-6103.

Washington's **Metrorail**, referred to locally as "the Metro," opened in 1976. It is inexpensive, convenient, clean, and safe. The stations are neat, cool, and pleasant; and the cars are quiet, air-conditioned, carpeted, equipped with picture windows, and furnished with upholstered seats. At the present time, 74 stations serve 89 miles of track, but nine more stations and 14 extra miles of track are yet to be added.

Metro passengers are served by five lines—Red, Blue, Orange, Yellow, and Green—and transferring from one line to another is easily accomplished. Entrances to the Metro stations are marked with tall brown columns with a large "M" on each side. Below the "M" is a colored stripe or stripes indicating which line or lines can be boarded there. Trains run from 5:30 am to midnight on weekdays and from 8 am to midnight on weekends. The base fare is $1.10 to $2.20 during off-peak hours (between 5:30 and 9:30 am and between 3 and 8 pm on weekdays); during peak hours, the fare increases to a maximum of $3.25. One-day passes that allow unlimited travel on any weekday after 9:30 am or at any time on weekends and holidays cost $5. Children four and under can travel free.

Vending machines near the Metro station entrance sell computerized "farecards." They accept nickels, dimes, quarters, $1 bills, and $5 bills (some of the newer machines also accept $10 and $20 bills and give you change). At the entrance gate, you insert the farecard into a slot on the turnstile, which records the time and location on the card's magnetic strip, then returns the card to you. *Be sure to look for it and take it with you* because you will need the card to go through the gate at the other end of your trip. The amount of the fare will be deducted automatically when you pass through that second gate, and if there's any value left on the card, it too will be returned to you. If there is not enough value left on the card to pay for your fare, you will have to make up the difference at the Addfare machine near the exit gate. (Note: Some travelers have reported that the magnetic strip on the Metro farecard has interfered with the strips on their credit cards and ATM cards. To be safe, keep your farecard in a separate pocket.)

If you plan to transfer to a Metrobus after you leave the subway, *pick up your transfer at the start of your trip*, not after you have reached your destination station. The transfers, which cost a quarter, are good for the full fare within the city and entitle you to a discount on fares within Maryland and Virginia.

The **Metrobus** operates almost around the clock, seven days a week. There are 15,800 stops on a 1,500-sq mi route, enabling travelers to reach all of the major arteries within the city and some places that cannot be reached by Metrorail, such as Georgetown. The Virginia and Maryland suburbs also are served by Metrobus.

Bus stops are identified by red, white and blue signs. Unfortunately, the signs don't tell you where any of the buses are going. Routing information can be obtained by calling 202/637-7000 from 6 am to 10:30 pm on weekdays and from 8 am to 10:30 pm on weekends and holidays.

On the Metrobus, the base fare within the District is $1.10. Trips into Maryland and Virginia cost somewhat more. Senior citizens can ride for a reduced fare (call 202/962-7000) as can people with disabilities (call 202/962-1245 or 202/962-1100). Up to two children under the age of five can ride free with a paying passenger. (Note: Metrobus drivers cannot make change, so you must either buy bus tokens in advance or carry the exact amount of change for your fare. If you will be in town long enough to use it, a two-week pass costs $20.)

Architecture

If you can name it, Washington, DC has got it. From the most modern designs of the 21st Century to the elaborate architectural facades of yesteryear—Art Deco, Gothic, Gothic Revival, Beaux Arts, Victorian, Queen Anne, French Renaissance, Romanesque Revival, Georgian/Italian Renaissance Revival—Washington has them all...and then some.

Row upon row of brownstones, blocks of traditional Eastern rowhouses, and gingerbread-style frame houses sitting on large, beautifully-manicured lawns line the residential streets of the nation's capital.

From exquisite mansions to lowly shanties, Washington is a living museum of past and present architecture.

Lodgings and Restaurants

Under LODGINGS, we will provide you with enough information to enable you to find a nice place to stay...close to the sights you most wish to see...and at a price that is suited to your budget. This information follows the description of each destination.

Prepare yourself. EVERYTHING in the Washington area is expensive. Lodgings and restaurants are no exception.

Naturally, a great deal depends on location. The farther out you are willing to stay, the less expensive the cost...but of course, that generally tends to increase your cost of transportation and shortens the amount of time that you have available for sightseeing. Everything is a trade-off.

On occasion, it is most convenient for tourists to stay near the airport, especially when they have just arrived or are just about to depart.

At Dulles Airport, we can recommend **Washington Dulles Airport Marriott** ($$$, 793/471-9500), and **Marriott Suites Washington Dulles at Worldgate** ($$$, 703/709-0400), 13101 Worldgate Dr, Herndon, VA 22070.

Near the **Ronald Reagan Washington National Airport**, there are the **Washington National Airport Hilton** ($$$, 703/418-6800), 2399 Jefferson Davis Hwy, Arlington, VA 22202, and the **Doubletree Hotel National Airport** ($$$, 703/416-4100 or 800/222-TREE), 300 Army-Navy Dr, Arlington, VA 22202.

At **Baltimore-Washington International Airport**, the choices include **Comfort Inn Airport** ($$, 410/789-9100), 6921 Baltimore-Annapolis Blvd; **Courtyard by Marriott-BWI Airport** ($$-$$$, 410/859-8855), 1671 W Nursery Rd; **Doubletree Guest Suites Hotel BWI** ($$-$$$, 410/850-0747), 1300 Concourse Dr; **Hampton Inn BWI Airport** ($$, 410/850-0600), 829 Elkridge Landing Rd; and a string of others.

Many people prefer to book their lodgings through one of the services that specialize in that sort of thing, particularly when the region is unfamiliar. There are several such organizations in Washington, including **Capitol Reservations** (202/452-1270 or 888/VISIT-DC, www.visitdc.com), 1730 Rhode Island Ave NW, Suite 1114, Washington, DC 20036; and **Washington, DC Accommodations** (202/289-2220 or 800/554-2220, www.dcaccommodations.com), 2201 Wisconsin Ave NW, Suite C110, Washington, DC 20007. For something a little bit different, **Bed & Breakfast League/Sweet Dreams & Toast** (202/363-7767), PO Box 9490, Washington, DC 20016, can book you into a charming little B&B.

We know too that no trip is enjoyable unless you can eat well. So, under the heading of FOOD & DRINK, we will suggest some restaurants that we think you might enjoy. We also will tell you why we have recommended them, and (once again) tell you what you can expect to pay when you eat there, so you won't strain your budget. The dining section follows the LODGING section associated with each destination.

Various publications, many of them available free of charge, offer discount coupons that can provide a considerable savings in certain hotels, motels, restaurants, and other attractions. In addition, many places offer discounts to senior citizens or to members of the American Automobile Association (AAA).

Entertainment (248/637-8400), 2125 Butterfield Rd, Troy, MI 48084, fax 247/637-9771, is another excellent place to look for discount opportunities. The company publishes reasonably-priced coupon books for virtually every major American city.

Price/Standards for Lodgings
The prices cited under the heading of LODGING are based on the rate for a standard double room. They are coded as follows:

$	under $50
$$	$50-$100
$$$	$101-$150
$$$$	over $150

Price/Standards for Restaurants
Once again, prices are coded to indicate the price of a dinner that includes an appetizer, main course, and dessert, but does *not* include beverages, tax, or tip.

$	under $15
$$	$15-$20
$$$	$21-$30
$$$$	over $30

Miscellaneous
Experienced travelers realize that *things do change* from time to time. Restaurants change chefs. Hotels add more rooms. Companies go out of business...move to a different address...or change telephone numbers. Old roads are widened and new roads are built. Prices change. For these reasons, we encourage you to plan your trip as far in advance as you can and to confirm all of your arrangements at the time of your departure. Use all of the information at your disposal. Generally speaking, a knowledge-able traveler is a happier traveler.

Please write
With the information contained in this book, we hope to help you enjoy a more interesting, informative, enjoyable trip. If so, please let us know about it. That is our job...and it's nice to know if we've been successful at it.

We appreciate your feedback, both positive and negative, so that we can create books of even greater benefit to our readers. If you have a favorite walk or if you have discovered a walk, a restaurant, or a hotel that we haven't encountered as yet, please let us know. We'll check it out. Also pass along any corrections, errors, or omissions that you may find so that we can see that they don't appear in later editions of our book.

You can write us at Out There Press, PO Box 1173, Asheville, NC 28802 or e-mail us at jim@outtherepress.com.

The White House
&
Its Neighbors

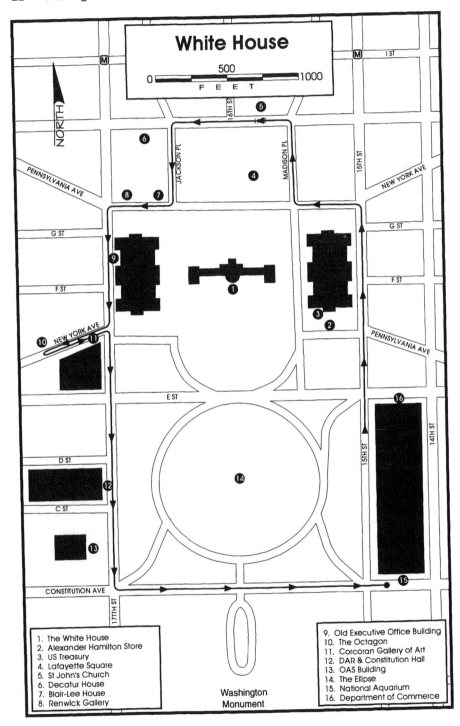

White House

Washington Monument

The White House & Its Neighbors

To many people, the most memorable part of their visit to Washington is a tour of the White House. As many as 5,000 people tour the president's home during the peak season, and tickets often are difficult to come by.

Situated at 1600 Pennsylvania Ave, the White House has been the home of every US President except George Washington. Washington selected the site and laid the cornerstone in 1792, but he never actually lived in the building.

To determine the style of the building, a national competition was held. Entrants were challenged to create a "presidential palace [with] a grandeur of conception, a Republican simplicity, and...true elegance of proportion." The $500 prize went to James Hoban, an Irish architect living in Charleston, SC, who based his design on Leinster Hall in Dublin, the country estate of an Irish duke.

When Pierre L'Enfant laid out the city, Pennsylvania Avenue was designed to be the shortest distance between the White House and the Capitol. For many years, it was the business and social center of the city—the venue for presidential inaugurations, six presidential funeral processions (including Lincoln's and Kennedy's), wartime victory celebrations, and a number of public and official demonstrations. The portion between 15th St and 17th St NW is now closed to vehicular traffic as a safety precaution.

Not long after John Adams moved into the then-incomplete building, the War of 1812 erupted and the British destroyed the mansion by fire, requiring extensive repairs. The South Portico was added in 1824; the North Portico in 1829. Electricity was added in 1891 during Benjamin Harrison's presidency.

In 1902, half a million dollars were spent to renovate the building. The West Wing, in which the Oval Office is located, was added that year. Between 1948 and 1952, the White House received even greater renovation, including some major structural improvements (Margaret Truman's piano had punched a hole through the dining room ceiling). While the renovations took place, the Truman family took up residence elsewhere.

Today's White House has 132 rooms and sits on 18.5 acres landscaped with trees, lawns and flower gardens. On the west side of the South Lawn is the Children's Garden, which contains imprints of the hands and feet of all the White House children and grandchildren, preserved in bronze.

Information

The White House (202/619-7222, 800/717-1450, or for a recorded message, 202/456-7041; www.whitehouse.org). The **White House Visitors Center** (202/208-1631) is at 1450 Pennsylvania Ave NW, opposite small, triangular Pershing Square. Look for three American flags and some blue awnings.

The Visitors Center issues tickets to the White House on a first-come, first-served basis. It begins to distribute the tickets at 7:30 am and continues to do so until noon, although the facility itself remains open until 4 pm daily—later during summer.

Apart from White House tickets, the Visitor Center contains a number of interesting attractions. The 30-minute videotape helps to prepare you for a tour of the White House. Maps and brochures describing many of Washington's other attractions are available, most of them free of charge, and the facility includes exhibits describing the Architectural History of the White House, Symbol & Image, First Families, The Working White House, Ceremony & Celebration, and White House Interiors—Past and Present. There also are some restrooms in the building.

Those who have a greater interest in the history of the White House may contact the White House Historical Assn (202/737-8292) at 740 Jackson Pl NW.

Getting there

Metro stations close to the White House are located on the Federal Triangle and at McPherson Square.

First Steps

Passes for the White House can be obtained by writing to your representative (c/o US House of Representatives, Washington, DC 20515) or senator (c/o US Senate, Washington, DC 20510). Tickets can be reserved no more than three months in advance, and normally no more than five tickets per family will be issued to visit any one facility.

Without a Congressional ticket, timed tickets are required from mid-March to mid-September. From Labor Day to mid-March, they may not be required, but it would be wise to phone ahead (202/456-7041), just to be sure. Phoning ahead is an excellent idea in any case, because tours are sometimes cancelled *without notice* if some official function is taking place.

We strongly recommend contacting your congressman or senator to enlist his or her aid in obtaining tickets to tour the White House. Apart from the convenience of not having to stand in a long line to acquire a ticket, there is another advantage to doing so: The "VIP tours" are more extensive than the regular tours, and the guides provide a running commentary as you make your way through the building. On the regular tours, people are available throughout the building to answer questions, but they do not escort you through nor do they provide you with those added insights into what you have seen, are seeing, or are about to see.

Seasonal highlights

Washington thrives on festivals, celebrations, parades, diplomatic functions, and a lively social scene. There are kings and queens, princes and princesses, emperors, emirs, pashas, and ambassadors to be entertained. There are causes to be advanced...and victories to be celebrated, along with a calendar full of national holidays.

Every fourth year, the **Inauguration Day Celebration** is held on January 20 on the west front side of the Capitol. The president of the United States is sworn into office and then a parade travels from the Capitol to the White House.

The **White House Easter Egg Roll & Hunt** (202/456-2200) is held either at the end of March or in early April. This annual event was held on the grounds of the Capitol until Rutherford B Hayes moved it to the White House in 1879. It is now held on both the White House lawn and on The Ellipse out front, and is staged once at 10 am and again at 2 pm. Tickets are required and may be obtained at the visitors' pavilion on the Ellipse as early as 7 am on the day of the hunt. (CAUTION: Two-hour waits are not uncommon.)

The **White House Spring & Garden Tour** (202/456-2200) is held in mid-April, and **White House Fall Garden Tours** (202/456-2200) are held in October.

White House Christmas Candlelight Tours are held in late December. So too is the month-long **National Christmas Tree Lighting & Pageant of Peace** celebration, held on the Ellipse, and the **US Navy Band Holiday Concert** (202/433-6090), held in Constitution Hall, 1776 D St NW.

All of the events mentioned above are free to the public, although reservations may be required in some cases.

Tours

If your congressman has not provided you with tickets to tour the White House, you should start your day *as early as possible* at the **White House Visitors Center**.

The congressional tours are conducted from Tuesday through Saturday at 8:15 am, 8:30 am, and 8:45 am. Each ticket indicates when and where you are to join the line waiting to get into the executive mansion, and is good only for the day on which it is issued. One person may acquire up to six tickets.

The White House. *This tour includes a visit to the White House and several of the buildings in the immediate vicinity. Plan on a full day to fully appreciate the tour's many stops. Visitors to the White House are asked to line up prior to admission at the East Visitors Gate, located on E Executive Ave. (Note: Baby strollers are not allowed in The White House.)*

The rooms inside the White House are functional, yet they serve as mini-museums of American history, art and culture.

The State Dining Room can seat 140 people. It is modeled after a late 18th-century neoclassical house, and a quotation from John Adams has been carved into the mantel: "I Pray Heaven to Bestow The Best of Blessings on THIS HOUSE and on All that shall here-after Inhabit it. May none but Honest and Wise Men ever rule under This Roof." During Theodore Roosevelt's term, a moose head hung over that fireplace and other of his hunting trophies adorned the walls. Be sure to look for GPA Healy's portrait of Abraham Lincoln, which hangs in this room.

The Blue Room, furnished in the manner of the James Monroe administration, is used as a place to receive guests. Grover Cleveland, the only president to be married in the White House, was wed in this room, and this is the customary location of the White House Christmas tree. The Blue Room also contains the portraits of five past presidents, including GPA Healy's portrait of John Tyler and Rembrandt Peale's portrait of Thomas Jefferson.

Peale's father, Charles Willson Peale, 1741-1827, was America's leading portrait painter, and produced paintings of such notables of the day as George and Martha Washington, Thomas Jefferson, Benjamin Franklin, and John Hancock. Peale had 17 children by three wives and they included Rembrandt Peale, Titian Peale and Raphaelle Peale, all of whom became artists. In addition, his daughters Anna Claypoole Peale and Sarah Miriam Peale became respected artists as well, and Peale's brother James became America's first important still-life painter.

The White House's gold-and-white East Room contains Parquet Fontainebleu oak floors, and its white painted wood walls are decorated with fluted pilasters and classical relief inserts. Nellie Grant, Alice Roosevelt and Lynda Bird Johnson were all married in this room, and it is in this room that every President who has died in office has been laid in state. This also is the room in which Richard Nixon delivered his resignation speech. Look for Gilbert Stuart's famous portrait of George Washington in the East Room. (When the British sacked and burned Washington during the War of 1812, Dolley Madison demonstrated remarkable courage in remaining behind to salvage a number of items, including this portrait of Washington, which she carefully cut out of its frame, rolled up, and carried with her to the Blair House.)

The Green Room, now used as a sitting room, served as the dining room during Thomas Jefferson's presidency. Paintings by Gilbert Stuart and John Singer Sargent adorn the green watered-silk fabric on the walls.

In the aptly named Red Room, the satin-covered walls and most of the Empire period furnishings are in red. The room is now used as a reception room, particularly for afternoon teas. Its walls contain portraits of past presidents, Gilbert Stuart's portrait of Dolley Madison, and Albert

Bierstadt's painting *View of the Rocky Mountains.*

Other parts of the White House that are open to public view are the Vermeil Room, the ground-floor Library, Cross Hall, and the North Entrance Hall.

Leave the White House, return to the East Visitors Gate and turn left onto 15th St NW. When you reach Pennsylvania Ave, instead of turning right toward the Visitors Center continue north for one block. On your left will be the **United States Treasury.** *The building should be entered through the Appointment Center doors on 15th St between F St and G St NW; a photo ID will be required. Free, guided 90-minute tours, for which reservations are required (202/622-0896), are available on Saturday mornings except on holidays.*

A statue of Alexander Hamilton, the nation's first Secretary of the Treasury, stands just South of the Treasury building. Hamilton was killed in a duel with Aaron Burr on July 11, 1804.

The **United States Treasury** is situated next to the White House on Pennsylvania Ave between E Executive Ave and 15th St NW. The building was designed by Robert Mills after two previous buildings had been destroyed by fire. Mills is the man who also designed the Washington Monument.

In 1855 and in 1869, wings were added to the T-shaped, Greek Revival building, which has an interior Greek colonnade containing 30 columns, each 36 feet tall and carved from a single block of granite. The north lobby features a gilded entablature and a stunning ceiling medallion, and the four exquisite corner domes can be accessed by magnificent staircases ornamented with oak and olive branch balustrades. Portraits of former Treasury Secretaries line the corridors.

Open to the public is the former office of Salmon P Chase, Secretary of the Treasury during the Civil War—the office used by President Andrew Johnson after the assassination of Abraham Lincoln. Also of interest is the Marble Cash Room, in which Ulysses S Grant held his inaugural reception in 1869.

Exit the Treasury Building as you entered it, returning to 15th St NW. Turn left for one block. Pennsylvania Ave will be on your left, New York Ave will be angling away from you on your right, and McPherson Square will be two blocks ahead of you. Turn left onto Pennsylvania Ave and walk one block to Madison Pl. Ahead of you on your right will be Lafayette Square.

Although a small park, **Lafayette Square** (202/755-7798) is one of the best-known squares in the city. It is located at the south end of 16th St NW and extends from Pennsylvania Ave to H St and from Jackson Pl to

Madison Pl, directly opposite the White House. Meticulously landscaped, it is named for the Marquis de Lafayette, who visited the United States in 1824 and drew large crowds to this park. Within the park are a number of statues, notably one of Andrew Jackson astride a horse, produced by Clark Mills. This was the first equestrian statue in the United States. Other statues in the park honor Rochambeau, Steuben, Kosciuszko, and of course, Lafayette himself.

In 1859, Congressman Daniel Sickles of New York, a resident of the area, discovered that his wife Teresa was having an affair with their friend, Philip Barton Key, son of Francis Scott Key, the author of *The Star Spangled Banner.* When Sickles spotted Key trying to signal Teresa through their window one night, he rushed outside and shot Key to death in this park.

In 1917, the park acquired another moment of infamy when women suffragists demonstrated there, got arrested, and were charged with "obstructing traffic." Since then, Lafayette Park has become known for its numerous protests, and is also known as a popular hangout for some of the city's homeless. The park is open from dawn to dusk.

Going north on Madison Pl for one block will take you to H St. Turn left and stroll one more block to 16th St NW where, on the northeast corner, you will find St John's Church

An Episcopal church designed in the Greek Revival style by Benjamin Latrobe, **St John's Church** (202/347-8766) has a dome and a colonnaded portico entrance. In 1883, architect James Renwick added a Palladian window over the altar and the church has become noted for its exquisite stained glass windows, which include *The Last Supper, The Adoration of the Magi,* and *Sower's Window,* which commemorates William H Seward, Abraham Lincoln's secretary of state. Another window was presented by President Chester A Arthur in memory of his wife, who had been a member of the church choir.

Every President since James Madison has worshiped in this church. Madison was a parishioner, as were James Monroe, Andrew Jackson, Martin Van Buren, William Henry Harrison, John Tyler, Zachary Taylor, Franklin Pierce, and Chester A Arthur. The morning after President Kennedy was assassinated, Lyndon Johnson went to this church for a moment of silent prayer. Presidents Ford and Bush attended services here almost every Sunday when they were in town.

The church is open daily in the summer from 8 am to 3 pm (to 4 pm the rest of the year), and a guided tour is conducted on the first Sunday of every month following the last morning service. Summer services are held

Monday through Friday at 12:10 pm and on Sunday at 8, 9 and 11 am (Sunday services are held at 8:30 and 10:30 am during the remainder of the year).

Next door to the church is the Parish House, which served as the residence of British Minister Lord Ashburton during the round of negotiations held in 1892 to work out the boundaries of Canada. Secretary of State Daniel Webster represented the United States' interests and Ashburton the British interests. Apart from the serious business at hand, the event was associated with a flurry of dinners, balls, parties, and receptions, for which Ashburton provided the wines and desserts, prepared by his French chef, and Webster personally shopped the local markets to select the finest and freshest of foods.

Continue walking west for one block, where you will find Jackson Pl entering H St. On the southwest corner, you will find the Decatur House. A National Historic Landmark at 748 Jackson Pl NW, the **Decatur House** (202/842-0030; www.nthhp.org/main/sites/decatur.htm or www.decaturhouse.org), a lovely three-story brick mansion facing Lafayette Square. When it was built in 1819, it was the first private residence built on Lafayette Square, thereby providing the President and his family with their first neighbors.

The house was designed by Benjamin Latrobe for Commodore Stephen Decatur, America's foremost naval hero, who lived there for the last 14 months of his life. Decatur had distinguished himself nobly in the Tripolitan War and in the War of 1812, but was then killed in a duel with an old enemy, Capt James Barron. Susan Wheeler Decatur, Decatur's widow, then moved to Georgetown.

Subsequent residents of the house included Henry Clay, Martin Van Buren, Judah Benjamin, and a host of foreign diplomats and American politicians. Gen Edward Fitzgerald Beale and his wife Nancy bought the house in the 1870s and had it remodeled in a Victorian manner. During the Civil War, the house served as a supply depot.

Today, the period rooms are decorated in both the Victorian and Federal styles. The first floor is furnished in the style of Decatur's occupancy, while the second floor reflects the Victorian decor favored by the Beales. For three weeks every December, period Christmas decorations are put up.

The house is open between 10 am and 3 pm from Tuesday through Friday and between noon and 4 pm on Saturday and Sunday. It is closed on Mondays, New Year's Day, Thanksgiving, and Christmas. Admission is $4, reduced to $2.50 for seniors and students. Children under 12 are admitted free. A gift shop is on the premises.

Guided tours lasting from 35 to 40 minutes depart every half-hour. Walking tours of Lafayette Square are conducted by appointment.

Walk south along Jackson Pl to the next corner (Pennsylvania Ave) and take a right. The first building on your right will be the historic Blair-Lee House.

It was in the **Blair-Lee House** that the Truman family resided during the period between 1948 and 1952 when the White House was under extensive renovation. The Lee House is the oldest of the two houses, having been built in 1824. The Blair House was built in 1858. Of the two, the Blair House is the more historic, for it was the home of Montgomery Blair, who served as the attorney for Dred Scott, a slave who felt he should be declared a free man because he had lived in a free territory. When the case reached the Supreme Court in 1857, Chief Justice Roger B Taney, a southerner, delivered the majority opinion that a Negro had no rights that "a white man was bound to respect" and therefore argued that Scott's petition had no merit. The decision was one of the most significant events leading up to the Civil War.

It was in the Blair House that Robert E Lee was offered the command of the Union Army once the Civil War did break out, but he rejected the offer in order to support the Confederacy, an effort that created a furor in the nation's capital.

Since 1943, the Blair-Lee House has served as the President's official guest house.

Just past the Blair House on Pennsylvania Ave, you will find the Renwick Gallery on the northwest corner of 17th St.

A part of the National Museum of American Art, the **Renwick Gallery** (202/357-2700) occupies a building designed by architect James W Renwick in 1859 but not completed until 1874. Created in the French Second Empire style, the building was the original home of the Corcoran Gallery, which moved to its present location after it outgrew these facilities.

So badly did the building deteriorate after the Corcoran Gallery moved out, it was seriously considered for demolition until it was rescued by Jacqueline Kennedy in 1963 as part of the Lafayette Square restoration project. It then became a part of the Smithsonian Institution and was renamed for its architect, who had directed the design of the Smithsonian "castle."

The gallery's Grand Salon has been restored and refurnished in the style of the late 19th century, including wainscoted plum walls beneath a 38-foot skylight ceiling. The emphasis of the exhibits centers around

American crafts—glass, ceramics, wood, fiber, and metal. Admission is free and the gallery is open from 10 am to 5:30 pm daily except Christmas.

Ask at the information desk for a free schedule of events, which include demonstrations, lectures and films. A museum shop also is on the premises.

Two blocks north of the Renwick Gallery on 17th St is Farragut Square and a Metro station, but you will want to turn in the opposite direction (south) and stroll to the Old Executive Office Building, which will be on your left between G St and F St.

Huge, gray and ornately styled, the **Old Executive Office Building** (202/395-5895) was built between 1872 and 1888. When completed, it was the largest office building in the world and it originally served as the State, War and Navy Building. Its elaborate Victorian interiors are matched only by its beautiful stained glass rotundas. Locals call the building the "OEB."

It was in the basement of this building that Col Oliver North and his lovely blond secretary, Fawn Hall, shredded documents in an attempt to hide some of the details associated with the 1986 Iran-Contra scandal. The building is open Saturdays from 9 to 11:30 am, but tours are available only by appointment.

Back outside on 17th St, continue to head south until you reach New York Ave, then turn right. On your right, in the first block of New York Ave, you will find the Octagon.

The Octagon (202/638-3221; www.amerarchfoundation.com), is at 1799 New York Ave, and is now owned by the American Architectural Foundation. Originally designed in 1798 by Dr William Thornton, architect for the US Capitol and the Woodlawn Plantation, the Octagon was to be a summer retreat for the family of Col John Tayloe III, a wealthy Virginia planter and horse breeder and a close friend of George Washington. Thornton is said to have mastered the principles of architecture in just two weeks and then to have moved on into the fields of astronomy, medicine, philosophy, art, language, and finance.

The Federal-style townhouse was completed in 1801, and was one of Washington's hallmark social centers, in which guests such as Adams, Jefferson, Madison, Monroe, Webster, Clay, Lafayette, and Calhoun were lavishly entertained. After the British burned the White House in 1814, it became Madison's residence, it was in a second-floor parlor of this house that Madison signed the Treaty of Ghent in 1815, bringing that war to a close.

In 1902, the building was purchased by the American Institute of

Architects, which built its headquarters behind the house. Thus, it became the oldest museum in America dedicated to architecture.

The marble-floored circular entrance hall is adjacent to the dining room and the drawing room, each of which is furnished with period pieces. A sweeping oval staircase leads to the second floor, where the table on which the Treaty of Ghent was signed is on display. Two other second-floor rooms contain changing exhibits devoted to architecture, the decorative arts, and Washington history.

Beneath the stairs are the kitchen, the servants' hall, the housekeeper's room, and a wine cellar. The 19th-century kitchen contains a stew hearth, a range, and a period bake oven.

Guided tours are available from Tuesday through Sunday between 10 am and 4 pm. The building is closed on Mondays and on major holidays. At 10:30 am, free story times are offered to children of kindergarten-to-third grade ages with a museum admission. Admission is $3 for adults and $1.50 for seniors and students. Children under five are admitted free.

Across the street from the Octagon is the Corcoran Gallery of Art. Just one block from the White House, the **Corcoran Gallery of Art** (202/639-1700 or 202/638-1439 for a recording; www.corcoran.org) is located at 500 17th St NW at New York Ave. It houses Washington's oldest art collection and one of the three oldest collections in the country.

From 1874 to 1896, the creator of the collection, a wealthy and prominent banker named William Wilson Corcoran, housed his collection in the red brick-and-brownstone building a few blocks away, now known as the Renwick Gallery. When the collection outgrew those facilities, Corcoran commissioned Ernest Flagg to design the present building, completed in 1897, and the Corcoran collection was transferred into it. Later, Sen William Andrews Clark's collection of European paintings and sculpture also was included.

The first floor of the gallery features a double atrium and an imposing marble staircase. It is on this floor that the Clark collection of Dutch and Flemish masters, French impressionists, Barbizon landscapes, Delft porcelains, and the Louis XVI salon dore, a late 18th-century gilded French room transported in toto from Paris are located. As you enter, ask for a brochure at the information desk.

The Clark Landing is a small, walnut-paneled room that contains 19th-century French impressionist and American works of art.

In all, the gallery contains a room of Corot landscapes, a room of Medieval and Rennaisance tapestries, numerous Daumier lithographs donated by Dr Armand Hammer, the works of some of the first great American portraitists, pottery, and photography. Representing the works of 19th-century American artists are those by Bierstadt, Home, Easkins, Remington, Whistler, Sargent, and Cassatt. Examples of the 20th-century moderns include the works of Nevelson, Warhol, and Rothko.

On the second floor is a white marble female nude, *The Greek Slave* by Hiram Powers, considered so daring in its day that it was separately exhibited to men and women on alternate days.

The gallery is open Wednesday through Friday and Monday from 10 am to 5 pm. It remains open on Thursday until 9 pm, but is closed on Tuesdays, on Christmas, and on New Year's Day. Free tours of the permanent collection are offered daily except Tuesday at 12:30. On Thursday, tours also are offered at 7:30 pm. Group tours can be scheduled by appointment (202/639-1730). Admission is free, but donations of $3 for adults, $1 for seniors and students, and $5 for family groups are recommended.

Return to 17th St and continue South. After you cross D St, you will find the DAR Museum/Constitution Hall on your right. The national headquarters of the **Daughters of American Revolution** (202/879-3241; www.dar.org) are at 1776 D St NW. One of the few buildings west of the White House at the time ground was broken for construction in 1902, the four-story red brick beaux-arts building is built atop a cornerstone laid with the same trowel that George Washington used when he was laying the cornerstone for the US Capitol. The cost of construction was borne, in part, by revenues from the "sale" of 33 rooms, purchased (in name only) by various state chapters of the organization. Thus, within the building you will find a Victorian Missouri parlor and a New Hampshire "Children's Attic" containing 19th-century toys, dolls and furnishings. A New Jersey room resembles a 17th-century English Council chamber and has woodwork and furnishings created from the timbers of the British frigate *Augusta*, which sank in Red Bank in 1777.

The building also houses a 30,000-piece collection of pre-1840s furnishings that includes Chinese export porcelain, English pottery, quilts, coverlets, samplers, pewterware, glassware, and silver. Several notable paintings can also be found in the building.

There is a Children of the American Revolution Museum that contains dolls, dollhouse furnishings, tea services, school books, colonial household objects, and children's clothing of the period. Interesting too are the exhibits showing how candles were made and how glass is blown. There is a gift shop and the DAR Library (202/879-3229) contains over

120,000 books and 60,000 manuscripts, many of them dealing with genealogy. The library is open to the public on a daily-fee basis from 8:45 am to 4 pm on weekdays and from 1 to 5 pm on Sundays.

Constitution Hall, contained within the DAR building, is an auditorium decorated in federal blue and gold. It features a variety of popular nighttime entertainment.

There is no admission charge for the building; hours are 8:30 am to 4 pm Monday through Friday and 1 to 5 pm on Sunday. The building is closed on Saturdays, New Year's Day, Thanksgiving, Christmas, and during the week-long DAR Congress held in April. Tours of the facility are offered from 10 am to 2:30 pm Monday through Friday, and from 1 to 5 pm on Sunday.

South of the DAR Museum on 17th St is the Organization of American States (OAS) Building, which sits between C St and Constitution Ave. The **Organization of American States** (202/458-3751) was founded on April 14, 1890 (Pan American Day) as a union of 35 different North and South American republics and is headquartered in one of Washington's most beautiful buildings. Topped by a terra cotta-tiled roof and bearing black wrought-iron balconies, the building has a garden patio that contains palms and tropical plants arranged around a rose-colored fountain. The Peace Tree, part fig tree and part rubber tree, was planted by President Taft when the building was dedicated.

Inside the building are palatial staircases and beautiful arched doorways. The Hall of Heroes contains the flags of all member nations, and pedestals bear the busts of such heroes as Jose Marti, Simon Bolivar, and George Washington.

High-ranking dignitaries are received in the Hall of the Americas, which features magnificent Tiffany chandeliers and has 24 Corinthian columns that support a vaulted ceiling 45 feet high. The Council Room adjoins the Hall of the Americas and displays bronze relief panels depicting the exploits of Cortes, Bolivar, Balboa, and others. Now used for committee meetings, it contains a magnificent conference table which, along with the accompanying set of chairs, was carved from a single mahogany tree. The new Council Room, the Simon Bolivar Room, is located on the first floor of the building.

The building is open Monday through Friday from 9:30 am to 5 pm, but closed on Federal holidays. Admission is free, but tours are available only by appointment.

On the southwest corner of 17th St and Constitution Ave, across from the OAS building, is a tiny stone house. In the late 1700s, Pierre L'Enfant's plan for Washington included "a canal through Tiber Creek"—a canal that would wander along Constitution Ave from the Potomac River in Georgetown, through the Ellipse, eastward through the remainder of the district, and then south to the Anacostia River. That canal was indeed built and was utilized until the 1870s, when the coming of the railroads made it obsolete. The little stone house, once the canal lock- keeper's house, is all that remains.

Across 17th St from the OAS building is the large garden-like expanse known as the Ellipse. The Ellipse stretches from E St on the north all the way to the Tidal Basin on the south. At the northern end of the Ellipse are monuments to the historic First and Second Divisions, the Zero Milestone, and beyond that, the White House itself. To the south are the Washington Monument and the Sylvan Theatre, both of which are described in the section devoted specifically to Washington's monuments and memorials.

Head East on Constitution Ave, cross the Ellipse, and then turn left onto 14th St. Immediately on your left will be the National Aquarium. Located on the lower level of the Department of Commerce building, the **National Aquarium** (202/482-2825) is the oldest public aquarium in the country. (NOTE: There is an aquarium in Baltimore that also is known as the National Aquarium, but the two attractions are quite different in content and scope.)

Established in 1873 by the Federal Fish Commission, the aquarium's original mission was the "propagation of desirable fishes." Today, more than 1,200 fish and other creatures are on display, representing 250 species of fresh- and saltwater life. Eighty tanks ranging in size from 50 to 6,000 gallons contain rare sea turtles, American alligators, eels, Japanese carp, tropical clownfish, and more. A popular touch tank contains horseshoe crabs, hermit crabs, starfish, snails, sea urchins, and other marine life that visitors may actually touch and examine.

Exhibits are arranged geographically (African lakes, South American rivers, Caribbean reefs) and thematically (stream life versus pond life), while a mini-theater offers visitors a continuous 20-minute videotape about aquatic life.

Sharks are fed at 2 pm on Mondays, Wednesdays and Saturdays, while piranha are fed at 2 pm on Tuesdays, Thursdays and Sundays. A special Shark Day is held on a Saturday in late July or early August. Included in the activities are a shark feeding, special exhibits, films, and (for the children) face painting.

The aquarium is open daily from 9 am to 5 pm, but closed on

Christmas. Admission is $2 for adults and 75 cents for children and seniors. A gift shop and a cafeteria on the premises are open until 2:30 pm on weekdays.

Occupying the same building as the aquarium is the **Department of Commerce** (202/482-4883; www.doc.gov), the federal agency responsible for promoting American business, developing economic statistics, conducting the census, issuing patents and trademarks, setting industrial standards, and forecasting the weather. The department has some 35,000 employees, roughly half of whom work in Washington, and an annual payroll of $150 million.

Created by congress in 1903, the Department of Commerce originally was named the Department of Commerce & Labor. Commerce and Labor became two different departments, each with its own cabinet-level secretary, in 1913. Past secretaries of commerce have included Herbert Hoover, a past president; Henry Wallace, once a vice president; and W Averell Harriman, a highly ranked statesman during the administration of Franklin Roosevelt.

Exit the Department of Commerce building onto 15th St and turn right (north). Just past Pershing Square, you will find yourself back at the White House gate where you began.

Lodging

When you stay within walking distance of the White House, you're talking about prime real estate...and the cost reflects it. On the other hand, it's generally true that you get what you pay for.

Within easy walking distance of the White House, the **Hay-Adams** ($$$, 202/638-6600 or 800/424-5054), One Lafayette Square, is one of Washington's most historic hotels. Located just across Lafayette Square from the White House, the hotel has played host to such celebrities as author Sinclair Lewis, aviator Charles Lindbergh, aviatrix Amelia Earhart, and actress Ethel Barrymore. Built in the 1920s by the same individual who built the Jefferson and Carlton hotels, the Hay-Adams is a moderately-sized hotel that contains just 143 rooms, but none of the luxuries are excluded...things like a complimentary morning newspaper, a relaxing robe, and turn-down service are all included. If you can manage it, get a room between the fifth and eighth floors on the H St side of the hotel, from which you will get a magnificent view of the White House and, in the distance, the Washington Monument.

Another excellent choice just one block from the White House is the **Hotel Washington** ($$$, 202/638-5900 or 800/424-9540; www.hotelwashington.com) at 515 15th St NW. This historic building, built in 1918 and extensively renovated in 1980, is listed on the National Register. Twelve stories tall, it contains 340 rooms, and the Two Continents restaurant ($$$), located on the lobby level, is open daily.

Two blocks from the White House is the **Willard Inter-Continental** ($$$, 202/637-9100 or 800/327-0200), located at 1401 Pennsylvania Ave. The 342-room hotel was built along beaux-arts lines in 1901 on the site of the earlier (1815) City Hotel. When it was purchased by the Willards, the name was changed. The hotel was designated a National Landmark in 1974. A restored Edwardian structure, it is sometimes referred to as the "Hotel of Presidents." Abraham Lincoln stayed here on the eve of his inaugural, and Julia Ward Howe was staying here when she wrote "The Battle Hymn of the Republic." During the Civil War, there were separate entrances for those who were pro-Union and those who had secessionist feelings. Marble columns line the lobby, where the ceiling contains huge globe chandeliers and 48 state seals (the state seals for Alaska and Hawaii can be found in Peacock Alley). The tastefully-done promenade is lined with potted palms, and the informal dining room, Cafe Espresso ($$, 202/628-9100), is open daily.

Food & drink

Washington has some magnificent restaurants...and the variety of food that is available is simply beyond belief, undoubtedly due to the ebb-and-flow of individuals from every nation that passes through the city on a regular basis.

Les Halles ($$, 202/347-6848), 1201 Pennsylvania Ave NW, is a French/American steakhouse that is open for lunch Monday through Friday, dinner daily, and a brunch on the weekends. Check out the cassoulet and blood sausage.

Provence ($$, 202/296-1166), 2401 Pennsylvania Ave NW, specializes in the foods of southwestern France. Lunch is served from noon to 2 pm on weekdays. Dinner is available from 6 to 10 pm Monday through Thursday, 5:30 to 11 pm on Friday and Saturday, and until 9:30 pm on Sunday. Chef Yannick Cam provides a variety of entrees including fish, fowl, game, and meat (the leg of lamb is marinated in Syrah wine, grilled over an open wood fire, and served with spinach and toasted peppers, while the grilled pigeon is accompanied by a celeriac-and-capers stew scented with thyme).

Good ol' Southern-style cookin' can be found at **Georgia Brown's** ($$, 202/393-4499), 950 15th St NW, where lunch is served Monday through Friday, dinner is served daily, and there is a mouth-watering Sunday brunch.

For Mediterranean-style food, try **Isabella** ($$, 202/408-9500) at 809 15th St NW, which is noted for its unusual decor.

Other excellent choices include the **Occidental Grill** ($$, 202/783-1475), 1475 Pennsylvania Ave NW, which has been serving Washingtonians with American cuisine since 1906 (hours: 11:30 am to 11 pm Monday through Saturday and noon to 9:30 pm on Sundays); the California-style **White House Connection** ($-$$, 202/842-1777), 1714 G St NW, a casual place that is open only on weekdays; and **Old Ebbitt Grill** ($-$$, 202/347-4801), 675 15th St NW between F St and G St (hours: 9:30 am to midnight on Sundays, 7:30 am to midnight Monday through

Friday, and 8 am to midnight on Saturday), and its on-site fast-food deli, **Ebbitt Express** (hours: 7:30 am to 8 pm Monday through Thursday and 7:30 am to 6 pm on Friday).

The Hay-Adams' **Lafayette Restaurant** ($$$), which faces the White House, serves gourmet American cuisine. You may recognize it as the place in which Dustin Hoffman and Robert de Niro did much of their plotting in the movie *Wag the Dog*. Afternoon tea is served; evening entertainment is available. At the Corcoran, the **Cafe des Artistes** ($, 202/639-1786) sits in a lovely garden-like setting. The cafe serves several cold main dishes, sandwiches, soups, salads, an outstanding key lime pie, and a childrens' favorite, fruit slushes. The cafe is open from 11:30 am to 4:40 pm daily and until 8 pm on Thursdays. Reservations are recommended on weekdays. A jazz brunch is held on Saturday from 11 am to 2 pm (202/638-1590).

Nightlife

A sure bet is the **Willard Room** ($$-$$$, 202/637-7440) in the Willard Inter-Continental Hotel (see LODGING above), which offers live music and is a very popular Washington nightspot. See how many Congressmen, Senators, and other celebrities you are able to spot. Reservations are highly recommended.

Events

At the Corcoran there are free Saturday Family Days featuring live music, and free Sunday Traditions Workshops (202/638-3211, ext 321 or 202/638-1439) held from 3 to 4:30 pm for the purpose of introducing children between the ages of four and 12 to various aspects of the museum's architecture and exhibitions. (Note: The Sunday Workshops are not held every week and reservations are recommended.) Ask for a complete schedule of the gallery's events, which include temporary exhibits, talks, concerts, art auctions, and more.

There also is a Corcoran School of Art, which offers a four-year program for students of the fine arts and photography. The school also provides studio classes for children (202/628-9484 for a catalog).

Capitol Hill

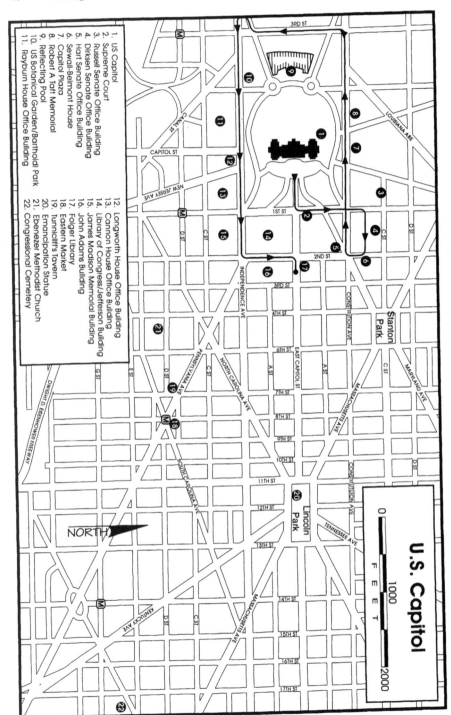

1. US Capitol
2. Supreme Court
3. Russell Senate Office Building
4. Dirksen Senate Office Building
5. Hart Senate Office Building
6. Sewall-Belmont House
7. Capitol Plaza
8. Robert A Taft Memorial
9. Reflecting Pool
10. US Botanical Garden/Bartholdi Park
11. Rayburn House Office Building
12. Longworth House Office Building
13. Cannon House Office Building
14. Library of Congress/Jefferson Building
15. James Madison Memorial Building
16. John Adams Building
17. Folger Library
18. Eastern Market
19. Tunnicliff's Tavern
20. Emancipation Statue
21. Ebenezer Methodist Church
22. Congressional Cemetery

U.S. Capitol

Capitol Hill

Mindful of the difficulties associated with living under a monarch, the founders of our country decided to distribute the power of the new government among three separate and distinct branches: the Executive, the Legislative, and the Judicial. The President heads the Executive branch and is generally conceded to be the leader of the nation, but it is our Legislature which creates the rules (laws) under which we live, and it is the Judiciary that makes sure that those laws are enforced. The Legislature is divided into two bodies, the House of Representatives and the Senate, and both bodies meet in the US Capitol. The Judiciary meets in the Supreme Court, directly across the street.

When George Washington selected the site destined to become the nation's first permanent capital, the area consisted of marshy bogs surrounding a small hill, then known as Jenkins Hill. Today, Jenkins Hill is known as Capitol Hill, and it is surrounded by a mixture of gigantic government buildings, Victorian architecture, Queen Anne rowhouses, Italianate mansions, townhouses, restaurants, and shops.

Broadly speaking, Capitol Hill extends from the Capitol building on the west to the RFK Memorial Stadium on the banks of the Anacostia River to the east. Since that covers a very considerable area, Capitol Hill, for the purposes of this book, is defined simply as the area immediately surrounding the US Capitol.

When Pierre L'Enfant, a French native who fought for the Colonies during the Revolution, told George Washington of his desire to help plan the nation's capital, the focal point of his plan was to be the "Congress House." Subsequently, Congress held a public competition to select the best design for the building, and the contest was won by an amateur architect, Dr William Thornton.

The **United States Capitol**, located in a 221-acre park, has become one of the most recognizab'e, most important symbols of the country, comparable to the White House itself. The city's street numbering system originates from here, north, south, east and west.

The first wing of the building was completed in 1800, and that year John Adams became the first president to address a joint session of Congress there. Congress had recently moved to Washington from Philadelphia, and at the time, the Capitol was still unfinished -- the mere brick-and-sandstone skeleton of the grand structure it was to become.

Congress moved into small, cramped quarters in the north wing—the House into a large room on the second floor, eventually intended to house the Library of Congress, and the Senate into a chamber on the ground floor.

By 1807, a second (South) wing of the Capitol was completed and the House of Representatives moved into it. A wooden walkway that ran across the yard linked the two wings of the Capitol until a connecting center structure could be completed. That is how the building looked at the time the War of 1812 began.

After the British burned the Capitol buildings in 1814, it took five years to restore the two original wings. The connecting center portion, originally covered by a low wood-and-copper dome, wasn't completed until 1826.

By 1850, so many new states had joined the Union that additional space was needed, and Congress decided to expand both the north and the south wings of the Capitol building. The House occupied the new south wing in 1867; the Senate occupied the enlarged north wing in 1869. All that remained of the original structure was the west side of the facade, which included the cornerstone originally laid by George Washington in 1793. (During a reconstruction done during the 1950s, that cornerstone was misplaced and has never been relocated.)

While the Capitol building was being built, a construction superintendent foolishly removed a critical support, causing part of the building to collapse. Architect Benjamin Latrobe was killed in the accident.

Information

The US Capitol is open daily from 9:30 am to 8 pm between March 1 and August 31 (the peak season) and from 9 am to 4:30 pm from September 1 to February 28. The building is closed on New Year's Day, Thanksgiving and Christmas. Admission to the building is free.

You can can call 202/225-3121 to see what House and Senate committee meetings are planned for the day or you can check the weekday "Today in Congress" column in the Washington Post for that information. You also can check the Washington Post "Supreme Court Calendar" to see what the court has scheduled for the day you plan to attend.

The Supreme Court building is open Monday through Friday between 9 am and 4:30 pm, but it is closed on the weekends and on all Federal holidays. Admission is free and no ticket is required. Visitors may see a case being argued in the upstairs courtroom (202/479-3211), but seating is limited to about 150 and visitors are admitted on a first-come, first-served basis. No cameras or recording devices are allowed.

On the ground floor, there are displays, a 20-minute film that explains court proceedings, and a gift shop.

The **Library of Congress** (202/707-8000 or 202/707-9956 recording; www.loc.gov/exhibits). **James Madison Memorial Building** has first-floor exhibit areas open Monday through Friday from 8:30 am to 9:30 pm and on Saturdays from 8:30 am to 6 pm. Other exhibit areas are open Monday through Friday from 8:30 am to 5 pm. The building is closed on Sundays and all Federal holidays. A 22-minute video describing the Library and its services is shown every half-hour in room LM-139.

The Thomas Jefferson Building is open Monday through Saturday from 10 am to 5:30 pm except on legal holidays, and admission is free. Tickets can be obtained at the information desk inside the West entrance on 1st St. A 12-minute introductory film is offered in the Visitors' Center, and visitors can rent equipment that will guide them on an audio tour of the facilities.

You can call for info about the **Folger Library** or 202/544-7077 or check out their web site at www.folger.edu. It's open Monday through Saturday from 10 am to 4 pm, but closed on Sundays and all Federal holidays. Admission is free and free 90-minute guided tours are offered daily at 11 am, on Tuesdays at 10 am, and on Saturdays at 1 pm.

Getting there

Metro stations close to the Capitol building include Capitol South and Union Station.

First Steps

Since this walk covers a considerable amount of ground, it would be a good idea to get an early start. In so doing, you not only will allow yourself sufficient time to see all that you wish to see but you will be much more likely to be at the head of the line when the other tourists arrive.

A helpful and informative brochure describing the United States Capitol is available to visitors. Pick one up on your way in.

Seasonal highlights

The **People's Christmas Tree Lighting** ceremony (202/224-3069) is held annually on the west side of the Capitol building.

Truly "seasonal" are the displays in the **US Botanic Garden**. If you like poinsettias, plan your trip for Christmas; chrysanthemums, for the fall; and lilies, tulips, hyacinths, and daffodils, for the spring. Flower shows are offered throughout the year (202/225-7099).

Shakespeare's birthday is celebrated on April 26 each year at the **Folger Library**, and a free open house is held there every September.

At the **Robert A Taft Memorial** near the Capitol building, selections are played on the bell tower's electronic keyboard at 2 pm on the Fourth of July.

A session of the **Supreme Court** generally runs from the first Monday in October through the month of April. Between mid-May and late June, visitors can attend brief sessions at which the Justices release their orders and opinions. These sessions are held on Mondays at 10 am.

Tours

Free 20-minute guided tours (202/224-4048 or 202/225-6827 recorded) of the US Capitol leave every 10 to 15 minutes except on Saturdays and Sundays during the peak season, when the last tour leaves at 3:45 pm. Sunday tours, which are offered *only* during the peak season, are available after 1:30 pm.

Once again, expect long lines, especially in the mornings during spring and summer. That is why it is advisable to write ahead to obtain passes from your congressman or senator, if at all possible. Address your request to: (Name of Congressman), US House of Representatives, Washington, DC 20515, or (name of Senator), US Senate, Washington, DC 20510. If you don't get the tickets by mail, ask for some at the congressman's or senator's office when you get to Washington.

Non-citizens should take their passports to the first-floor appointment desk on the Senate side of the Capitol or to the third-floor House gallery and request a pass. Guided tours are offered at the **Voice of America** building, in the **Library of Congress** Thomas Jefferson Building, and at the **Congressional Cemetery**.

US Capitol & Capitol Hill. *Start your visit in the Capitol Plaza on the east side of the US Capitol building, adjacent to the intersection of E Capitol St and 1st St NE.*

Enter the Capitol from the east front of the building, where presidential inaugurations have been held since James Monroe was inaugurated in 1817. If you are taking a guided tour, use the steps leading up to the Rotunda. If you are planning to tour the building on your own, enter through the ground-level Law Library or Document Doors that flank the front steps and you will find yourself on the ground floor of the building.

Massive bronze doors at the entrance to the US Capitol depict events in the life of Christopher Columbus. The Capitol Rotunda is a 96-foot wide circular hall, capped by a 180-foot high dome, which replaced the original copper-and-wood dome in 1863 during Abraham Lincoln's presidency. The present dome has a diameter of 100 feet, weighs 9 million pounds, and is one of world's largest.

Atop the dome is the bronze figure of *Freedom*, created by sculptor Thomas Crawford. The figure is 19.5 feet tall and weighs 14,985 pounds. Originally, the female figure was to have been nude but, due to the moral standards of the period, Crawford was required to drape it in a flowing robe instead. The statue remained atop the dome for 130 years until it was temporarily removed for restoration in 1993, cleaned and then replaced.

Crawford also created the bas reliefs in the pediments above the Corinthian-columned main entrance and at the entrance to the US Senate (to the right of the dome as you face it). They are named *Genius of America* and *Progress of Civilization* respectively.

Inside the dome is an allegorical fresco by Constantino Brumidi. *Apotheosis of Washington* is symbolic of George Washington, surrounded by Roman gods and goddesses Liberty, Victory and Fame, watching over the progress of the nation. The 13 figures in the fresco are crowned with stars representing the original 13 states. Like Michelangelo working on the Sustine Chapel, Brumidi worked on his back for 11 months as he created this work.

Beneath the dome, directly below Brumidi's painting of George Washington, is the figure of a woman, *Armed Freedom*, said to have been modeled after Lola Germon, a young actress with whom the 60-year-old Brumidi had a child. When he died, Brumidi was painting the frieze that rings the Rotunda and other artists had to finish his work. The frieze depicts events in American history from the arrival of Christopher Columbus through the Wright Brothers' flight at Kitty Hawk.

Hanging in the Rotunda are four giant canvases by John Trumbull, an aide-de-camp to George Washington who recorded scenes of the American Revolution. Also on the walls are eight large oil paintings of events in American history, such as the signing of the Declaration of Independence and the surrender of Cornwallis at Yorktown.

A statue by Adelaide Johnson pays tribute to three pioneers of women's suffrage: Lucretia Mott, Elizabeth Cady Stanton, and Susan B Anthony.

Another woman, Vinnie Ream, sculpted the life-sized marble statue of Lincoln that also stands in the Rotunda. Ream worked from sketches she had made of Lincoln during half-hour sessions with the President during the last five months of his life. She was only 19 when she received a commission to do the statue, and 23 when the work was completed.

The Rotunda has long been the venue for state funerals, including those of Presidents from Abraham Lincoln to Lyndon Johnson, members of Congress, military heroes, and a variety of prominent citizens.

Just off the Rotunda is **National Statuary Hall**, which houses 38 of the building's 95 statues of famous Americans. From 1807 to 1857, when the House represented just 32 states, it met in this space. John Quincy Adams, who served nine years as a Congressman after completing his term as President, suffered a stroke while delivering a speech here in 1848. A bronze plaque marks the spot where he fell. Adams died in an adjoining room two days later. The space became Statuary Hall in 1864 after the House moved to larger quarters. Each state was invited to submit two statues of famous residents. Those statues, each weighing a ton, include those of such prominent Americans as Ethan Allen, Henry Clay, Daniel Webster, and William Jennings Bryan. Five statues have never been received.

As more states joined the Union, space for the statues dwindled and eventually ran out, making it necessary to move some of the art to other parts of the Capitol building.

The Hall also contains two statues by Vinny Ream. They represent Samuel Jordan Kirkwood of Iowa and Sequoya, the famous Oklahoma Cherokee leader. Ream also produced the statue of Lincoln which stands in the Rotunda.

As you exit the National Statuary Hall, turn right and go down the stairs. Head to the ground-floor level of the House, where you will enter the Hall of Columns. The **Hall of Columns** was so named because it is lined with 28 magnificent marble columns. It contains some of the statuary that could not be accommodated in the National Statuary Hall on the floor above. There are three other corridors in this part of the building named the **Hall of the Capitals**, the **Great Experiment Hall**, and the **Westward Expansion Hall**.

On the lower floor below the Rotunda is the Crypt. Intended to be the burial place of George and Martha Washington, **The Crypt** contains exhibits associated with the Capitol building and its builders. (The Washingtons preferred to be buried at Mount Vernon.) The Crypt also is used to store the catafalque on which the nation's heroes lie in state in the Rotunda above. Thus far, nine Presidents have been so honored.

The Crypt also contains a large sculpture of Abraham Lincoln done by Gutzon Borglum, the man who designed Mount Rushmore. Notice that one side of Lincoln's face looks more haggard than the other—Borglum's attempt to portray the toll that the presidency took on Lincoln's life. The omission of Lincoln's left ear symbolizes the President's incomplete life. Legend has it that a cat appears in the catafalque when there is a change in the administration or before a national tragedy occurs.

Around a corner from the Crypt is the **original Supreme Court chamber**, used from 1810 to 1860. Fully restored, including hooks on which to hang the justices' robes, the room contains marble busts of many of the country's first Chief Justices.

John Marshall presided during much of the time the Supreme Court (then known as the Great Chief Justice) was housed in this room. It was from this office too that Samuel FB Morse sent out the world's first telegraph message in 1844. The umbrella vault ceiling was designed and built by Benjamin Latrobe.

Directly upstairs is the old Senate Chamber, used between 1810 and 1859. this is where Daniel Webster, Henry Clay, and John C Calhoun delivered many of their most colorful orations. When the Senate moved out of that chamber, the Supreme Court moved in and continued to meet there until 1935, when it moved to its present building across the street.

For 97 years, the Capitol building also housed the Library of Congress.

On the Senate side of the ground floor can be found the Refectory and the Brumidi Corridors. In the **Brumidi Corridors**, the vaulted ceilings and crescent-shaped spaces over the doorways display Brumidi's paintings of flowers, fruits, animals, and 40 different kind of birds, along with portraits of famous Americans and Revolutionary War heroes.

The third floor in both the south and north wings of the Capitol contains the current chambers of the Senate and House, and you can visit both. If sessions are in progress, you must obtain a pass from your congressman or senator in order to get in. (You can tell if either body is in session from outside the Capitol. If a flag is flying above the south wing, the House is in session; above the north wing, the Senate is in session.)

The Congressional Chambers can be accessed by stairs or elevators located at the ends of the hall on the first floor. On the wall over the west stairway of the House wing is *Westward the Course of Empire Takes Its Way*, a 20x30-foot fresco painted in 1862 by Emanuel Leutze, best known for his painting *Washington Crossing the Delaware.*

Visitors are asked not to take photographs in the Congressional Chambers. Men may not wear hats except for religious reasons. Guests must remain seated and refrain from reading, writing, smoking, eating, drinking, or applauding. Children under six may attend sessions in the House Chamber, but are not permitted in the Senate Gallery.

The **House of Representatives** is the largest legislative chamber in the world. This is where the president delivers his annual State of the Union address. First occupied in 1857, the chamber underwent a complete remodeling and structural renovation between 1949 and 1951. It is paneled in walnut and has pilasters of gray marble. The ceiling contains the seals of 50 states, four territories, and the District of Columbia, plus a carved glass eagle outlined in bronze. The walls flanking the Speaker's rostrum bear portraits of George Washington and the Marquis de Lafayette.

A law passed in 1911 limits the number of representatives to 435. Until 1913, the representatives sat at desks; today they sit on benches. Members are not assigned to individual seats, but may sit wherever they wish—the Republicans sitting to the left and the Democrats to the right of the House Speaker.

The offices of individual Congressmen are located in the series of House Office Buildings along Independence Avenue, south of the Capitol.

In the east staircase of the Capitol's **Senate** wing is *Battle of Lake Erie*, a 20x30-foot painting by William Powell that depicts the moment when Oliver Hazard Perry transferred the colors of his flagship to a ship in better condition during the War of 1812.

US senators originally were selected by their states' legislators, rather than the general public. That changed in 1913, when the Seventeenth Amendment called for the public election of senators. In the Senate Gallery, remodeled about the same time as the House Chamber, the members sit behind individual mahogany desks constructed in 1819. As new states have joined the Union, similarly-styled desks have been added. As they do in the House, the Republicans sit on the left and the Democrats sit on the right.

Niches in the gallery walls below the ceiling house the busts of 20 vice presidents (Dan Quayle and Al Gore are not included—yet). In the ceiling is a representation of the Great Seal of the United States.

The senators' offices are located in the Senate office buildings on Constitution Avenue north of the Capitol. To locate a congressman or senator, call 202/224-3121.

Leave the Capitol as you entered it, onto the Capitol Plaza. Take the sidewalk to 1st St NE, where you will see the Supreme Court building on the northeast corner of 1st St and E Capitol St. The third branch of our government, co-equal to the Executive and Legislative arms, is the **United States Supreme Court** (202/479-3000 or 202/479-3211), which is charged with the responsibility of seeing that the Executive and Legislative Branches do not overstep their authority or exercise that authority inequitably. It is our nation's highest tribunal. Some 6,500 petitions are received from lower courts each year and the Supreme Court Justices hear about 120 of them each year. Four of the nine Justices must agree to review a case before it can be taken up by the court.

Before you enter the Supreme Court building, stop at the top of the entrance steps and enjoy a marvelous view of the US Capitol.

The court moved into this marble structure, designed by architect Cass Gilbert, in 1935. Over the Corinthian-columned entrance notice the motto

"Equal Justice Under Law." When the court is in session, it generally alternates approximately every two weeks between "sittings" and "recesses." Sittings are sessions at which the Justices hear cases and deliver decisions. Recesses are times during which they consider other business that comes before the court. These meetings take place from Monday through Wednesday between 10 am and 3 pm, with an hour's recess at noon. Public lectures are offered every hour on the half-hour 9:30-3:30 when the court is not in session.

Leave the Supreme Court building, turn right (north) and follow 1st St NE for one block to Constitution Ave. On the northwest corner ahead of you is the **Russell Senate Office Building.** On the northeast corner is the **Dirksen Senate Office Building,** and just east of that along Constitution Ave is the **Hart Senate Office Building.** Unless you wish to drop in to say hello to your Senator, there is little in the buildings that is of much interest.

That said, the Russell Senate Office Building does have a gorgeous rotunda and there is a magnificent circular Corinthian colonnade on the second floor. The building is a duplicate of the Cannon House Office Building on the other side of the Capitol.

The Dirksen Senate Office Building, named for Illinois Senator Everett McKinley Dirksen, has a facade that shows motifs of laborers at work. The extra-long windows give the eight-story building the appearance of having just four floors. The building is connected by a walkway with the Hart building next door.

The Hart Senate Office Building, named for Michigan Senator Philip Hart, has an atrium containing Alexander Calder's *Mountains and Clouds,* the only work by Calder that combines both statuary and a mobile. The piece was completed in 1976, the year Calder died.

Senate offices are open Monday through Friday from 8 am to 6 pm and on Saturdays from 9 am to 1 pm. Visitors arriving after 6 pm must register.

Private subways connect all of these buildings with the Capitol building.

Just east of the Hart Senate Office Building is the Sewall-Belmont House. A repository for suffragist and feminist history, the **Sewall-Belmont House** on the northwest corner of 2nd St NE and Constitution Ave is open to the public Tuesday through Friday from 10 am to 3 pm and on Saturdays and Sundays from noon to 4 pm, March through October only.

Headquarters of the National Woman's Party, whose members have included such noted feminists as Kathryn Hepburn, Gloria Swanson, Margaret Mead, Mary Pickford, and Georgia O'Keefe are on the ground floor. The tourist entrance in on the second floor, where docent-guided tours are available throughout the day on request. Admission is free. On the right as you enter is a drawing room, which has silver-hinged doors that came from the home of Daniel Webster. Also on display is Susan B Anthony's rolltop desk, along with a great many paintings and statues.

The Federal/Queen Anne-style house is one of the oldest houses in Washington. One portion dating from 1680 was incorporated into the present house, which was built by Robert Sewall in 1800. Albert Gallatin, Secretary of the Treasury under Madison and Jefferson, rented the house from 1803 to 1813. It was Gallatin who arranged the financing that enabled the United States to make the Louisiana Purchase, effectively doubling the size of the country. Some damage to the house occurred when it was set afire by the British in 1814, but the property remained in the Sewall family for 123 years. The Belmont designation pays homage to Alva Belmont, who was once married to Cornelius Vanderbilt II. She was a major benefactor to the National Woman's Party. Alice Paul, founder of the National Woman's Party in 1913 and the author of the Constitution's original Equal Rights Amendment, lived in this house from 1929 to 1972. Paul was jailed seven times in the United States and Great Britain for her efforts on behalf of women's suffrage.

After touring the Sewall-Belmont House, return westward along Constitution Ave. You will pass the row of Senate Office Buildings before coming to a charming park called Capitol Plaza (not to be confused with the plaza of the same name where you started your tour of the Capitol area).

On the western side of the plaza is the **Robert A Taft Memorial**, which consists of a statue and a bell tower. Concerts take place here on an irregular basis.

Continuing west on Constitution Ave, you will come to 3rd St NW, which leads south past the Capitol Reflecting Pool (on your left). Just past the Reflecting Pool, two streets enter 3rd St from the right, Jefferson Dr and Maryland Ave. Angle to the southwest along Maryland Ave for one short block to Independence Ave and there, on the opposite side of the street, you will see the headquarters for Voice of America.

The **Voice of America** (202/619-3919), housed in the same building as the US Information Agency, 330 Independence Ave SW, broadcasts programming designed not only to entertain America's Armed Forces but to provide information and hope to oppressed peoples in countries throughout the world. The largest radio station in the world, its programs are broadcast worldwide over 26 channels in 42 languages. Admission is free, and a 45-minute tour enables you to see the control room, hear part of a feature show, and view a short film. Tours are given at 10:40 am, 1:40 pm, and 2:40 pm Tuesday through Thursday.

Turn left onto Independence Ave and at the next street (1st St) you will find the US Botanic Garden on the northwest corner of the intersection. Admission is free to the **US Botanic Garden** (202/225-8333), which is open daily from 9 am to 5 pm except New Year's Day, Yom Kippur and Christmas. First proposed by George Washington, the garden opened in the center of the Mall in 1820. Today, it occupies a site on the West side of the US Capitol, housed in a conservatory built between 1931 and 1933 along the lines of a 17th-century French orangerie. A series of connected glass-and-stone buildings and greenhouses, the garden is entered through a room centered around two reflecting pool fountains under a skylight. Inside are tropical, subtropical and desert plants, including a large array of orchids. Benches give visitors a place to rest and absorb the beauty around them.

Surrounding the building on three sides is the flagstone Summer Terrace, which overlooks the Capitol's reflecting pool and is graced by white canvas umbella-tables from spring through fall. Soon, a three-acre National Garden is to be added. This new feature is to include an Environmental Learning Center with interactive exhibits, a rose garden containing over 200 varieties, a regional plant collection, and a water garden dedicated to the nation's First Ladies.

A part of the Botanic Garden is **Bartholdi Park**, a mini-park about one city block in size. The centerpiece of the park is a 30-foot cast iron "fountain of light and water" designed by French sculptor Frederic Auguste Bartholdi, creator of the Statue of Liberty. Intended for the 1876 International Exposition in Philadelphia, the fountain was later moved to Washington.

Bartholdi's fountain is crowned by three young sea gods, shown kneeling to catch water in seaweed. Supporting the basin are three classical bronze sea nymphs clad in headdresses of leaves and clinging drapery, clasped at the waist by scallop shells. At the feet of the sea nymphs, water-spouting sea monsters, shells and fish encircle the fountain's base.

Originally lighted by 12 gas lamps, the fountain's lights have been powered by electricity since 1915. Surrounding the fountain are petunias, sunflowers, lilies, morning glories, roses, zinnias, cosmos, and phlox. The park contains tall ornamental grasses, and there are benches sheltered by vine-covered bowers. There also is a touch-and-fragrance garden containing such herbs as pineapple-scented sage.

As you continue walking east along Independence Ave, you will encounter the Rayburn, Longworth and Cannon House office buildings, in that order. Again, unless you have a reason to see your congressman, these buildings are much like any other office buildings and hold little that is of interest to a tourist. House offices are open from Monday through Friday between 8 am and 6 pm and on Saturdays between 8 am and 1 pm. Visitors arriving after 6 pm must register.

The block-long **Rayburn House Office Building** has colorful Ionic columns flanked by two seated statues entitled *Majesty of the Law* and *Spirit of Justice*. If you're ready for a snack, there's also a cafeteria inside.

At the corner of Independence Ave and 1st St SE is the James Madison Memorial Building, one of the three buildings that constitute the Library of Congress.

The **Library of Congress** is the world's largest library. In three separate buildings, over 110 million items are stored on 532 miles of shelves, including over 17 million catalogued books printed in virtually every language. It contains the largest collection of books printed prior to 1500 in the Western Hemisphere, 48 million manuscripts, and 95 million maps and atlases that date from as far back as the mid-14th century. There are 22 reading rooms.

Established by an act of Congress in 1800, the Library now employs a staff of more than 4,000 people. Its Congressional Research Service answers 500,000 requests for information from members of the House and Senate each year. Its Law Library is the research arm of Congress in matters related to foreign law.

Millions of the Librarys records, including its entire card catalog, are now easily accessible via the Internet at www.loc.gov.

The Library of Congress was originally housed in the Capitol building, which was burned and pillaged by the British in 1814. A month later, Thomas Jefferson offered to replenish the loss by offering the Library his own 50-year collection of books, at that time one of finest collections in the United States. Congress accepted the offer in January 1815 and purchased Jefferson's 6,487-volume collection for $23,950.

The Library continued to grow, and when Congress decided to erect a new building to house the expanding collection, a competition was conducted to select the design. The $1,500 prize was awarded to architects John L Smithmeyer and Paul J Pelz for their Italian Renaissance plan in 1886, and the building was built between 1888 and 1897. Horse-drawn wagons then transferred 800 tons of materials from the US Capitol to the new Library. The building was expected to serve the

Library's needs for the ensuing 150 years. Instead, it was filled in just 13. The newest of the Library's three buildings, the **James Madison Memorial Building** is one of the three largest buildings in Washington. The Copyright Office (202/707-3000 or 202/707-6737), a part of the Library of Congress since 1870, is on the 4th floor of the Madison Building. Ainsworth Rand Spofford, the Librarian of Congress, was responsible for Congress' adoption of a copyright law in 1870. The Copyright Office handles 600,000 new registrations each year, and its 45-million card catalog is the largest in the world. An interesting exhibit featuring such things as an original Maltese falcon, masks from *Star Wars*, Bert and Ernie puppets, Barbie dolls, posters, and similar items is open to the public daily from 8:30 am to 5 pm.

Just north of the Madison Building is the Thomas Jefferson Building, the first of the Library's three buildings to be built. Until 1980, the **Thomas Jefferson Building**, 10 1st St SE, was known simply as the Main Building. After a 10-year, $81.5 million renovation, the Jefferson Building was reopened to the public in 1997. It stands on grounds originally landscaped by Frederick Law Olmstead and is set off by the Neptune Plaza and fountain, installed in 1898. Three massive bronze doors, *Tradition, Writing* and *Printing*, protect the front entrance. There are floor mosaics of Italian marble and allegorical paintings on the overhead vaults. The building contains more than 100 murals and 42 granite sculptures.

The Main Reading Room rests beneath a 160-foot, 23-carat gilded dome. Creamy Italian marble, rosy Algerian marble, and gray Tennessee marble offset the building's terra cotta walls. Columns capped by female figures representing art, commerce, religion, law, poetry and philosophy are flanked by statues of Shakespeare, Homer, Bacon, Beethoven, Newton, and Moses.

The marble Great Hall rises 75 feet to a stained glass ceiling and exhibits more than 200 of the Library's rarest and most interesting items in an exhibit called "Treasures of the Library of Congress." There is one of the three perfect vellum copies of the 1455 Gutenberg Bible in the world, the Giant Bible of Mainz, and manuscripts by Bach, Beethoven and Brahms. Thomas Jefferson's rough draft of the Declaration of Independence is there with marginal notations by Benjamin Franklin and John Adams. Tours of the Great Hall are given Monday through Saturday at 11:30 am, 1 pm, 2:30 pm, and 4 pm.

Other exhibits include the first book ever printed in the United States, the earliest surviving American photographic portrait, the first Disney comic book, and the first baseball cards. The Library has the magic books of Harry Houdini, two drafts of Lincoln's Gettysburg Address, some of George Washington's letters, and the papers of such famous personalities as Sigmund Freud, Alexander Graham Bell, Orville and Wilbur Wright, and Groucho Marx.

Visitors can listen to the voice of Theodore Roosevelt and hear the music of Duke Ellington. There are transcriptions of thousands of hours of radio programming dating from 1926. In all, there are over two million audio discs, tapes, and talking books, plus 3.5 million pieces of music, plus musical instruments from the 1700s that include Stradivarius violins, violas, and cellos. Visual matter includes 13 million prints and photographs, as well as 700,000 movies and videotapes, including the earliest motion picture print made by Thomas Edison in 1893. More items are being added to the Library's collection at the rate of 7,000 items every working day.

To the east of the Jefferson Building, on the northeast corner of 2nd St and Independence Ave, is the John Adams Building, the third building currently occupied by the Library of Congress.

Younger than the Jefferson Building but older than the Madison Building, until 1980 the Library of Congress' **John Adams Building** was known simply as "The Annex." An art deco building faced with white Georgia marble, the building was built in 1939 to absorb the overflow from the original Library building next door.

Now walk north along 2nd St. At the next intersection (E Capitol St), turn to the right. To your right will be the Folger Library.

The **Folger Library** is between 2nd St and 3rd St SE at 201 E Capitol St. Built in 1930 and opened in 1932, the library was founded by Henry'Clay Folger, a Standard Oil executive, and his wife Emily, who together gathered the world's largest collection of Shakespeare's printed works. The collection includes some 250,000 books, 100,000 of which are quite rare.

The building has a neoclassical Georgian marble facade decorated with nine bas-relief scenes from Shakespeare's plays. The oak-paneled Great Hall terminates at an Elizabethan innyard theater that is used for concerts and similar events. The 243-seat theatre is an authentic model of an Elizabethan theatre. The venue for Washington's Shakespeare Theatre group until it moved to larger facilities in the Lansburgh Building at 450 7th St NW in 1992, the theater continues to host a selection of smaller works that are performed here.

There are exhibits of costumes, Renaissance musical instruments, and playbills. A statue of Puck is located in the west garden, and the

Elizabethan garden on the east side of the building contains many plants and herbs of the Shakespearean era, including many that were mentioned in Shakespeare's plays. Docent-led tours identify the plants...and the plays in which they are mentioned...at 10 and 11 am on the third Saturday of each month from April to October.

Exit the Folger Library onto E Capitol St and turn left. That will take you back to the Capitol Plaza, where you began your walking tour of the nation's Capitol and its environs. If your legs have enough strength left in them, there are a number of other interesting sites located just south and east of the Capitol.

The red brick **Eastern Market** (202/546-2698) at 7th St SE and C St has been a tradition in Washington since 1873. It is open from Tuesday through Sunday. One of the city's oldest farmers' markets, it features fresh meats, produce and baked goods, and is held every Saturday morning during the season. A flea market is held every Sunday.

Directly across the street from the market at 222 7th St SE, is **Tunnicliff's Tavern** ($$, 202/546-3663). Named for an earlier tavern that operated in the area around 1796, the present tavern opened in 1988, serving breakfast, lunch, and dinner. There is an outdoor cafe and a partly set-apart dining room that is often frequented by local dignitaries. The restaurant cultivates a Mardi Gras atmosphere and serves such New Orleans favorites as po' boys, gumbo and fried oysters. Live music is provided on Saturday nights.

The **Emancipation Statue** at the West end of Lincoln Park on E Capitol St between 11th St and 13th St NE depicts Arthur Alexander, the last slave captured under the Fugitive Slave Law, breaking the chains of slavery while Abraham Lincoln reads the Emancipation Proclamation. Created by Thomas Ball, the statue was paid for by emancipated slaves and was dedicated in 1876 with Frederick Douglass in attendance.

The Mary McLeod Bethune Memorial, the first memorial honoring a black American in Washington, also is located in Lincoln Park.

Ebenezer Methodist Church (202/441-1415) at 420 D St SE is open Monday through Friday between 8:30 am and 3 pm. In 1863, this was the site of the first public school for African-Americans. The church now houses the school's archives.

The **Congressional Cemetery** at 1801 E St SE (202/543-0539) was the capital's first cemetery (Metro: Stadium-Armory). Covering 30 acres, it dates from 1807 and contains a great many pieces of Victorian statuary. John Philip Sousa, photographer Matthew Brady, Indian chiefs Pushmataha and Taza, and one-time FBI Director J Edgar Hoover are among those who are buried there.

Guided tours are conducted by appointment.

Lodging

For a convenient place to stay, it's hard to top the **Hyatt Regency Washington on Capitol Hill** ($$-$$$, 202/737-1234 or 800/233-1234; www.hyatt.com), 400 New Jersey Ave NW, which is just two blocks from the Capitol and two blocks from Union Station. The 11-story hotel has 834 rooms and 31 suites, and the lobby features a five-story atrium. There are glass elevators and a number of other niceties, including a gift and sundries shop, a lobby lounge featuring music videos and a pool table, a business center, a health club, and a heated indoor pool. Indoor valet parking is provided.

A more economical choice would be the **Best Western Downtown on Capitol Hill** ($, 202/842-4467 or 800/242-4831) at 724 3rd St NW. This is a smaller establishment (58 rooms) and a little less convenient (four blocks to Union Station and the Capitol), but it does offer a complimentary continental breakfast, free parking, and a free morning newspaper. The house restaurant, **The Nuwadee** ($) serves Asian food for lunch and dinner, and it offers both live music and dancing.

Priced in the mid-range is the **Capitol Hill Suites** ($-$$, 202/543-6000 or 800/424-9165) at 200 C St SE. There are 152 units, all suites, and the location is excellent—right next door to the Library of Congress, two blocks from the Capitol, and only one block from the Metro station. Kitchens and kitchenettes are available for added economy, and complimentary coffee, juice and muffins are provided each morning, along with the newspaper. There also are laundry facilities on the premises, as well as valet parking.

A little more pricey is **Holiday Inn on the Hill** ($$-$$$, 202/638-1616 or 800/638-1116), 415 New Jersey Ave NW. Located just two blocks from Union Station, the inn has 341 rooms, some located on non-smoking floors. There are an exercise room, a large outdoor rooftop swimming pool, a cocktail lounge, a coin-operated laundry, and underground parking. An all-you-can-eat breakfast is served every morning.

Arts & culture

The **Library of Congress** offers a year-around program of concerts (202/707-5502), lectures and poetry readings (202/707-5394), and a folklife program (202/707-6590). Classic, rare, and unusual films are shown in the Library's **Mary Pickford Theater** (202/707-5677).

The **Folger Library**, although no longer serving as the venue for Washington's Shakespeare Theatre group, continues to present smaller works in its charming Elizabethan innyard theater.

Food & drink

If you enjoy Greek food, you will love **Taverna—The Greek Islands** ($$, 202/547-8360) at 305 Pennsylvania Ave SE. The menu offers such classical Greek dishes as lamb, moussaka, spanakopita, seafood, and various vegetarian dishes.

Banana Cafe & Piano Bar ($$, 202/543-5906), 500 8th St SE, has a Caribbean atmosphere—Cuban music, mango margaritas, Latin artwork, and "criollo" Cuban and Puerto Rican cuisine, although Tex-Mex cuisine "with an upscale flair" is also available. Dancing is featured in the piano bar. Lunch is served on weekdays from 11:30 am to 2:30 pm, and dinner from Sunday through Thursday between 5 to 10:30 pm and on Saturday until 11:30 pm. A Sunday brunch is offered from 11 am to 3 pm, and outside seating is available in season.

Sherrill's ($, 202/544-2480), 233 Pennsylvania Ave SE, accepts no credit cards but it has been pleasing customers with home-cooked meals since 1922. It is open Monday through Friday from 6 am to 7 pm and on Saturdays, Sundays and holidays from 7 am to 6:30 pm. Enjoy the vintage soda counter, where you can still get a good, old-fashioned milk shake.

Inside the Hyatt Regency (see lodging) is the **Park Promenade** restaurant ($$), which serves American-style food at breakfast, lunch and dinner, while the rooftop **Capitol View Restaurant** ($$-$$$) offers beautiful views of the Capitol building nearby.

Visitors can get a bite to eat in the **House of Representatives Restaurant** ($, 202/225-6300), also called the Members' Dining Room, which is located in Room H118 in the south end of the Capitol.

In the basement of the Supreme Court building is the little **Supreme Court Cafeteria** ($, 202/479-3246), which serves breakfast and lunch. Open Monday through Friday between 7:30 and 10:30 am and between 11:30 am and 2 pm, the cafeteria serves a different ethnic cuisine each Wednesday. Reservations and credit cards are not accepted.

In the Dirksen Senate Office Building, the **South Buffet Room** ($-$$, 202/224-4249) at 1st St and C St NE is a marble-colonnaded art deco dining room with leather chairs and white-linened tables that serves an excellent buffet from Monday through Friday between 11:30 am and 2:30 pm.

The **Library of Congress Cafeteria** ($, 202/554-4114 or 202/707-8300) is is open Monday through Friday from 9:30 to 10:30 am and from 12:30 to 2 pm (lighter fare can be purchased up to 3:30 pm) and has a wall of windows overlooking the city. There always is a salad bar at lunch time, plus hot main dishes, deli sandwiches, and desserts. Reservations and credit cards are not accepted.

Events

The **Folger Library** presents occasional concerts, literary readings, lectures, and family programs throughout the year. The Folger Consort continues to work there, and the library remains the venue for the annual Pen-Faulkner Awards.

Union Station

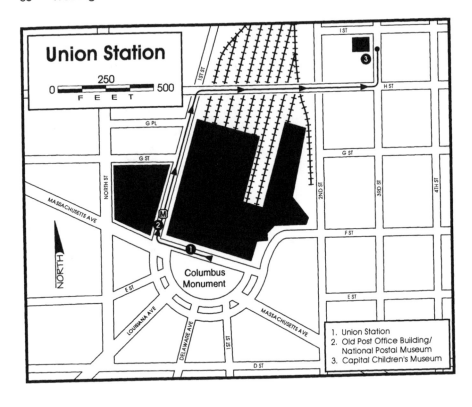

Union Station

0 — 250 — 500
FEET

NORTH

G PL

G ST

NORTH ST

MASSACHUSETTS AVE

1ST ST

2ND ST

3RD ST

4TH ST

I ST

H ST

G ST

F ST

E ST

M

2

1

Columbus
Monument

E ST

LOUISIANA AVE

DELAWARE AVE

1ST ST

MASSACHUSETTS AVE

D ST

1. Union Station
2. Old Post Office Building/
   National Postal Museum
3. Capital Children's Museum

Union Station

Many of the locals consider Union Station to be a part of Capitol Hill, and while that may be true geographically, it also can be argued that the area around Union Station seems more like the barrio on the edge of town than a part of the town itself.

When the station was built in 1907, railroads were at their peak...and it was the largest, most awesome railroad station in the world. But over the years, as rail travel diminished in popularity and air travel came to the fore, Union Station and the neighborhood in which it sits began a process of slow deterioration. So bad did the situation become that parts of the building actually began to collapse, and in 1981, the place was shut down and closed to the public. Only then did Congress take steps to restore the gigantic old structure.

Now, Union Station is again one of the must-see sites in the nation's capital, particularly if one likes to shop, is interested in stamp-collecting, has young children in tow, or is looking for a good restaurant in the area. Highlights in the area immediately outside the station include the **National Postal Museum**, located in the **Old Post Office Building**, and the **Capital Children's Museum**.

Information
Union Station is located at 50 Massachusetts Ave NE (202/289-1908, www.lasalle.com/union). A Visitor Information Center is located in the center of the Union Station's Main Hall. The main hall is open between 10 am and 9 pm Monday through Saturday and between noon and 6 pm on Sundays.

The **National Postal Museum** (202/357-2700 or 202/357-1729 TDD; www.si.edu) is open daily from 10 am to 5:30 pm except for Christmas; admission is free.

The **Capital Children's Museum** (202/675-4120; www.ccm.org) at 800 3rd St NE is open daily from 10 am to 5 pm, but closed on New Year's Day, Easter, Thanksgiving, and Christmas. Admission is $6 ($4 for seniors), but free for children under two.

Getting there
The best way to arrive is of course by train. The Metro stop is called—logically enough—Union Station. If you arrive by car, park in the lot at the back of the station; merchants inside will validate your ticket for up to two hours of free parking.

First steps
Stop at the information desk in the **National Postal Museum** to get free copies of *A Self-Guided Tour for Very Young Visitors* and *Check It Out!* Both booklets contain a great deal of useful and interesting information.

Tours
The **National Postal Museum** offers free guided tours at 11 am, 1 pm and 2 pm daily.

Seasonal highlights
A Halloween Monster Bash (202/675-4125) is presented in the **Capital Children's Theater** every year on October 31.

Union Station. *Begin your walking tour where Louisiana Ave, Delaware Ave and 1st St NE all converge on a semicircular plaza. Before you stands the entrance to the Union Station.*

Chicago architect Daniel H Burnham modeled his beaux arts "Temple of Transport" after the Baths of Diocletian and the Arch of Constantine in Rome. A hundred stone eagles decorate the facade, while the interior is ornamented with graceful 50-foot Constantinian arches, rich Honduran mahogany, marble walls and floors, and coffered ceilings that are embellished with half a million dollars' worth of 22-karat gold leaf.

The Main Hall has a 96-foot barrel-vault ceiling and a balcony that is adorned with 36 sculptures of Roman legionnaires created by August Saint-Gaudens. This is the place where Gen John J Pershing was welcomed on his return from France, where Rear Adm Richard Byrd was greeted on his return from the South Pole, and where thousands of mourners met the train bearing President Franklin Delano Roosevelt's body on its return from Georgia.

More than 65,000 people a day pass through the station, which once again serves railroad passengers from every section of the country. In the main hall you'll find 130 upscale shops on three levels. The shopping facilities also include a bank, ATMs, an international money exchange, an Amtrak ticket counter, a car-rental agency, and a flower stand. On the lower level is a nine-screen movie theater and an international food court.

Located near Gate C is a bronze statue of A Philip Randolph, founder of the Sleeping Car Porters Union and the civil rights activist who organized the 1963 March on Washington.

Exit Union Station onto Massachusetts Ave and turn right. Step across 1st St NE and you will find yourself in front of the Old Post Office Building.

Built in 1914, the **Old Post Office Building** presents an exterior embellished with fancy stonework, massive arches, and turrets inspired by the Romanesque cathedrals of 12th-century France.

On the lower level of the Old Post Office Building is the **National Postal Museum**, one of the Smithsonian Institution's dazzling specialized museums. Opened in 1993, the museum consists of five major galleries, all on one floor. It's a wonderful place to wander about on your own, but if you are interested in a free guided tour, inquire at the information desk. The interactive museum specializes in postal history and philately, and there are more than 40 hands-on interactive exhibits that trace America's postal history from 1673, roughly 170 years before there were such things as stamps, envelopes and mailboxes.

More than 16 million objects are on display in the museum, including an almost-overwhelming 55,000 postage stamps from countries all over the world. The museum's Library Research Center (202/633-9370) contains over 40,000 volumes and manuscripts, but is open by appointment only. Nickelodeon films show train wrecks and train robberies. There are video games and some 40 videos related to postal matters. Visitors can create their own postcards.

The central gallery has an enormous exhibit called "Moving the Mail" which includes an 1851 mail/passenger coach, railway mail cars, three vintage mail planes hanging from the 90-foot atrium ceiling, and a Ford Model A mail truck equipped with skis. Also included is a WW I bomber that was converted to a mail plane.

Several of the museum's exhibits deal with the Pony Express, a popular and fascinating piece of postal history that was actually only in operation for only two years. A display in the Civil War section tells about Henry "Box" Brown, a slave who had himself "mailed" from Richmond, VA to a Pennsylvania abolitionist in 1856. Another describes the life of Owney, the Postal Dog.

Docents in period attire play the roles of Aaron Montgomery Ward or LL Bean, who talk about the benefits of ordering merchandise by mail (85% of everything that goes into the mailbox is classified as direct mail sales material).

The building also contains a Post Office, a restaurant, and a museum shop.

Exit the museum onto 1st St NE and turn left. Go two short blocks to H St and turn right. At 3rd St NE, turn left for another short block. On the southwest corner of 3rd St and I St NE, you will find the Capital Children's Museum.

Interesting enough to fascinate people of all ages, the **Capital Children's Museum** is extremely popular with kids between 2 and 14, who are welcomed at the front door by a giant cootie bug. Here, kids can touch, smell, taste, and sometimes wear many of the exhibits. They can produce their own TV show, star in their own cartoon, make kid-sized bubbles in the Bubble Room, or slide down a fire pole. They can hide in an Ice Age cave, explore beneath a city street, drive a bus, or climb a Mayan pyramid. They can send a message on a ship's blinker or explore with chemistry, using everyday objects such as bananas and shaving cream. Or they can don Mexican clothes, make a tortilla, grind Mexican chocolate beans, and dance in a Mexican plaza.

In the Tatami Room, children take off their shoes, sit at a *kotatsu* (a low wooden table), and eat "pretend" octopus and seaweed with chopsticks. A docent gives a 20-minute talk about twice an hour, and a video ("My Day") describes a day in the life of a Japanese schoolboy.

Other museum activities include crafts, computer projects, and cooking.

Lodging

The **Phoenix Park Hotel** ($$-$$$, 202/638-6900 or 800/824-5419), 520 N Capitol St NW, is a delightful European-style boutique hotel containing 150 rooms, which include nine suites. Located one block from Union Station and two blocks from the Capitol, it is convenient to the sites on the tour, and amenities include a complimentary morning newspaper, robe, valet garage parking, a small fitness center, and an on-site restaurant.

Washington Court on Capital Hill ($$-$$$, 202/628-2100 or 800/321-3010), 525 New Jersey Ave NW, is larger (264 rooms), but equally convenient. Located just two blocks from the Capitol, its amenities include a full American breakfast, three telephones, TV in a marble bathroom, the morning newspaper, a multilingual staff, valet parking, a business center, a fitness center, and an on-site restaurant.

Arts & culture

Performances are staged throughout the year in the **Capital Children's Museum**'s Storyteller Theater (202/675-4120).

Food & drink

Inside Union Station you'll find an international food court and five full-service restaurants. In the West Hall, **America** ($-$$, 202/682-9555), features six dining rooms on four levels. The food is American-style and features over 200 dishes associated with various regions of the country, such as Kansas T-bone steak and fries, Navajo fry bread, New Mexico's blue corn chicken enchiladas, chicken "lips," Sonoma Valley vegetarian pizza, and Vermont goat cheese salad. Back-lit maps of states decorate the walls, while some of the windows provide lovely views of the

Capitol. A balcony table provides an interesting view of Union Station's Main Hall. The restaurant is known as a great place to spot celebrities.

B Smith's Restaurant ($$-$$$, 202/289-6188), is in the east hall of the station. Lunch and dinner are served between 11:30 am and 4 pm and again from 5 pm to midnight Monday through Saturday. A Sunday brunch is offered between 11:30 am and 8 pm. Once the Presidential Suite in which various dignitaries were entertained, the restaurant has an elegant 29-foot domed ceiling hung with chandeliers, mahogany doors, white marble floors, gold-leaf moldings, and towering Ionic columns. Mellow background music is provided to accompany the Southern-style cuisine "with Cajun-Creole nuances," such as jambalaya, ribs, grilled lamb chops, and the "Swamp Thing," which is a medley of fresh seafood tossed with Southern-style greens. Live jazz entertainment in the evenings makes this a popular after-hours haunt as well.

La Brasserie ($$, 202/546-9154), 239 Massachusetts Ave NE, occupies two floors of adjoining townhouses. Outdoor dining is available in season. The house specialty is French cuisine.

La Colline ($-$$, 202/737-0400), 400 N Capitol St NW, is directly across from Union Station and is open for breakfast and lunch from Monday through Friday and for dinner from Monday through Saturday. Noted as one of city's best French restaurants, the menu stresses Chef Robert Greault's seafood, duck, and veal with chanterelle mushrooms. Seating is in comfortable high-backed leather booths that lend privacy to your meal. Complimentary garage parking is provided after 5 pm.

Cafe Berlin ($$, 202/543-7656), 322 Massachusetts Ave NE, is located just three blocks from the Union Station Metro and has the style and atmosphere of old Germany, reflected in such German dishes as herringstrip, gently marinated herring tidbits with apples, onions and sour cream; rahmschnitzel, the tender center cut of veal; and jagerschnitzel Cafe Berlin, tender pork steak sauteed and topped with spicy bacon and mushroom sauce. The restaurant occupies two nicely-decorated rooms on the bottom level of a Capitol Hill townhouse, and during the Summer months, the front terrace provides outdoor service. Hours are 11 am to 10 pm from Monday through Thursday, from 11 am to 11 pm on Friday and Saturday, and from 4 to 10 pm on Sunday.

2 Quail ($$, 202/543-8030), 320 Massachusetts Ave NE, is next door to the Cafe Berlin. Elegant and romantic like a quiet country inn, it features such delicacies as an appetizer of mushroom caps stuffed with crab and artichokes, blue cheese and apple salad and an entree of baked chicken breast stuffed with cornbread and pecans. Steak and quail also can be found on the menu. The restaurant is open from 11:30 am to 10 pm Monday through Thursday, 11:30 am to 11 pm on Friday, noon to 11 pm on Saturday, and 4 to 10 pm on Sunday.

Nightlife

Exercise caution walking the streets in this area after dark.

Capitol City Brewing Company ($, 202/842-2337), 2 Massachusetts Ave NE, is Washington's original and only microbrewery restaurant. Its outdoor terrace is reminiscent of the old German biergartens. American food is served, but the house specialty is a variety of English-style ales and German lagers.

The Dubliner ($$, 202/737-3773), 520 N Capitol St NW, is located in the Phoenix Park Hotel. A wood-paneled pub, it offers live Irish music nightly and calls itself "the nation's largest purveyor of Guinness Stout." Breakfast (weekends only), lunch and dinner also are served.

Events

Special weekend activities are offered at the Capital Children's Museum, and various workshops and classes are held in the museum's Media Works Center.

The National Mall

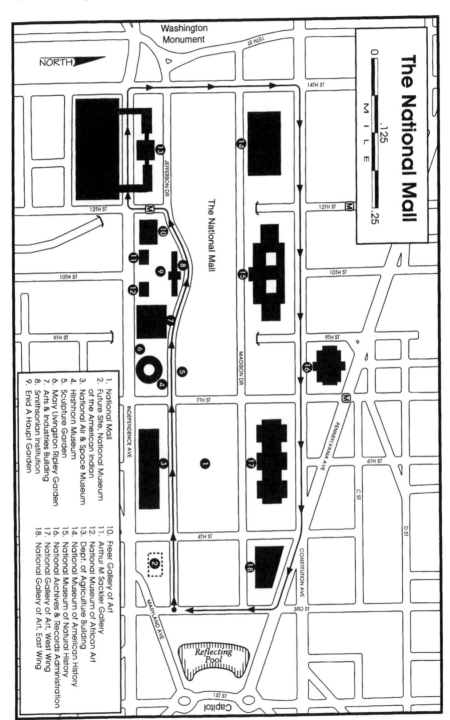

The National Mall

NORTH

Washington Monument

The National Mall

MILE

0   .125   .25

1. National Mall
2. Future Site, National Museum
   of the American Indian
3. National Air & Space Museum
4. Hirshhorn Museum
5. Sculpture Garden
6. Mary Livingston Ripley Garden
7. Arts & Industries Building
8. Smithsonian Institution
9. Enid A Haupt Garden
10. Freer Gallery of Art
11. Arthur M Sackler Gallery
12. National Museum of African Art
13. Dept. of Agriculture Building
14. National Museum of American History
15. National Museum of Natural History
16. National Archives & Records Administration
17. National Gallery of Art, West Wing
18. National Gallery of Art, East Wing

Reflecting Pool

Capitol

The National Mall

Stand beside the US Capitol reflecting pool at 3rd St and Jefferson Dr NW and look to the west. The green expanse before you is The National Mall. In the distance, you can see the Washington Monument, which effectively divides the Mall into two parts: the Smithsonian museums on the eastern side and the nation's vast collection of monuments and memorials on the western side. It is the site of frequent concerts, celebrations, picnics, softball games, and Frisbee contests.

Pierre L'Enfant's "Grand Esplanade" is two and one-half miles long and 300 feet wide, a gigantic swath of green that links Constitution Ave and Independence Ave SW. At the end nearest the Capitol building, The Mall is lined with 200-year-old American elm trees.

At 100 Jefferson Dr SW, more or less in the middle of the eastern portion of The Mall stands the headquarters of The Smithsonian Institution. It was founded in 1829 with a bequest from James Smithson, a wealthy Englishman who never set foot in the United States. Smithson wanted "to found at Washington...an establishment for the increase and diffusion of knowledge," and for that purpose left the United States 105 bags of gold sovereigns worth $508,318.46—an enormous fortune at that time.

Typically, it took the American government a decade to decide what to do with Smithson's gift. Turn it down? Build a university? Build an observatory...a library...a teachers' college? In 1846, Congress finally decided on the program that is in place today, and the cornerstone for the first building was laid in 1847.

Today, there are 14 Smithsonian museums in Washington, DC and two in New York City. Nine of the museums in Washington are located on The Mall; the other five include the National Zoo, the Anacostia Museum on the southeastern edge of town, the National Museum of American Art, the National Postal Museum, and the Renwick Gallery. The Smithsonian has been around for such a long period of time that it is interesting to discover that many of the museums in Washington are relatively new. The Hirshhorn Museum & Sculpture Garden, for example, was opened in 1974, the National Air & Space Museum opened in 1976, and both the Arthur M Sackler Gallery and the National Museum of African Art opened in 1987.

According to the Greater Washington Board of Trade: "If all the treasures of the Smithsonian Institution were lined up in one long exhibit, and you spent one second looking at each item, it would take you more than 2.5 years of around-the-clock touring to see them all." Obviously, there is no way a person can do justice to all of the museums on The Mall in a single visit. Indeed, a day is hardly enough to see all that any one of the 14 museums has to offer. Be selective. You will get a great deal more out of your trip if you identify the subjects that interest you the most, concentrate on them, and defer the rest for (hopefully) another visit.

Information

Virtually all of the Smithsonian museums are open from 10 am to 5:30 pm during most of the year, but the Summertime hours are extended each year by a vote of Congress—not surprising since 15 million people visit the museums during the months of June, July and August alone. Almost all of the museums are closed on Christmas.

The **Smithsonian Institution** (202/357-2700, 202/357-2020 recording, 202/633-9126 Spanish, or 202/357-1729 TDD; www.si.edu) is at 1000 Jefferson Dr SW.

The **National Air & Space Museum** (202/357-1400 or 202/357-1505 TTY) is at 6th St and Independence Ave SW.

The **Hirshhorn Museum & Sculpture Garden** (202/357-3235 or 202/357-1729 TDD) is at 7th St and Independence Ave SW is

The **Arts & Industries Building** (202/357-2700 or 202/357-1729 TTY) is at 900 Jefferson Dr SW.

The **Enid A Haupt Garden** (202/357-2700) is 10th St and Independence Ave SW.

The **Freer Gallery of Art** (202/357-4880 or 202/786-2374 TTY, www.si.edu /asia) is at Jefferson Dr and 12th St SW.

The **Arthur M Sackler Gallery** (202/357-3200 or 202/357-1729 TDD) is at 1050 Independence Ave SW.

The **National Museum of African Art** (202/357-1300 or 202/357-4814 TTY) is at 950 Independence Ave SW.

National Museum of American History (202/371-6671 or 202/357-1729 TTY)

The **National Museum of Natural History** (202/357-2747 or 202/633-9287 TTY) is at 10th St and Constitution Ave NW.

The **Enid A Haupt Garden** (202/357-2700) is open between 7 am and 8 pm from Memorial Day until Labor Day, and from 7 am to 5:45 pm the rest of the year.

The **National Archives & Records Administration** (202/501-5000 and 202/501-5404 TDD). The Central Research and Microfilm Research rooms are open Monday through Saturday except on holidays. Hours are 8:45 am until 5 pm on weekends (9 pm on Tuesdays and Thursdays) and 8:45 am to 4:45 pm on Saturdays. Those who are interested should use the entrance at Pennsylvania Ave and 8th St NW and stop in Room 460 for guidance before they start. A photo ID also will be required. A museum shop is in the lobby.

Archives II (301/713-6800) was built in 1994 to house the Archives' overflow. It occupies a 33-acre site in College Park, MD near the University of Maryland and is open on Mondays and Wednesday from 8:45 am to 5 pm; on Tuesdays, Thursdays and Fridays from 8:45 am to 9 pm; and on Saturdays from 8:45 am to 4:45 pm.

The **National Gallery of Art** (202/737-4215 or 202/842-6176 TDD; www.nga.gov) occupies two buildings on Constitution Ave

The **Department of Agriculture** (202/720-2791 or 202/720-5505).

Getting there

The Mall and the numerous Smithsonian museums cover a substantial portion of midtown Washington. A number of Metro stations serve the area quite well. In order of convenience to the average tourist, they include the Smithsonian, L'Enfant Plaza, Federal Triangle, Archives/Navy Memorial, and Judiciary Square stations.

First steps

The *Washington Post Weekend Magazine*, published on the third Friday of every month, always carries a "Smithsonian Sampler" section—a full page listing the special events to be coming up at the Smithsonian.

There is an information kiosk on **The Mall** and there are information desks in many of the **Smithsonian** buildings, including the Smithsonian "Castle," the Institution's main building. As you enter the Castle, ask for a copy of *10 Tips to Visiting the Smithsonian With Children*, which includes a map, family highlights, a quiz, and other interesting material. It's a worthwhile guide, even if you don't have any children with you.

At the **Freer Gallery**, ask for a free copy of their colorful workbooks *Peacocks, Patterns, and Paint; Ganesha's Guide to the Galleries*, which features an elephant-headed Hindu god explaining how museums work; *The Princess and the Peacocks*, which tells the story of the famous Peacock Room; and *Arts of China*, which explains some of the art that was created thousands of years ago.

In the **Arthur M Sackler Gallery**, ask for the free family guide *Getting to Know the Hindu Gods*. The **National Museum of African Art** also has a free gallery guide.

The **National Museum of American History** will give you *Hunt for History*, which outlines a self-guided tour of the facility for families.

Both wings of the **National Gallery of Art** offer free guidebooks. The one in the West wing is called *West Building Highlights*, and the one in the East wing is called *Shapes + Patterns*.

The information desk at the **National Air & Space Museum** can provide you with a floor plan and a list of events, and there also is an information center in the **Arts & Industries Building**.

You can pick up a schedule listing all of the upcoming films, lectures, and workshops to be held in the **National Archives & Records Administration** building at the information desk.

Other sources of information in The Mall and in the various Smithsonian museums can be found in the **Hirshhorn Museum & Sculpture Garden**, and in the **National Museum of Natural History**, which provides visitors with a free floor plan of the facility.

Seasonal highlights

At Easter, a special Easter Egg Hunt for Blind Children is held at the Washington Monument in the middle of The Mall. Children hunt for beeping eggs that they can exchange for prizes.

From September through July, the Discovery Theater (202/357-1500) in the Arts & Industries Building highlights storytelling, music, mime, and puppets for children 12 years old and younger. The programs are held Tuesday through Friday at 10 and 11:30 am and on Saturdays at 11:30 am and 1 pm. Reservations are required and there is a $5 admission charge.

The **National Fourth of July Celebration** (202/619-7222) is held on The Mall and includes a parade, concerts, special events, and fireworks bursting over the Washington Monument.

In late July, a **Latin-American Festival** is held on The Mall.

National Archives & Records Administration stages a multifaceted celebration on September 17, Constitution Day. The US Constitution is put on display, an honor guard ceremony is staged, and a naturalization program is conducted.

The Smithsonian stages an annual **Holiday Celebration** (202/357-2700) in December.

Tours

Tours of the **Smithsonian "Castle"** are provided in English from Friday through Sunday, while Spanish-language tours are offered on the first Saturday of each month.

The **National Air & Space Museum** offers guided tours daily at 10:15 am and at 1 pm. If you prefer, you can rent an audio tour tape ($4.75, $4 for students and seniors) and wander through the museum on your own.

Tours of the **Hirshhorn Museum & Sculpture Garden** are conducted on weekdays at 10:30 am and at noon, and on Sundays at noon and 2 pm.

At the **Enid A Haupt Garden**, free guided tours are conducted on Sundays at 9:30 am during the warm-weather months, weather permitting.

Docent-led tours of the **Arthur M Sackler Gallery** are featured daily, as are daily tours of the **Freer Gallery of Art**.

Similarly, docent-guided tours of the **National Archives & Records Administration** building are offered at 10:15 am and 1:15 pm on weekdays. Children under 16 must be accompanied by an adult, and reservations are required to take the tour (202/501-5205).

Free guided tours of the **National Museum of American History** are offered daily at 10 am and 1 pm, and audiotape tours are available for those who like to stroll about on their own.

At the **National Museum of Natural History**, self-guiding audiotape tours are available for $4.75.

The **National Gallery of Art** offers tours of the West Wing on weekdays at 11:30 am and 3:30 pm, on Saturdays at 10:30 am and 12:30 pm, and on Sundays at 12:30, 2:30 and 4:30 pm. Tours conducted in French, Spanish, German, and Japanese are offered on Tuesdays and Thursdays. Self-guided tour tapes can be rented for $4 (seniors and students $3.50). Tours of the East Wing are available at 10:30 am and 1:30 pm on weekdays and at 11:30 am and 1:30 and 3:30 pm on Saturdays and Sundays.

The National Mall. *A walk along The Mall and a tour of The Smithsonian Institutions are so closely interwoven that we do not attempt to separate them here. Obviously, there is far too much for a person to see in one day...one week...or an entire lifetime. Suffice it to say that the visitor may pick and choose, cramming as much as possible into each day, and returning the next to pick up wherever he or she left off. Start your tour beside the Capitol building at 3rd St and Jefferson Dr and follow Jefferson Dr west.* On your left you will see the future site of the **National Museum of the American Indian,** due to open in 2002 containing exhibits that are temporarily being housed in the Arts & Industries Building.

Next, you will come to the **National Air & Space Museum** at 6th St and Independence Ave SW. Opened in time for America's Bicentennial celebration in 1976, this is the most visited museum in the world. Longer than two football fields, the pink marble structure holds exhibits that center on the history, science and technology of aviation and space flight, as evidenced by the two-level gallery just inside the entrance where a "Milestones of Flight" display exhibits Wilbur and Orville Wright's actual 1903 *Flyer*, Charles Lindbergh's *Spirit of St Louis*, John Glenn's *Friendship 7*, *Gemini 4*, *Apollo 11*, the command module *Columbia*, Chuck Yeager's *Bell X-1*, and a selection of moon rocks.

Also to be found in this museum is *Vega*, the plane flown by Amelia Earhart, the first woman to fly across the Atlantic Ocean; *Chicago*, used to make the first around-the-world flight (which took nearly six months); and the flight suit of Guion "Guy" Bluford, the first African American in space. At the northwest corner of building is the *Enola Gay*, from which the United States dropped the first atom bomb on Hiroshima in 1945.

As you make your way through the museum, you can enter the nose section of an American Airlines DC-7, learn about the evolution of the spacesuit, inspect the Mars landscape, or climb into a full-size Cessna 150 and handle the controls that operate the wings and the tail. On the second floor, three short films make the education process entertaining. The museum also contains a gift shop, a large bookstore, and two restaurants.

Next door at 7th St and Independence Ave SW is the **Hirshhorn Museum & Sculpture Garden**. Built in 1974, it is housed in a cylindrical building with floor-to-ceiling windows and is entered through glass doors near the plaza fountain.

The collections in this museum began with that of a Latvian immigrant, Joseph Hirshhorn, who donated 2,000 pieces of sculpture and 4,000 paintings and drawings to the Smithsonian. The fifth most visited art museum in the United States, the museum now contains one of the finest collections of modern art in the country and one of the best collections of 20th-century sculpture in the world.

There are galleries on the two upper floors of the Hirshhorn. Paintings hang in the galleries of the outer circle while sculptures and comfortable seats fill the inner circle (known as the "ambulatory"). The second floor generally is given to changing exhibits. On the third floor is a gallery containing the works of Francis Bacon, while elsewhere can be found Calder's *black stabile* as well as some works from such noted artists as Jean Dubuffet, Georgia O'Keefe, Jackson Pollock, and Auguste Rodin.

Across Jefferson Dr from the museum is the sunken **Sculpture Garden,** featuring works of the major artists of the 20th century in stone, bronze, and other metals. Next to the garden is the carousel, which operates year-around from 10 am to dusk, weather permitting. Rides cost $1.50.

Between the Arts & Industries Building and the Hirshhorn Museum is the **Mary Livingston Ripley Garden**, which features seasonal plantings and a miniature bulb collection.

More than 200 varieties of herbaceous and woody perennials, numerous shrubs and a number of trees are contained in the garden, as well as seasonal annuals.

Next in line at 900 Jefferson Dr SW is the Smithsonian's **Arts & Industries Building** , an 1881 brick-and-sandstone that was the nation's first national museum. Originally intended to house the exhibits from the country's first World's Fair, the International Exhibition held in conjunction with the Centennial in 1876 (and recreated for the Bicentennial in 1976), the building contains one of the world's foremost collections of Victorian Americana. In the North Hall are items that would have been found in a Victorian home, such as samples of 19th-century clothing, copies of *Uncle Tom's Cabin*, and some of the cookbooks of the day.

The rotunda features changing floral displays and a fountain, while the West Hall contains old-time items like an ice-cream machine, an old telegraph, and a vintage printing press. Also on display are a 45-foot model of the cruiser *USS Antietam*, a restored 1876 Santa Cruz Railroad locomotive engine, actual pieces of Plymouth Rock, and some Lincoln memorabilia.

Changing exhibitions deal with African American and Native American cultures. The museum also contains a retail shop.

Continuing to 1000 Jefferson Dr SW, the next building you will encounter is the **Smithsonian Institution Building,** an enormous red sandstone building known as "the Castle." This building, designed by architect James Renwick, is the headquarters of the Smithsonian Institution.

If you enter from Jefferson Dr, you will see the crypt of the organization's founder, James Smithson, on your left. Smithson was originally buried in Genoa, Italy, but when that cemetery became endangered in 1904, his remains were transfered here.

Helpful is the 20-minute indoctrination video that is shown throughout the day. There are two orientation theatres, as well as scale models of the city, an interactive touch-screen program in six languages, and two large electronic wall maps. There is a 1902 Children's Room in the South Tower, and the building contains a museum shop.

Outside the south side of the building at 10th St and Independence Ave SW is the **Enid A Haupt Garden,** an elegant 4.2-acre Victorian-style garden which may be entered through cast-iron carriage gates flanked by four red sandstone pillars. The garden features elaborate flowerbeds, plant-filled urns, 1870s cast-iron furnishings, flower-filled baskets that hang from 19th-century lampposts, and an ornamental handmade brass sundial. The ornate Downing Urn that sits in an appealing, shaded rest area is a memorial to American landscape artist Andrew Jackson Downing.

On one side of the garden, you can enter through a 9-foot moongate to the Asian "Island Garden," where there are benches and a shaded still pool. On the other side is the "Fountain Garden," inspired by the gardens of Shalimar, where visitors sit on granite seating walls to watch a waterfall cascade into a small pond and there are tiny water channels fed by fountains. Three small shaded terraces are located near the Arts & Industries Building—a haven during the heat of summer.

Although the Haupt Garden is at ground level, it literally provides a rooftop for two adjacent Smithsonian museums: the Sackler Gallery and the African Art Museum, both of which occupy three-story facilities *totally underground*. Both underground museums can be entered through doorways leading off the garden, the entrance to the Sackler Gallery located near the "Island Garden" and the entrance to the African Art Museum near the "Fountain Garden."

Continue walking west along Jefferson Dr to the Freer Gallery. At Jefferson Dr and 12th St SW is the **Freer Gallery of Art**, the first art museum in the Smithsonian, built in 1923. This Italian Renaissance-style building is usually adorned with a number of colorful banners that greet you as you emerge from The Mall exit of the Smithsonian Metro station.

Focusing on the Asian arts, the Freer Gallery began with the donation of a collection by Detroit industrialist Charles L Freer, one of the primary patrons of artist James McNeill Whistler. Its collection of Whistler's works—over 1,200 pieces—is the largest in the world.

Particularly noteworthy is Whistler's *Harmony in Blue and Gold: The Peacock Room*. The actual dining room that you see was painted by Whistler between 1876 and 1877 for Frederick Leyland, a British businessman who commissioned Whistler to decorate the room around Whistler's painting *The Princess from the Land of the Porcelain*. Over the years, the room was moved, piece by piece, from London to Detroit to Washington. Look for Whistler's trademark butterfly signature, located in four places throughout this room.

In addition to the 19th and 20th century American art on display, the gallery contains one of the world's best collections of Near and Far Eastern art. Spanning a period of 6,000 years, the exhibits display Japanese art, Korean ceramics, Buddhist art, South Asian art, Islamic art, and Chinese art. There is a large collection of blue-and-white Oriental porcelain, bronzes, paintings, pottery, ceramic objects, manuscripts, and lacquerware. The building also contains a museum shop.

A new underground exhibition area connects to the Arthur M Sackler Gallery and The National Museum of African Art. *Instead of taking the indoor route, take the opportunity to catch a breath of fresh air and go outside. At the first corner, turn left (south), go one block, and make another left onto Independence Ave. Beneath the Enid A Haupt Garden (described above) you will find entrances to both the Sackler Gallery and the National Museum of African Art.*

At 1050 Independence Ave SW is the entrance to the **Arthur M**

Sackler Gallery, a three-story underground museum opened in 1987 that displays changing exhibitions of Asian art from major collections around the world

Amid plants, fountains and skylights, the exhibits cover Asian art from ancient times to the present including Chinese bronzes, Southeast Asian sculpture, Persian manuscripts, paintings, Japanese lacquerware, a Chinese jade hound, and Iranian silver. Also check out the museum shop.

At 950 Independence Ave SW, also underground, the National Museum of African Art is the country's only national museum dedicated exclusively to African art. Like the Sackler Gallery, it can be entered through a pavilion located in the Haupt Garden.

After being housed in cramped Capitol Hill quarters for a number of years, the museum was moved to its present location in 1987. It is devoted to the collection, study and exhibition of African art from south of the Sahara, which includes carved wooden masks, fertility dolls, Cameroon court figures, royal Benin art, and works from the ancient Nubian city of Kerma. On display are sculptures, textiles, and utilitarian objects of wood and metal, ivory, gold, fired clay, and fiber. The museum also houses the Eliot Elisofon Photographic Archives.

The facility also contains a museum shop and the Warren M Robbins Library (202/357-4875), which is open to researchers by appointment from 10 am to 5 pm on weekdays.

Exit the museum onto Independence Ave, turn right, and walk to 14th St. On the south side of Independence Ave is the Department of Agriculture Building. Exhibitions are often staged here on the Jamie L Whitten Patio. Unless you have an interest in agriculture, however, there's little here to hold your attention.

Go north on 14th St for three blocks to Constitution Ave. The first building on your right will be the National Museum of American History. The National Museum of American History is devoted to the history of science, technology, society, and culture in America. The museum contains some three million objects, including such diverse items as coins, quilts, cars, trains, and computer gadgetry. Also included is one of the country's first Teddy bears, a Victorian dolls' house, Archie Bunker's chair from the *All in the Family* television show, one of Muhammad Ali's boxing gloves, Dorothy's ruby slippers from the *Wizard of Oz* movie, and Nancy Reagan's inaugural gown.

Near the Constitution Ave entrance is a working Post Office that has been relocated from an old-time country store in Headsville, WV.

The first-floor exhibits are geared to science and technology and include, among other things, a 280-ton steam locomotive. On the second floor is material related to America's social and political history. The third floor deals with money, musical instruments, printing, the graphic arts, and the history of the armed forces. On display is the *Philadelphia*, a gunboat built and sunk during the Revolutionary War when Benedict Arnold's fleet of 16 small craft was soundly beaten by the British in 1776, but was raised from the bottom of Lake Champlain in 1935. Also on exhibit are four rare Stradivarius musical instruments, various military medals, and a number of ship models plus an early Thomas Edison lightbulb, and an Edison phonograph.

In the Hands on Science room on the first floor, children over the age of five can don safety goggles and experiment with dry ice, do some DNA profiling, and check the pH levels of various liquids. The room is open Tuesday through Saturday from noon to 3 pm. On the second floor, a Hands on History room contains 30 activities related to life in America between 1780 and 1850. Children can ride (in place) on a high-wheeler bike, harness a (fiberglass) mule, and gin raw cotton on a reproduction of the Eli Whitney cotton gin. This room also is open between noon and 3 pm from Tuesday through Saturday.

Next door as you head east along Constitution Ave is the National Museum of Natural History. A dinosaur topiary will greet you as you arrive at the **National Museum of Natural History** at 10th St and Constitution Ave NW. Opened in 1993 and billed as the place "where natural history lives," the museum has a 4-story, marble-pillared rotunda on the first floor. Also on the ground floor is a display of 300 birds that are native to the eastern United States.

The O Orkin Insect Zoo allows children to crawl through a replica of an African termites' mound, inspect cockroaches and an Amazon walking stick, see bees swarming around a hive, watch ants build a colony, and see giant millipedes. Tarantula feedings are staged on most days. Over a million visitors a year examine such wonders as Big Bob, a tarantula as big as a dinner plate; shrunken heads; and the world's largest bush elephant, standing over 13 feet tall and weighing 8 tons. In all, the museum contains more than 120 million objects.

The Fossil Collection describes ocean creatures from 600 million years ago, exhibits a 70-million-year-old dinosaur egg, and displays skeletons of 100-million-year-old dinosaurs, while the Dinosaur Hall, which has a quetzalcoatlus, the largest known flying reptile, suspended from ceiling, displays a number of juvenile dinosaurs.

In the Sea Life Hall, a life-size (92-foot) blue whale is suspended from the ceiling. You'll also see a model of the giant squid and two 3,000-gallon aquariums, one that demonstrates life on a Caribbean reef and another that shows the sea life in the subarctic waters off Maine. Be sure to watch the accompanying video.

The museum's Janet Annenberg Hooker Hall of Geology, Gems and Minerals opened in 1997 after a two-year, $13 million renovation. Consisting of seven different areas, the exhibition is centered around gemstones, jewelry, and minerals. A video and supporting displays explain such things as mining and plate tectonics. Four mines have been recreated.

Arguably, the centerpiece of the exhibit is the 45.5-carat Hope diamond that is on display in a revolving glass case in the Harry Winston Gallery. Donated in 1958 and valued at $100 million, this "bad luck diamond" was once owned by Evalyn Walsh McLean, a Washington socialite. Visitors also can examine the diamond earrings that were worn by Marie Antoinette on her journey to the guillotine, a necklace containing 374 diamonds and 15 emeralds, moon rocks that were brought back by the Apollo astronauts, and a 1,371-pound meteorite.

The hall contains interactive stations and monitors, while a world map records the activity of every volcano and earthquake that has occurred over the last 40 years.

Another exhibition, *Western Civilization: Origins and Traditions*, has murals, dioramas, and films that explain the beginnings and the legacies of ancient civilizations.

The Ocean Planet exhibit involves a narrated video tour beneath the ocean, with several stops on the way to a descent to 25,000 feet. Plays and puppet shows are a part of the exhibit, helping to make the information more entertaining and memorable for the children. On the East side of the building is a Butterfly Garden.

Other features of the museum include a recently-expanded ground-floor museum shop, a nice bookstore, and a newly-added on-site restaurant called the **National Museum of Natural History Cafeteria** (202/357-2700).

Leaving the museum, continue east along Constitution Ave to the next intersection (9th St). On the northeast corner is the building that houses the National Archives. The **National Archives & Records Administration** occupies a Beaux-Arts building designed by John Russell Pope, architect of the National Gallery and the Jefferson Memorial. Each of the bronze doors at the entrance weighs 6.5 tons and the building contains 72 Corinthian columns. In the Rotunda, armed guards surround the original

Declaration of Independence, portions of the US Constitution, and the Bill of Rights, displayed in helium-filled cases that are lowered into a bomb- and fire-proof, 55-ton steel-and-concrete vault each night for safekeeping.

Over 4 billion paper documents, 6 million photographs, and 91 million feet of motion picture film are stored in this building, including a 1297 version of the Magna Carta.

What will the Archives display next? Believe it or not, the Archives' officials are currently negotiating with the Special Prosecutor's Office to obtain Monica Lewinsky's semen-stained dress.

Although less spectacular perhaps, thousands of old newsreels can be screened in the motion picture, sound and video branch of the Archives, which is located on the ground floor. A prior appointment is necessary.

A central depository where two centuries of Census figures, military records, immigrant passenger lists, and other valuable records are stored, the Archives are often used for genealogy research (202/501-5402). Alex Haley began to research his roots here...and others can do the same.

Cross back to the south side of Constitution Ave and turn left. Between 3rd St and 7th St on Constitution Ave NW are two buildings that constitute the **National Gallery of Art.** The first building, the 500,000 sq ft. **West Wing** was constructed in 1941. Designed by John Russell Pope, the mid-19th-century Greek Revival building was funded by Pittsburgh financier Andrew Mellon, who also donated his personal collection to the gallery.

One of the world's greatest art museums, the National Gallery attracts more than 6 million visitors a year. More than 35,000 works exhibited within the Gallery represent over two centuries of American art. George Catlin's 19th-century American Indian paintings are particularly popular. Exhibits are presented chronologically, beginning on the main floor of the West Wing.

A Micro Gallery containing 13 interactive computer screens can be found near The Mall entrance. A bronze statue of *Mercury* is located in the rotunda. Two colonnaded garden courts with upholstered chairs are located under arched skylights, where they overlook some fountains.

Along with the American art that is included in the collection are numerous European paintings and some sculpture of the 13th through 19th centuries. Some of the more notable works include Botticelli's *Portrait of a Youth*, Raphael's *St George and the Dragon*, Holbein's portrait of *Edward VI as a Child*, and Renoir's *a Girl With a Watering Can*. Also shown are the works of Titian, Rembrandt and Anthony van Dyck., as well as the only Leonardo da Vinci painting outside of Europe. And yes, there are shops where you can buy some souvenirs.

A new (1997) six-acre outdoor sculpture garden is on 7th St opposite the West Wing. It includes works by Calder and Noguchi, plus a 24-ft bronze spider by Louise Bourgeois.

Across the street from the West Wing at 4th St and Constitution Ave NW is the East Wing of the National Gallery. Its only above-ground entrance is on 4th St. Designed by IM Pei, the architect who constructed a gigantic glass pyramid next to the Louvre in Paris, the building is a marble trapezoid divided into two interconnected triangles. Opened in 1978, it features the bronze sculpture *Venus and Cupid*. The ground-level central court has a 3-story Alexander Calder mobile and Joan Miro's enormous tapestry *Woman*.

Along with 20th-century works by Alexander Calder, Pablo Picasso, and Jackson Pollock, the building contains Lichtenstein's *Look Mickey* and Matisse's *Large Composition With Masks*. There is a magnificent research library and an extensive photographic archives.

From the upper level, climb the 25 steps to the Tower level, where special works are hung.

Leave the museum by the Pennsylvania Ave exit and turn right. At the first intersection, make another right and you will find yourself back in front of the Capitol reflecting pool where you began.

Lodging

At 550 C St SW, **Holiday Inn Capitol at the Smithsonian** ($$, 202/479-4000 or 888/TRIP2DC), fax 202/488-4627, offers 529 rooms including 19 suites. Located just one block from the National Air & Space Museum, the inn is newly-renovated, has a bar, a restaurant, and a deli. Also available is underground parking, an exercise room, and a rooftop pool.

The larger **JW Marriott** ($$-$$$, 202/393-2000 or 800/228-9290) at 1331 Pennsylvania Ave NW, fax 202/626-6915, www.marriott.com, has 772 rooms including 34 suites. It is located at the northeast end of The Mall near the White House. It features the **Celadon** restaurant, **Allie's American Grill** (on the lower level), valet parking, an indoor pool, and a health club. The **Garden Terrace** lounge offers a Sunday brunch, sometimes featuring a Dixieland band, and there is a connecting mall that contains 85 shops, restaurants, a car rental facility, a gift shop, and a business center.

One of the newest—and most hip—spots in town is the **Hotel George** ($$, 202/347-4200 or 800/576-8331) at 15 E St NW, www.hotelgeorge.com, a little gem that contains only 139 rooms including the 8 suites.

Arts & culture

The **Samuel P Langley IMAX Theater** (202/357-1686) at the National Air & Space Museum offers several shows a day on a screen five stories high. Double features generally are shown after the museum closes ($5 for adults, $3.75 for youths under 21 and seniors).

The **National Museum of Natural History** also has an IMAX theater. This one offers 487 seats and a six-story screen.

The **Albert Einstein Planetarium**, also at the National Air & Space Museum, presents a free program on the constellations daily at 3 pm.

The **National Gallery of Art** features talks from Tuesday through Sunday, and some 20 special exhibits are held in the East Wing annually, including concerts, lectures, and films.

Food & drink

Many of the galleries and museums have cafe's where you can sit down, take a break, and refuel.

In the Air & Space Museum is the **Flight Line Cafeteria** (202/371-8750), which has 800 seats, is of tubular construction and has large windows that overlook The Mall. Credit cards are accepted, but reservations are not. **Wright Place** (202 /371-8777) is suspended in air above the Flight Line. Offering a spectacular view of the Capitol, it serves hot lunches, fast food, sandwiches, salads, beverages, beer and wine from 11 am to 3 pm daily. Reservations are recommended and credit cards are accepted.

In the Hirshhorn is the **Full Circle Cafe** (202/357-3235), a self-service outdoor cafe that is open from Memorial Day to Labor Day between 11 am and 3 pm daily, weather permitting. No reservations or credit cards are accepted.

In the Museum of American History you'll find an old-fashioned cafe and ice cream parlor called the **Main Street Cafe** ($, 202/371-6671). It's located on the first floor of the museum across from the museum shop and bookstore and is open from 10 am to 5 pm daily; credit cards accepted. Other places in the museum to grab a snack include **Smithson's Deli, All American Grill, Grab-n Go, Eastern Shore and Pizza Parlor,** and the **Palm Court Cafe and Ice Cream Parlor,** which is located on the first floor and is open daily from 11 am to 4 pm daily.

In the West Wing of the National Gallery is the **Garden Cafe** (202/347-9401), open Monday through Saturday from 11 am to 4:30 pm and on Sunday from noon to 5 pm. Seat yourself at a fountainside table surrounded by ferns and admire the bronze sculpture *Venus and Cupid*. Credit cards are accepted. In the East Wing try the **Cascade Espresso Bar**, which accepts credit cards, is open from 10 am to 4 pm Monday through Saturday and from 11 am to 5 pm on Sunday. On the upper level is the **Terrace Cafe** (202/789-3201), which also accepts credit cards. The hours there are 11:30 am to 4 pm Monday through Saturday and noon to 4 pm on Sunday.

Away from all the culture are a few other restaurants worth mentioning. **Bertolini's Authentic Trattoria** ($$, 202/638-2140) at 801 Pennsylvania Ave NW, serves northern Italian food at lunch and dinner.

Two blocks away at 601 Pennsylvania Ave NW, is another northern Italian restaurant, **Bice** ($$-$$$, 202/638-2423). Also open only for lunch and dinner, this charming little restaurant with a large bar is open from 11:30 am to 2:30 pm and from 5:30 to 10 pm on weekdays and from 5:30 to 10 pm on Saturdays.

If you're more in the mood for Spanish, there's **Jaleo** ($$, 202/628-7949) at 480 7th St NW, where the specialty is tapas—the little dishes of Spain. Lunch and dinner are served daily in a colorful, music-filled atmosphere. Reservations are recommended; credit cards are accepted.

Also worth noting is **701** ($$, 202/393-0701) at 701 Pennsylvania Ave NW, where the portions are large and the service is exceptional. Carry your calendar with you because the hours vary almost daily: 11:30 am to 3 pm every weekday *plus* 5:30 to 10 pm on Mondays and Tuesdays, 5:30 to 11 pm on Wednesdays and Thursdays; 5:30 to 11 pm on Saturdays; and 5 to 9:30 pm on Sundays.

Nightlife

The park-like atmosphere of The National Mall does not lend itself too well to nightclubs and "hot spots." Not too far away, they are numerous, but they are described in other sections of the book. We will, however, mention one, the **District Chophouse & Brewery** at 509 7th St NW, where the specialties are handcrafted lagers and ales. Billiards also is available...and it's a great place for steaks, chops, and seafood.

Events

At the **Hirshhorn Museum & Sculpture Garden** information center, ask about the films that are shown from time to time. Both childrens' films and art films are presented in the first-floor auditorium. If you have children, also inquire about the children's workshops (202/357-3235) that are held on selected Saturdays.

If you have children in the 6 to 12 age bracket, look into ImaginAsia (202/357-4880), held in the **Arthur M Sackler Gallery** on Saturdays at 1:30 pm from March through October and on Mondays and Wednesdays in July and August. The program is free for both children and their parents and gives participants an opportunity to create a work of art that they can take home.

On one or two weekends each month, the **National Museum of African Art** hosts a storytelling period for children (202/357-4860) that focuses on an individual country or a special subject.

A Discovery Room for children is open in the **National Museum of Natural History** from September through May, Monday through Thursday from noon to 2:30 pm and Friday through Sunday from 10:30 am to 3:30 pm. Between Memorial Day and Labor Day, the hours are from 10:30 am to 3:30 pm. Free passes are available at the door.

In the **Smithsonian Institution Building**, the Smithsonian Associates Resident Program (202/357-3030) regularly presents special after-hours performances, lectures, films, and tours. Prices vary, so ask at the information desk, open from 9 am to 5:30 pm daily, about the prices and the schedule of activities.

Monuments & Memorials

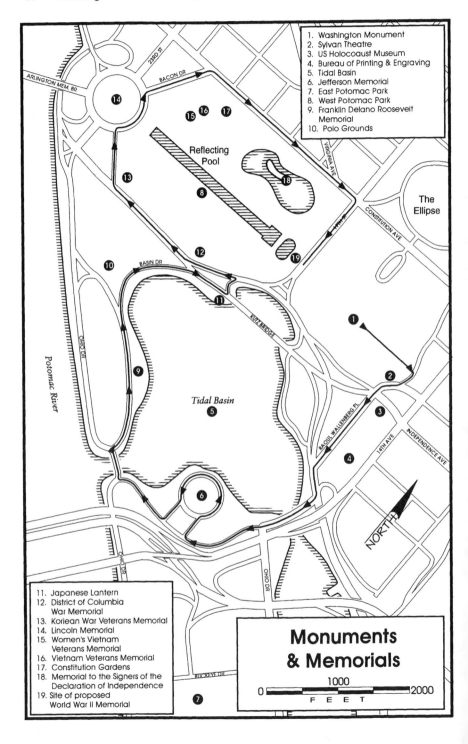

1. Washington Monument
2. Sylvan Theatre
3. US Holocoaust Museum
4. Bureau of Printing & Engraving
5. Tidal Basin
6. Jefferson Memorial
7. East Potomac Park
8. West Potomac Park
9. Franklin Delano Roosevelt Memorial
10. Polo Grounds

11. Japanese Lantern
12. District of Columbia War Memorial
13. Korlean War Veterans Memorial
14. Lincoln Memorial
15. Women's Vietnam Veterans Memorial
16. Vietnam Veterans Memorial
17. Constitution Gardens
18. Memorial to the Signers of the Declaration of Independence
19. Site of proposed World War II Memorial

Reflecting Pool

The Ellipse

Potomac River

Tidal Basin

NORTH

Monuments & Memorials

0 — 1000 — 2000

FEET

Monuments & Memorials

Along the south side of Constitution Ave at the east end of The Mall are most of the magnificent monuments and memorials that the United States has erected to celebrate its most cherished heroes and icons. Most of them are located in East Potomac Park and West Potomac Park.

Bordered on the southwest by the Potomac River, the area combines with East and West Potomac Park to provide the venue not only for the nation's most prestigious monuments but for a never-ending series of special events. It is a serene setting, conducive to a sense of reverence...remembrance...gratitude...contemplation. It is also, unfortunately, jam-packed with people, automobiles, buses, trolleys, and bicycles...perhaps the biggest "pedestrian traffic jam" in all of Washington.

But for all of the turmoil and congestion, the capital's monuments and memorials are a must-see for every visitor. Not surprisingly, the young and the foreign-born, who best appreciate the differences between life in America and life in other parts of the world, are among those who treasure them the most. This is the legacy that Washington, Jefferson, Lincoln, and the others who are celebrated here worked so hard to create. It is their ultimate reward.

To date, four former Presidents have been honored with monuments in the nation's capital—George Washington, Abraham Lincoln, Thomas Jefferson, and Franklin Delano Roosevelt. Their monuments serve as the nucleus for the many other memorials that also have been erected here.

Information

Except where noted, all of the memorials are open 24 hours a day, but are staffed only until midnight.

The **Washington Monument**: 202/426-6839 or 202/426-6841.

US Holocaust Memorial Museum: 202/488-0400 or 202/448-0406 TDD; www.ushmm.org. The museum is open daily from 10 am to 5:30 pm (until 8 pm on Thursdays), but no visitors are admitted after 3:30 pm. The building is closed on Yom Kippur and Christmas. Tickets are required to view the permanent collection, which is housed on three floors and is not particularly suitable for small children. Tickets are not required, however, for the museum, the Wexner Learning Center, the Hall of Remembrance, or special exhibits.

Bureau of Printing & Engraving: 202/874-3188 or 202/874-2330. The building is open weekdays from 9 am to 2 pm except for federal holidays, and the holiday period between Christmas and New Year's. The hours usually are extended from June through August.

Jefferson Memorial: 202/426-6822.

Franklin Delano Roosevelt Memorial: 202/619-7222 or 202/376-6704
Korean War Veterans Memorial: 02/619-7222 or 202/426-6841
Lincoln Memorial: 202/426-6895 or 202/426-6841)
Womens' Vietnam Veterans Memorial: 202/426-6841
Vietnam Veterans Memorial: 202/634-1568
World War II Memorial: 800/639-4992, www.wwiimemorial.com

Getting there

The Metro's Smithsonian station is a 10-minute walk from the midst of Washington's memorials. Also worth considering are the Independence Ave and Foggy Bottom stations. If you're driving to the Washington Monument, there is a limited amount of free 2-hour parking at the 16th St Oval. There is free one-hour parking at the Jefferson Memorial.

First steps

Most of Washington's monuments and memorials are under the guardianship of the Park Rangers, 202/426-6842. Additionally, there is an information kiosk on 15th St at the base of the Washington Monument.

The National Park Service maintains a Visitors' Center in **East Potomac Park**, and the **Bureau of Printing & Engraving** has a Visitor Center that remains open from 8:30 am to 3:30 pm. There also is an Information Center near the South end of the **Franklin Delano Roosevelt Memorial** and an information booth at the **Lincoln Memorial**.

Seasonal highlights

The **National Cherry Blossom Festival** (202/547-1500 or 202/789-7000) is held at the end of March or in early April each year in West Potomac Park. Public art contests, tree plantings, concerts, family gospel celebrations, sushi cooking demonstrations, and a parade (202/728-1137) are regular features of the celebration.

During the Fourth of July celebrations each year, the Washington Monument makes a dramatic backdrop for the fireworks. In addition, the **Sylvan Theatre**, which is located on the grounds of the monument, provides the venue for an all-afternoon Fourth of July celebration (202/426-6841).

Each fall, Park Service gardeners hand-plant 10,000 Dutch tulip bulbs near the **Tidal Basin**. In April, the flowers burst forth into a dazzling panorama of color. After the tulips fade, they are replaced by annuals.

In November, a special Veterans Day ceremony is held at the **Vietnam Veterans Memorial** (202/619-7222), complete with speeches and wreath-laying.

Tours

For those who wish to ascend the **Washington Monument**, free timed passes are required. The passes can be obtained at a kiosk at the base of the monument, but long line are not uncommon. To avoid waiting in line, visitors can reserve passes in advance through TicketMaster (800/505-5040) for a fee of $1.50. Atop the monument, Rangers give 30-minute talks throughout the day. A "Down the Steps" tour also is offered, usually at 10 am and 2 pm. Those who join the tour walk the 897 steps from the observatory room to the ground level. Along the way, they see the 192 carved stones that were incorporated into the interior of the building, which include 50 from the various states, some from other countries, some from various organizations, and one from the Parthenon in Greece. The tours generally are limited to the first 25 persons who apply. (CAUTION: Think carefully before you volunteer for this tour. Once the tour has started, there is no turning around. There are no windows along the descent, and space is tight near the top where the tour begins.)

The number of tickets to tour the **US Holocaust Memorial Museum** is restricted to 2,000 per day. They are available at a box office on 14th St, where a second entrance to the building is located. Advance tickets may be obtained for a small additional fee from either ProTix (703/218-6500 or 800/400-9373) or from TicketMaster (202/432-7328).

Free tickets to the **Bureau of Printing & Engraving** can be obtained at the kiosk on 15th St SW, which opens at 8 am except during the winter, when tickets are not required. With an average of 5,000 visitors parading through the facility each day, however, the tickets often are gone before noon. Forty-minute guided tours begin every 10 minutes and start with an introductory film.

Rangers offer 20- to 30-minute programs throughout the day at the **Jefferson Memorial** and at the **Lincoln Memorial**, and tours are offered daily on request.

Monuments and Memorials. *Start your tour at the Washington Monument, which is located due south of the White House in the center of The Mall.* The **Washington Monument** (202/426-6839 or 202/426-6841) is located between 15th St and 17th St off Constitution Ave NW, and it is to Washington what the Eiffel Tower is to Paris or Big Ben is to London—the city's most distinguishing feature. If you arrive by air at National Airport, be sure to watch for the monument as you approach for a landing, particularly if you are coming in at night.

When the Continental Congress first approved a monument in 1783, an equestrian statue was planned, but not until the early 1830s (the 100th anniversary of Washington's birth) was any real action taken. In 1830, Horatio Greenough was commissioned to create a memorial statue that would sit in the Capitol Rotunda, but his creation, a bare-chested Washington wrapped in a Greek toga, was so repulsive to Washingtonians that the statue was soon relegated to a museum in the Smithsonian.

The present monument was designed, after a few minor alterations, by Robert Mills, the architect who designed the Treasury building and the Old Patent Office building. A cornerstone was laid in 1848, but the Civil War soon brought construction to a halt, leaving an ugly 150-foot "stump" protruding from the ground. It soon became known as the Beef Depot Monument because cattle were allowed to graze on the grounds before being taken to slaughter. In 1878, President Grant finally approved the funds to complete the project, but the long delay made it impossible to match the original color of the marble. To this day, you can see a marked difference in the color at the 150-foot level (about a third of the way up).

The 555-foot marble-and-granite obelisk now stands surrounded by 50 American flags. Its walls taper from 15 feet wide at the base to 18 inches wide at the top. It was formally dedicated in 1885 and opened to the public in 1888, the tallest free-standing masonry structure in the world. A $9.4 million restoration of the monument was initiated early in 1998, and since then, the exterior has been cleaned from top to bottom and a new glass-doored elevator has been installed. Closed for most of the renovation, the monument was scheduled to reopen to the public in February or March 2001.

Visitors no longer are allowed to ascend the stairs, but the free 70-second elevator ride carries visitors to an observation room at the 500-foot level from 9 am to 5 pm daily except on Christmas (from April to Labor Day, the elevator operates from 8 am to 11:45 pm). From the top, you can get a spectacular panoramic view of the city. If anything, the Washington Monument is even more beautiful after dark.

Exit the Washington Monument grounds onto 15th St and turn right (south). Just past Independence Ave, the street will become Raoul Wallenberg Pl SW and there, on the southeast side of the street, you will find the US Holocaust Memorial Museum. At 100 Raoul Wallenberg Pl SW (formerly 15th St), the **US Holocaust Memorial Museum** is the nation's memorial to the 6 million Jews and additional millions of Jehovah's Witnesses, Gypsies, homosexuals, political prisoners, and others who became victims of Nazi Germany between 1933 and 1945. Approved by a unanimous act of Congress in 1980 as a means of educating the public about the dangers of prejudice and authoritarian rule, the memorial is adjacent to The Mall and next to the Bureau of Engraving & Printing.

Opened in April 1993, the Holocaust Memorial attracted over 2 million visitors the first year, and 2 million visitors have been visiting the site every year since then. At the entrance to the museum are some cobblestones that once were a part of the Warsaw Ghetto. Upon entering, each visitor is given an identity card bearing the name, picture and family history of some Holocaust victim.

To tour the permanent collection, visitors enter the Hall of Witness and take an elevator to the fourth floor, where the tour begins. Flash photography and video cameras are not permitted. The fourth floor contains exhibits devoted to the rise of Nazism from 1933 to 1939. Walls nearly 5-feet high shield the youngest children from many of the most vivid exhibits. The exhibits include artifacts, lifelike re-creations, films, photographs, and oral histories, many accessed via touch-screen computers. A video shows the Dachau prison camp outside of Munich. American newspaper stories published as early as 1933 tell of Hitler's plans for genocide. Other exhibits document the liberation of many camps by US troops in 1945. Descending to the third floor, visitors learn about the persecution of minorities, life in a ghetto, and life in the death camps from 1940 to 1944. Only a portion of the second floor is devoted to the museum's permanent collection. There, exhibits illustrate the liberation of the prisoners from their camps; show how many European non-Jews helped to save many Jews, even at great personal risk; show many of the resettling efforts that were required following the liberation, including the use of Displaced Persons camps and the immigration of numerous Jews to Israel and America; and describe the infamous Nuremberg trials for Nazi war criminals.

Among the other exhibits is the Tower of Faces, which shows the pictures of more than 100 families taken near Vilna (now Lithuania) between 1890 and 1941, an Anne Frank exhibit, a rail car that once stood on the tracks outside Treblinka, artwork created by many of the children who were imprisoned at Auschwitz, and thousands of shoes that were left behind by death camp victims. An audio presentation, "Voices from Auschwitz" is based upon the memories of some of the actual survivors of Auschwitz. Also located on the second floor is the Wexner Language Center, where an interactive computer system provides access to photographs, videotapes, and oral histories of Holocaust victims. The tour ends in the Hall of Remembrance, a six-sided, 60-foot tall structure that is illuminated through a skylight. A 30-minute film, "Testimony," shows holocaust victims telling their own stories.

For those who do not wish to take the tour, the first-floor exhibit "Daniel's Story: Remember the Children" deals with a fictional but historically accurate German youth's odyssey from a comfortable and secure home in Frankfurt in the 1930s to a 1941 ghetto and then to the gates of Auschwitz. The exhibition concludes with a short film.

The museum's Wexner Learning Center offers 24 touch-screen

computer workstations to use for accessing Holocaust information. On the lower level opposite the Resource Center, the Wall of Remembrance (also called the Children's Wall) displays 3,300 hand-painted tiles created by students from across the United States and dedicated to the memory of the 1.5 million children who were murdered by the Nazis during the war.

The fifth floor of the museum has a library and an archives, both of which may be used for scholarly pursuits. They are open daily from 10 am to 5:30 pm. There is a museum shop offering books, audio tapes and videotapes.

The building just south of the Holocaust Museum houses the Bureau of Printing & Engraving, an interesting diversion from the dizzying tour of monuments and memorials located in this part of the city. If you have wondered where Washington gets all of its money, stop at the **Bureau of Printing & Engraving** at 14th and C Sts SW. This is where most of the nation's currency is printed, as well as our postage stamps, US Treasury bonds, and invitations to various White House functions. Some 2,600 employees work in shifts around the clock to print about 22.5 million notes a day at the rate of 7,000 sheets per hour. How much does this amount to? More than $100 billion worth of currency and as many as 25 billion postage stamps *each year.*

Why do we need so much? It's hard to imagine, but the dollar bill has a life expectancy of just 18 months. That's one of the reasons Washington has introduced the new Sacagewea one-dollar coin. Coins last a great deal longer.

Exhibits include immense piles of money, counterfeit bills, a $100,000 bill that is intended solely for official transactions (since 1969, the largest bill in general circulation is the $100), and bills that no longer are in use. Want to take home a sack full of money to impress your friends? In the Visitor Center, you can buy a bag of old shredded bills to take away with you. You'll also see displays covering the history of money from Pieces of Eight to modern currency, a pile of bills containing *one million dollars,* some video displays, and some electronic games.

Head to the left as you exit the building and you will reach the Tidal Basin, beautifully lined with 1,300 Toshino cherry trees. Want a little diversion? Paddle boats can be rented on the Tidal Basin from March through September. Barring that, continue along the banks of the Tidal Basin toward the west and you will soon reach the Jefferson Memorial.

At the south end of 15th St SW, the **Jefferson Memorial** overlooks the Tidal Basin. Circular, with Ionic columns, the memorial was designed by architect John Russell Pope. Not surprisingly, the memorial bears a strong resemblance to the Pantheon in Rome, a design that was strongly favored by Jefferson himself. He employed a similar design for the Virginia State Capitol, the University of Virginia (which he founded), and Monticello (his home in Charlottesville, VA). The site selected for the memorial was originally a mosquito-infested swamp. In order to recover enough land to sustain the memorial, the swamp had to be dredged, a process that created what we now know as the Tidal Basin. Dedicated on April 13 (Jefferson's birthday) in 1943, the memorial stands in West Potomac Park with a clear view of the Capitol, the White House, the Washington Monument, and the Lincoln Memorial from its front steps. The memorial is particularly spectacular after dark.

Thomas Jefferson unquestionably was one of America's most outstanding public figures. He was an author of the Declaration of Independence. He was George Washington's Secretary of State, and John Adams' Vice President. He was the third President of the United States, the first to be inaugurated in the city of Washington, and the founder of the University of Virginia. When the British destroyed most of the original Library of Congress during the War of 1812, Jefferson replenished it with his own personal collection. So impressed with Thomas Jefferson was President Franklin Roosevelt that he had all of the trees between the White House and the Jefferson Memorial cut down so that he could have an unobstructed view of it.

Above the entrance to the memorial, Jefferson is shown standing before Benjamin Franklin, John Adams, Roger Sherman, and Robert Livingston, all members of the committee that was appointed to write the Declaration of Independence. The columned rotunda is inscribed with inspiring passages from Jefferson's writings (although 11 mistakes were made by workmen while transcribing portions of the Declaration of Independence). A 19-foot bronze statue of Jefferson stands beneath the domed rotunda atop a 6-foot pedestal of black Minnesota granite.

South and east of the Jefferson Memorial is the 300-acre **East Potomac Park**, *which contains one 18-hole and two 9-hole golf courses (202 /554-7660), picnic grounds, tennis courts (202/554-5962), a large swimming pool (202/727-6523), and riverfront hiking and biking paths. A permit is required to use the tennis courts.*

The Potomac River waterfront is lined with cherry trees. Although less-often publicized, East Potomac Park actually has more of them (1,800) than its neighbor, West Potomac Park, and more varieties (11) as well.

A long walk but an interesting side-trip by car or bicycle will take you along Ohio Dr (a one-way street) to the end of this man-made peninsula.

There, you will find a large playground and an area called Haines Point, which contains a memorial to the ill-fated Titanic, open daily from 6 am to midnight, plus a giant half-buried bronze statue named *The Awakening*.

From the Jefferson Memorial, circle the Tidal Basin in a clockwise direction, taking Ohio Dr North into West Potomac Park. **West Potomac Park** takes in the Lincoln, Jefferson, Roosevelt, Korean War, and Vietnam War Veterans Memorials as well as the Tidal Basin and Constitution Gardens. It also is the primary venue for the National Cherry Blossom Festival held each year. Of the 3,000 Yoshino cherry trees presented to the United States by Japan in 1912, only about 200 survive (marked with bronze plaques). More Yoshino trees have been added over the years, but they now co-mingle with two other varieties, the Akebonos and the Kwanzan. Unfortunately, the cherry blossoms last for only two weeks—and will prevail for even less if the weather is unkind.

Shortly after you cross a short bridge that links the Tidal Basin with the Potomac River, the Franklin Delano Roosevelt Memorial will appear on your right. Sitting on the banks of the Tidal Basin at 900 Ohio St SW, the **Franklin Delano Roosevelt Memorial** honors the only president to serve more than two terms. Actually, Roosevelt was elected to serve *four* terms, but he died during his final term, and was succeeded by his vice president, Harry Truman. Federal law now limits the president to two terms.

Authorized by Congress in 1955, Lawrence Halprin's design for the memorial was approved in 1958. Ground was broken in 1991, and the site was dedicated in May 1997. Directly across the Tidal Basin from the Washington Monument, the FDR memorial sits between the Jefferson Memorial and the Lincoln Memorial. The 7.5-acre site, which contains shade trees, plantings, waterfalls, and fountains, is the length of three football fields.

As you approach the south end of the memorial, you will find a book store (open 9 am to 9 pm) at the main entrance. Four outdoor "gallery" rooms feature 10 bronze sculptures of the 32nd President, First Lady Eleanor Roosevelt, and various events that transpired between the Great Depression and World War II. The first room contains a copy of the Great Seal, a life-size statue of Roosevelt, and quotations from his first inaugural address. The second room focuses on the Great Depression and contains three sculptures—*Despair*, depicting a weary rural couple; *Hunger*, portraying people in an urban breadline; and *Hope*, showing a man who is listening to one of Roosevelt's "fireside chats" on the radio. The third room is devoted to the events of World War II, and contains a 9-foot statue of the president with his dog Fala, while the fourth room contains a 30-foot bas-relief that depicts the Roosevelt funeral cortege. In front of the fourth room, a 39-ton statue of First Lady Eleanor Roosevelt stands before the Seal of the United Nations, making this the first presidential memorial to so honor a first lady.

By the exit is a bas-relief of FDR as Commander-in-Chief of the Armed Forces, standing on the bridge of a naval destroyer. In his earlier days, Roosevelt served as Assistant Secretary of the Navy. At this writing, a life-size bronze statue that shows FDR in a wheelchair is nearing completion, to be installed in front of the first gallery room. From the time he was afflicted with polio at the age of 39, Roosevelt was compelled to use a wheelchair, but he chose never to be seen in it, if at all possible. When the Roosevelt Memorial was designed, those wishes were taken into account and nothing representing a wheelchair was included among the exhibits, which angered some people, who felt that Roosevelt was an outstanding role-model for people with handicaps and should be depicted as such. The latter point of view eventually prevailed.

As you leave the memorial, continue heading north until you reach Basin Dr and turn right. Here, about midway between the Jefferson Memorial and the Lincoln Memorial, is the 4-acre site upon which a monument to Martin Luther King Jr will be erected. Approved by the National Capital Planning Commission in December 1999, the monument will stand on the south side of Basin Dr at the northwest end of the Tidal Basin.

Continue northeast along Basin Dr and take a right at the next intersection, which leads to the Kutz Bridge across the northern end of the Tidal Basin. There, you will see the 300-year-old stone Japanese Lantern, which was presented to the city by the governor of Tokyo in 1954. The lantern is lit as a part of the week-long National Cherry Blossom Festival each year.

Now carefully cross to the north side of the road toward the Reflecting Pool. Almost immediately, you will come across the **District of Columbia War Memorial.** *Head west to French Dr, which angles toward the Lincoln Memorial, but defer that experience long enough to look to your right, where you will find the* **Korean War Veterans Memorial.** The memorial stands near Daniel French Dr and Independence Ave southeast of the Lincoln Memorial. One of Washington's newer monuments, it was unveiled in July 1995 at a cost of $18 million, paid for exclusively with funds specifically donated for that purpose.

The memorial honors the 1.5 million Americans who served in the Korean "police action" of 1950-53. It sits on a 2.2-acre site adjacent to the Lincoln Memorial Reflecting Pool and consists of two primary elements, a circular "Pool of Remembrance," situated in a grove of trees, and a triangular "Field Of Service," which shows a 19-man column of 7-foot, battle-equipped soldiers plus a 164-foot wall inscribed "Freedom Is Not Free." Etched onto the black granite wall are 2,500 photo-images of nurses, chaplains, mechanics, cooks, and other personnel, vital to the support of our fighting men. The faces on the wall were culled from actual photos of Korean War veterans.

Just up the path, at the west end of The Mall at 23rd St NW, is the **Lincoln Memorial**, designed by Henry Bacon. Beyond it is the approach to the Arlington Memorial Bridge and Arlington National Cemetery. Planned as early as 1867, it took until 1912 to select a design for the memorial, which centers around a 19-foot statue of a seated Lincoln, flanked on both sides by limestone walls containing the Gettysburg Address on one side and Lincoln's Second Inaugural Address on the other. Above them under the 60-foot ceiling are two 60-foot allegorical murals by Jules Guerin. The one on the south wall shows the Angel of Truth freeing a slave, flanked by groups of figures that represent Justice and Immortality, while the one on the North wall depicts unity between the North and South, flanked by groups of figures meant to symbolize Fraternity and Charity.

The memorial to our 16th President was designed to look like a classic Greek temple, somewhat similar to the Parthenon. It took 28 blocks of white marble and four years of carving to complete it, and it was not ready for dedication until 1922. The memorial overlooks the 2,292-foot Reflecting Pool to the east, and Lincoln appears to be looking out over The Mall, the Washington Monument, and the US Capitol. There are 36 Doric columns, one for every state in the Union at the time Lincoln was in office.

Six million visitors a year come to the Lincoln Memorial, which has an underground mini-museum containing the Lincoln's Legacy exhibition, a collection of photographs and film clips of protests that have taken place here over the years. Among them are films of Marian Anderson's concert on Easter 1939 after she had been barred from the DAR's Constitution Hall and films of Martin Luther King Jr's "I Have a Dream" speech, delivered here on August 28, 1963. The museum is open daily from 8 am to midnight daily. A bookstore also is on the premises.

For a particularly stirring experience, visit the memorial at dusk and watch as the sun sets behind the memorial.

Located in a grove of trees just east of the Lincoln Memorial and just north of the Reflecting Pool is the **Womens' Vietnam Veterans Memorial**, dedicated in November 1993 to honor the 265,000 American women who served in that war. A one-ton bronze statue by sculptor Glenna Goodacre depicts three servicewomen and a wounded soldier supported by sandbags.

Nearby is the **Vietnam Veterans Memorial** (202/634-1568), which sits in Constitution Gardens near Constitution Ave and Henry Bacon Dr NW across from the Lincoln Memorial.

A long, low, V-shaped wall containing 140 panels of polished black granite appears to emerge from the earth. One wing of the wall points to the Washington Monument while the other wing points to the Lincoln Memorial. Shown on the wall are the names of 58,192 Americans who died in the war or are still missing. The names on the 492-foot wall are inscribed by platoon and listed chronologically from the first casualty in 1959 to the last in 1975. Directories are available to help visitors locate specific names on the wall, and name rubbings can be made on request.

The haunting, stark memorial was designed by the gifted sculptor and designer Maya Ying Lin when she was still a senior at Yale; it was erected in 1982. In 1984, a life-size Frederick Hart sculpture showing three Vietnam soldiers was installed near the entrance.

Exit the park onto Constitution Ave and turn right (east). Between Washington and Lincoln Sts on the south side of Constitution Ave, the lovely **Constitution Gardens** (202/485-9880) occupy 52 beautifully-manicured acres. The gardens include a one-acre flower garden, walks, bike paths, and a 6-acre lake full of ducks, turtles, fish, and frogs. Kids love to sail their boats here. In the middle of the lake is a small island, on which a **Memorial to the 56 Signers of the Declaration of Independence** (202/426-6841) has been erected. The large granite blocks, carved with replicas of the patriots' signatures, are set in a landscaped garden that can be reached via a short footbridge.

Continue down Constitution Ave in an easterly direction to the next through-street (17th St NW) and turn right. On the right-hand side of the street, directly opposite the Washington Monument, you will see a small reflecting pool in the center of Memorial Plaza, which stands at the eastern end of the larger reflecting pool that leads to the Lincoln Memorial. As soon as sufficient funding can be arranged, this will be the site of a new **World War II Memorial**, designed by Friedrich St Florian. The memorial will consist of two arches, one on the north side of the pool and one on the south side. When completed, this will be the nation's first monument to honor both the military veterans who served in a war and the countless civilians who served on the home front. President

Clinton dedicated the site for the memorial in 1995 and former Senator Robert Dole, a veteran of World War II, is chairman of the group that is attempting to raise the $100 million that it will cost to build the memorial.

Parenthetically, this will be the last memorial to be erected between the White House and the Jefferson Memorial or between the Capitol and the Lincoln Memorial. Fearing that the area is becoming over-crowded with monuments, the Joint Task Force on Memorials has banned any future proposals for memorials in that part of the city.

Across the street is the place from which you began, the Washington Monument.

Lodging
Parkland occupies this entire part of town. There are no hotels on The Mall or in Potomac Park, and excluding the few cafeterias and snack shops found in some of the memorials and public buildings, there are no eating establishments either.

For suggestions regarding lodging and dining, see the sections describing Foggy Bottom, the White House, and L'Enfant Plaza, all of which are close by and each of which is loaded with excellent places to stay and eat.

Arts & culture
On Summer evenings, the US Army, Navy, Marine, and Air Force bands play on a rotating basis in the **Sylvan Theatre**, which is located on the grounds of the Washington Monument.

Food & drink
There is a snack bar on the grounds of the **Washington Monument,** as well as a number of picnic tables for the use of those who bring their own lunches

The US Holocaust Museum Cafe, a cafeteria that serves sandwiches, fruit, desserts, and drinks daily from 9 am to 4:30 pm, occupies an annex adjacent to the **US Holocaust Museum.**

Nightlife
Once again, we refer you to other sections of the book for information about Washington's nightlife.

Events
Annually, a series of free summer festivals and outdoor concerts are staged on The Mall. To be able to schedule these things into the itinerary for your visit to Washington *before ever leaving home*, access the Internet at www.dcaccommodations.com

On the north side of Basin Dr are the **Polo Grounds**, where spirited matches are played on Sunday afternoons from late April through October except for the month of August.

Sidetrip—Arlington National Cemetery

Southwest of the Lincoln Memorial and across the Potomac River is "the nation's most sacred shrine"—Arlington National Cemetery. The first burial on these 612 hilly acres took place in 1864. Today, 250,000 members of the military, government officials, and their family members are buried in , and an average of 15 burials take place every day. It is estimated that the cemetery will be full by the year 2020.

Here can be found the graves of famous explorers (Adm Robert E Peary and Matthew Henson), scientists (Walter Reed), presidential hopefuls (William Jennings Bryan and Robert Kennedy), military heroes (Audy Murphy, the most decorated solider in World War II), and athletes (Joe Louis). Here too can be found the tombs of prominent generals (Philip Sheridan and John J Pershing), admirals (Hyman Rickover), and presidents (William Howard Taft and John F Kennedy).

Not to be missed are the Tomb of the Unknown Soldier and other monuments erected in honor of both past and present members of the United States armed forces.

A leisurely stroll through these hilly, well-manicured grounds can easily consume an entire day. Maps are available to help you locate the points of particular interest, and bus tours also are available.

Information
Arlington National Cemetery (703/607-8052) is open daily from 8 am to 5 pm except for April to September, when the grounds remain open until 7 pm. Admission is free. Inside the cemetery, Arlington House is open daily between 9:30 am and 6 pm from April through September and between 9:30 am and 4:30 pm the rest of the year. It is closed on Christmas and New Year's.

Getting there
Take the Metro to the Arlington station. If you arrive by car, you'll find a parking deck adjacent to the cemetery entrance.

Seasonal highlights
The new Memorial Amphitheater in Arlington National Cemetery is used for some 20 small ceremonies each year. Memorial services are conducted there on Memorial Day, Veterans Day, Easter Sunday, and other meaningful occasions, accompanied by military bands.

In May, Memorial Day Ceremonies at the **Tomb of the Unknowns** include a Presidential wreath-laying at 11 am. Similar Veterans Day Ceremonies are held there in November. Memorial Day services and Veterans Day ceremonies are held here, at the Amphitheater, and at the Kennedy gravesite each year.

Tours

Narrated Tourmobile tours (202/554-5100) leave the **Arlington National Cemetery** Visitor Center every 15 minutes, covering all of the major points of interest on the grounds. Passengers can get off the Tourmobile and reboard it as they wish for a $4 fare (children under 12 can ride for $2).

Park Rangers dress in period costume as they greet visitors to **Arlington House** on the grounds of Arlington National Cemetery and answer questions. Self-guided tours of the house are permitted (be sure to get a brochure as you enter).

Our tour begins at the Metro station. From there, look back toward the city of Washington. Before you is the **Arlington Memorial Bridge.** To the right of it stands the statue of a lone soldier on top of an inscribed base. The **United Spanish War Veterans Memorial,** *The Hiker,* was placed on that site in 1965.

Across the road stands another statue, that of a soldier holding the hand of a small child. This is the **Seabees Memorial,** designed to honor the US Naval Construction Battalion (CB or "Seabee") formed early in World War II. Behind the statue is a bas-relief containing the famous Seabee motto: "The difficult we do at once; the impossible takes a bit longer." The man who sculpted the statue, Felix de Weldon, also created the Iwo Jima Memorial.

Follow Memorial Dr toward the cemetery gate. On your left is the **Information Center.** Across from the Information Center is a statue of **Rear Adm Richard Byrd Jr,** Polar explorer and Congressional Medal of Honor winner. Created by Felix de Weldon, whose Seabees Memorial you have just seen, the statue was erected by the National Geographic Society. Byrd is buried in Arlington National Cemetery. Among the other admirals buried in Arlington cemetery is Adm Robert E Peary.

Pass through the gate and enter the cemetery. On your right is the **Schley Gate,** named for Rear Adm Winfield Scott Schley, who led American forces to victory in Santiago Harbor, Cuba, during the Spanish-American War. Opposite that is the **Roosevelt Gate,** named for Theodore Roosevelt, and on the lawn between the two gates is the **Women in Military Service for America Memorial,** Washington's newest. Erected in honor of the 1.8 million women who have served in America's armed forces, the memorial includes a bi-leveled terrace. The upper terrace provides stunning views of the cemetery grounds and the monuments of Washington across the river, while the lower terrace contains a fountain that flows through a black granite trough into a reflecting pool. On the lower terrace is a hemicycle wall, behind which is an Education Center, a Hall of Honor, a theater, a conference center, 14 exhibit alcoves, and a gift shop. There also is a computer register of 250,000 servicewomen that visitors can use to access information about individuals who have voluntarily submitted their recollections and their photographs.

When you reach a pathway to the right, take it and go down the steps. Four steps from the bottom, on the right-hand side, is a marker bearing the number 36-1431. This marks the grave of **Medgar Evers**. Evers took part in the Normandy Invasion on D-Day and won two Bronze Stars. Later, as field secretary for the National Association for the Advancement of Colored People (NAACP), he was killed outside his Jackson, MS home after a civil rights rally.

Return to the main road. On the far side, you will see two sets of stairs heading up the hill. Between the two sets of stairs is the grave of **Gen Omar N Bradley**, who led the largest American military force ever assembled during World War II. The last of America's five-star generals, Bradley succeeded Dwight Eisenhower as Army Chief of Staff in 1948 and later became chairman of the Joint Chiefs of Staff. He was promoted to five-star general, one of only five people to attain that rank.

Prior to 1948, burial sites throughout the cemetery were allotted according to rank. Some of the other generals buried in Arlington are Gen John J Pershing, Gen George C Marshall, Gen Jonathan Wainwright, Lt Gen Claire L Chennault, and Gen Hoyt S Vandenburg.

Stay to the right, heading uphill and pass a huge oak thought to be 400 years old. At the top of the path is a 14.5-foot rose granite marker identifying the grave of **President William Howard Taft** and his wife. Taft was the first civilian governor of the Philippines (1900-1912) and the only president to serve as Chief Justice of the Supreme Court (1921-1930). President from 1909 to 1912, Taft was the first president to throw out a ball to open the new baseball season, and his wife Helen was instrumental in bringing the famous cherry trees to Washington.

Backtrack along the road a few steps and take the other stairway to Custis Walk. Near the top of the steps, on your left, is a grove of holly trees surrounding the granite tomb of **Robert Todd Lincoln**, the eldest son of Abraham Lincoln, his wife Mary Harlan, and their son Abraham Lincoln II, who died at the age of 17. Robert Todd Lincoln's history, although little known, is as colorful as that of his father in many respects. The only child of Abraham and Mary Todd Lincoln to reach adulthood, Lincoln was saved from falling in front of a train as a young man by Edwin Booth, the actor-brother of the man who later would assassinate his father. During the Civil War, he served on the staff of Gen Ulysses S Grant, and after the war, he became a lawyer. He was named Secretary of War by President James Garfield, and in 1881, he witnessed Garfield's assassination. Twenty years later, he witnessed the assassination of another president, William McKinley. From 1889 to 1893, Lincoln served as our Ambassador to Great Britain, and from 1897 to 1911, he served as president of the Pullman Company of Chicago. Lincoln died in 1926 at the age of 78, but his wife lived until 1937, when she died at the age of 91.

Continue along Custis Walk to a paved road and turn left. On your right, you will soon see a large semicircular granite monument bearing the word "Weeks." **John Wingate Weeks** was both a congressman and a senator from Massachusetts and served as Secretary of War under two presidents, Warren Harding and Calvin Coolidge.

Up the grassy hill behind the Weeks monument is the grave of **Potter Stewart**, associate justice of the Supreme Court from 1958 to 1981. When he retired, Stewart was succeeded to the high court by Sandra Day O'Connor, the nation's first female Supreme Court Justice.

Next to Stewart's grave is that of **Thurgood Marshall**, the first black Supreme Court justice, and behind Stewart's grave on the right are the graves of **Adm Hyman Rickover** and his two wives. Rickover immigrated with his family from Czarist Russia to the United States when he was six years old and served in the US Navy until he reached the age of 82.

Other Supreme Court Justices buried at Arlington include Earl Warren, William O Douglas, and Oliver Wendell Holmes.

Take the first right and follow a curving granite walkway up the hill. At the entry to the grave of **President John F Kennedy** is an oval area and a low wall that bears seven of his best-known quotations. The eternal flame was lit by his wife on November 25, 1963, three days after the president's assassination. Two of their children, an unnamed daughter and a son, Patrick, died in infancy and were buried in Boston, but have been disinterred and are buried on either side of their father. Next to Kennedy's marker is that of his wife, Jacqueline Bouvier Kennedy Onassis, who died in 1994.

Facing JFK's gravesite, look to your left for a short path. The grave of **Robert F Kennedy** is marked with a simple wooden cross on the hillside beneath Arlington House. Opposite the grave is a fountain bearing quotations from two of his more famous speeches. During the presidency of his brother, Robert Kennedy served as US Attorney General, and he was assassinated while campaigning for the office of President in 1968. He was only 43 years old at the time.

Return to the main road and on to Custis Walk. Turn left onto Custis Walk and follow the long graded steps leading up the hill. As you near the top of the hill, look to your left for a marker in front of a grave that is enclosed by a brick wall. This is the grave of **Mary Randolph**, the first person to be buried at Arlington. A direct descendant of Pocahontas, Randolph was a cousin of Thomas Jefferson and of Robert E Lee. She died in 1828.

Look for a path to the left and take it to Lookout Point, which affords the best view of JFK's gravesite and the US Capitol far in the distance. The higher you climb up the hill, the better the view. To the right of the flagpole is the grave of **Pierre Charles L'Enfant**, the man who laid out the nation's capital but died penniless and forgotten in 1825. Originally buried in Maryland, L'Enfant's remains were recovered and moved here, overlooking the city he created, in 1909. A veteran of the Revolutionary War, L'Enfant is one of 11 Revolutionary soldiers interred at Arlington.

Atop the hill stands the Custis-Lee Mansion, most commonly called **Arlington House**. Built between 1802 and 1817 by Robert E Lee's father-in-law, George Washington Parke Custis, the grand portico faces the river. Custis was the son of Martha Custis Washington, adopted by George Washington, and subsequently raised at Mount Vernon. His only child, Mary, married Robert E Lee, a distant cousin whom she had known since childhood, in a military-style wedding in the front parlor of this house on June 30, 1831. Six of their seven children were born here.

On April 22, 1861, when his home state of Virginia seceded from the Union, Lee resigned his commission in the Union Army, accepted command of the Confederate forces, and left Arlington forever. A month later, the house was occupied by Union troops. Gradually, more and more of the soldiers who were killed during the war were buried on the estate.

Following the Civil War, Lee moved to Lexington, VA, where he lived until his death, but his eldest son, Washington Custis Lee, sued the United States government, asking for the return of the Arlington property. Although the US Supreme Court eventually ruled in his favor, Lee felt that he could no longer bear to live at Arlington, surrounded by gravesites, and the Supreme Court ordered the federal government to purchase the property from him for $150,000.

George Washington Parke Custis and his wife are both buried on the premises, and Arlington House has been proclaimed the **Robert E Lee**

Memorial. Outside the house are the old slave quarters and a small museum.

Outside, past the vegetable garden, is a museum dedicated to the family history of Robert E Lee. Among the displays are Lee's mess kit, the key to the tomb of the Unknown Soldiers of the Civil War, locks of Lee's hair, and some hair from the mane of Lee's favorite horse, Traveller.

Behind the main house is a bookstore, and on the far side of the garden is a brick path that leads through a hedge and into the **Tomb of the Unknown Dead of the Civil War,** where 2,111 Confederate and Union soldiers were buried in September 1866 after being killed at the battle of Bull Run and along the route to the Rappahannock River.

Walk to the end of the road that parallels the brick walkway and down the hill. The **Old Amphitheater** has a white colonnade, a latticed roof, and a center dais where memorial services and special ceremonies were conducted between 1868 and 1921. It could accommodate 1,500 people whereas the new amphitheater is capable of seating 5,000.

Follow Meigs Ave to the portion of the cemetery known as Section 1. Among the graves located in this section are those of Col Abner Doubleday, Brig Gen Stephen Vincent Benet, and Quartermaster Gen Montgomery Meigs. **Abner Doubleday** is the Civil War hero who is credited with inventing the game of baseball, and although that part of the story is a myth, Doubleday Field and the Baseball Hall of Fame in Cooperstown, NY are named for him. Doubleday also founded the nation's first cable car company in San Francisco. **Stephen Vincent Benet,** whose grave is marked by a tan obelisk, achieved fame as a poet and storywriter, while **Montgomery Meigs,** an engineer and architect, designed the Old Pension Building in Judiciary Square, the Old Executive Office Building near the White House, and the building that is now the Centennial Building of the Smithsonian Institution.

Continue along Meigs Ave to McPherson Ave and turn left. When the road divides, take the left fork. When you come to the junction of McPherson and Garfield Drs, bear left and walk past Farragut Ave. On your right at Jackson Circle, in Section 1b, is the Confederate Section of the cemetery and the **Confederate Monument,** a statue of a female figure holding a laurel branch. The monument was erected by the United Daughters of the Confederacy in 1914. Some 410 Confederate soldiers are buried here in concentric circles surrounding the monument, which was built in 1914 and formally dedicated on the anniversary of the birth of Jefferson Davis, president of the Confederacy. The monument's sculptor, Confederate veteran Moses Ezekiel, is buried at its base.

Continue along the same road. On your left, you will see the **Rough Riders Monument**, created in 1906. Properly called the First US Volunteer Cavalry, the Rough Riders fought during the Spanish-American War. Their most famous veteran, Theodore Roosevelt, attended the unveiling ceremony.

Go back to Farragut Ave and turn right. At Sigsbee Ave, turn right again. The **Mast of the USS *Maine***, a battleship that was blown up in Havana Harbor on February 15, 1898, commemorates the event that triggered the Spanish-American War. The mast protruded from Havana Harbor for 12 years before it was removed to Arlington and erected here, inscribed with the names of the 229 crewmen and officers (62 known and 167 unknown) who were killed aboard the ship. In the distance, you can see the Corinthian column of the **Spanish-American War Memorial**, topped with a globe and an eagle, and dedicated by Theodore Roosevelt in 1902.

Follow the walkway to the street. En route, you will pass a marker in honor of **Ignace Jan Paderewski**. An "artist, composer, musician, statesman, patriot, humanitarian, and friend of American war veterans" who requested that he be laid to rest in Arlington cemetery until his native country of Poland was freed from Communist domination. His body remained in the vault of the USS *Maine* Memorial from 1941 until June 1992, when it was finally removed and taken to his homeland. The marker was erected by the American Legion.

At the end of the path, there are two monuments on your left. One is a memorial to eight servicemen who died in an aircraft accident attempting to rescue 53 American hostages in Iran in 1980. The other is the ***Challenger* Memorial**, a tribute to the crew of the spacecraft *Challenger*, which exploded on takeoff in 1986.

Walk to the road, turn right, and proceed to a flagstone walk under a tall tree. Beside the path is the grave of **Audie Murphy**, marked by a simple headstone. As a major in the Texas infantry, Murphy was awarded 28 medals, including the Congressional Medal of Honor, making him the most decorated soldier in World War II *before he had even reached his 21st birthday!* Murphy went on to become a popular movie star, but died in an untimely plane crash at the age of 46.

Across the street is the new **Memorial Amphitheater**. President Woodrow Wilson laid the cornerstone of the white marble structure in 1915. The exterior wall contains the names of 44 battles in which American forces were engaged.

Next to the amphitheater is the **Tomb of the Unknowns**, attended around the clock by an honor guard—a solitary soldier who takes 21 steps in front of the tomb, pauses 21 seconds to face it, turns, pauses another 21 seconds, and then repeats the process in the other direction. Specially-selected members of "The Old Guard" stationed at nearby Fort Myer, the guards are changed every half-hour during the summer and every hour during the winter. At night, the guards are changed every two hours.

The die piece of the tomb is made of marble from Yule, CO. One of the largest blocks of marble ever quarried, the stone weighed 50 tons before the carving began. In a sarcophagus beneath the tomb is the body of an unknown American soldier who was brought back from France after World War I.

The Amphitheater next door has a special display hall that exhibits awards and tributes that have been given to America's unknown soldiers, as well as a pictorial history of their burials.

Take the flagstone path to the right of the tomb and circle to your left. Pass two main walkways leading to the tomb and turn right at Section 7A. Just before you reach Roosevelt Dr, look to your right to see the pink granite marker topped by the figure of a boxer in fighting stance. This is the grave of **Joe Louis**, who served during World War II in the same segregated Army unit as baseball star Jackie Robinson. Louis, "the Brown Bomber," retained the heavyweight boxing title longer than anyone before or since. *Turn left onto Roosevelt Dr and follow it back to the Visitors Center. The route is marked by blue signs.*

Midtown, Penn Quarter & Chinatown

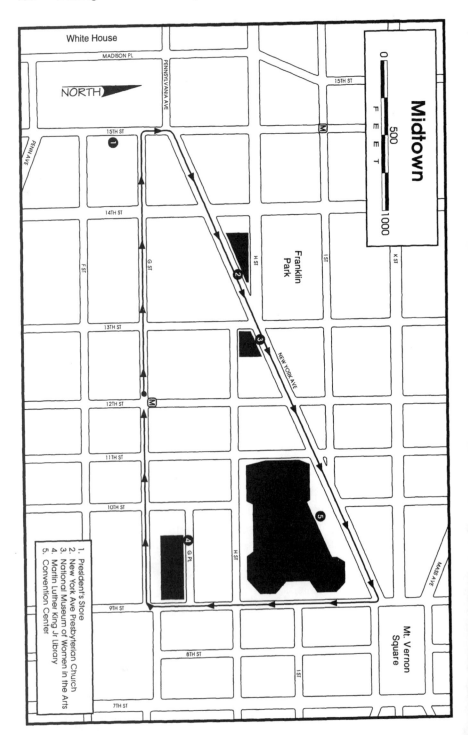

Midtown

NORTH

White House

MADISON PL

PENNSYLVANIA AVE

15TH ST

PENN AVE

15TH ST

14TH ST

F ST

G ST

13TH ST

12TH ST

11TH ST

10TH ST

9TH ST

8TH ST

7TH ST

H ST

Franklin Park

1 ST

K ST

NEW YORK AVE

G PL

H ST

1 ST

MASS AVE

Mt. Vernon Square

1. President's Store
2. New York Ave Presbyterian Church
3. National Museum of Women in the Arts
4. Martin Luther King Jr Library
5. Convention Center

0   500   1000
F E E T

Midtown, Penn Quarter & Chinatown

Like many other cities across America, Washington has seen its old downtown area slip into a pattern of decay over the past half-century. People have moved away from the center of town into the suburbs, and the merchants have followed them. Today, Washington is literally encircled with a series of huge shopping malls.

Fortunately, however, the old midtown section of Washington, stretching roughly from 9th St NW at the eastern perimeter to 15 St NW on the western perimeter and from G St on the South to M St and Thomas Circle on the North, has started a long-overdue comeback. More and more smart shops, pleasing restaurants, and refurbished hotels are starting to make their appearance.

Directing much of this recovery is the Business Improvement District and its "Downtown SAM," a group of public safety officers, dressed in bright red, that patrols the 110 square blocks of downtown Washington daily from 10 am to 11 pm. A portion of the team is devoted to crime prevention, but cleaning up litter, providing assistance to visitors, and helping individuals with personal emergencies is an equally-important part of their service.

Hecht's Department Store remains. The old Woodward & Lathrop's, located at 11th St and G St NW is the new home of the Washington Opera House.

A delightful and historic part of Washington's downtown area is the somewhat triangular wedge known as Penn Quarter. Running from the north side of Pennsylvania Ave to G St NW between 3rd St and 12th St NW, this area contains an interesting blend of historic old buildings and modern new government offices. It also is home to a number of the city's old theatres, including Ford's Theatre, where Abraham Lincoln was assassinated, several popular museums, a number of interesting government office buildings, and Washington's Chinatown.

Midtown

Generally speaking, the area covered in this chapter is that which lies North of Capitol St and The Mall, within easy walking distance of the White House, the US Capitol, and Union Station. In days past, this was the main shopping district for the people of Washington. It is still a place to go for a taste of "things the way they used to be."

Information

A Visitor Center is located near the corner of New York Ave and 13th St NW, close to the National Museum of Women in the Arts. Also helpful is the DC Chamber of Commerce office at 1301 Pennsylvania Ave, Suite 309, Washington, DC 20004, (202/789-7000).

National Museum of Women in the Arts: 202/783-5000. The museum is open from 10 am to 5 pm Monday through Saturday and from noon to 5 pm on Sunday. Admission costs $3 for adults and $2 for seniors and students.

Martin Luther King Jr Library: 202/727-1186. Library hours are 9 am to 9 pm from Monday through Thursday, 9 am to 5:30 pm on Saturday, and 1 to 5 pm on Sunday.

Getting there

McPherson Square and Metro Center stations are both convenient to Midtown.

First steps

Write, call or stop in the DC Chamber of Commerce at 1301 Pennsylvania Ave, Suite 309, and pick up maps and brochures, ask questions, and get directions, if necessary. Before leaving home, you can access the Chamber on the Internet at www.ci.washington.dc.us or www.dcchamber.org.

Seasonal highlights

On the third Thursday of each month, 10 galleries and culturally-oriented midtown organizations extend their evening hours to attract the public to the downtown area.

Tours

Guided 90-minute tours (202/639-0908) of the downtown area are conducted at 10:30 am and 1 pm. The tours leave the Discovery Channel Store at 7th St and F St NW and cost $7.50 per person ($5 for seniors and students). Included on the tour is the house in which John Wilkes Booth plotted the assassination of Abraham Lincoln.

Guided tours of the **New York Ave Presbyterian Church** are offered each week after the Sunday services.

Downtown. *Since the Metro Center is located at 12th St and G St NW in the downtown area, our tour begins there. From the Metro Center, walk east along G St to 15th St NW, three blocks away.* At 685 15th St NW, take a quick look into the **President's Store** (202/547-1871), almost directly across from the White House, a fitting location for a store that's devoted solely to the sale of authentic presidential memorabilia—books, videos, photographs, campaign buttons, banners, campaign posters, and the like.

If it was used during a presidential campaign, you're likely to find it here. This is a great spot for reliving old memories.

After you have finished browsing among the matchbook covers and other paraphernalia associated with past presidential campaigns, leave the store, turn right and walk one short block to New York Ave. Once there, make another right and go a block-and-a-half to H St NW. On the northwest corner across the street you will see an interesting Federal-style church. The **New York Ave Presbyterian Church** at 1313 New York Ave NW was organized in 1803 by the Scottish stonemasons who built the White House. Presidents John Quincy Adams and Abraham Lincoln were members of the congregation. The present building, built in 1951, contains 19 beautiful stained glass windows. On display at the church are Abraham Lincoln's pew, his hitching post, and the original manuscript of his proposal to abolish slavery. One of the church's ministers, Dr Phineas Gurley, preached Lincoln's funeral oration.

Another minister to serve the church was Dr Peter Marshall, who inspired the book *A Man Called Peter*, which later was made into a popular motion picture. In 1954, yet another minister, Dr George Docherty, delivered a Lincoln Day service that was attended by President Dwight D Eisenhower. The president was so moved by the sermon that it prompted him to suggest that the words "one nation under God" should be inserted into the Pledge of Allegiance. The church office is open Tuesday through Friday from 9 am to 5 pm and on Sunday from 9 am to 1 pm.

Leaving the church, continue walking northeast along New York Ave. On the southeast corner of New York Ave and 13th St NW stands an unusual museum. The **National Museum of Women in the Arts**, 1250 New York Ave, "celebrates the contribution of women to the history of art" and contains 1,500 works of art created by 400 female artists from 28 different countries. Opened in 1987 with a collection donated by Wilhelmina and Wallace Holladay, the museum is housed in a marvelous Renaissance Revival building designed by Waddy Wood in 1907 as a Masonic temple. It was the first such museum in the country. The building was expanded in 1997 with the addition of the Elizabeth A Kasser Wing which added two new galleries to the museum.

Stay on New York Ave and continue walking northeast. After you cross 11th St NW you will find yourself standing beside Washington's gigantic Convention Center. Depending on the event being held inside at the time of your visit, you may or may not stumble across something of interest, and you may or may not be allowed inside. Check at the front door to see what may be taking place.

A new convention center is under construction and is scheduled to open in March 2003. When completed, the new convention center will have 725,000 sq ft of exhibit space, 150,000 sq ft of meeting space, a 60,000-sq ft ballroom, and 44,000 sq ft of retail space.

Continue your journey along New York Ave for one more block and you will come to Mt Vernon Square, one of the many lovely street-intersection parks for which Washington is famous. Next, take a right onto 9th St NW and wander southward to G St. On your right will be Washington's main public library. The **Martin Luther King Jr Library**, 901 G St NW, was designed by the world-famous architect Mies van der Rohe and features a large mural that depicts many of the highlights of King's life.

As you exit the library, turn right on G St, walk three short blocks, and you will be back at the Metro Center where your walk began.

Penn Quarter & Chinatown

An extension of Washington's midtown area, Penn Quarter was one of the city's preeminent entertainment and cultural centers in years past. It was on the fringe of Washingtons "centers of power"...a place to unwind and relax after a day of tending to the nation's problems. Today, it is easy to close one's eyes and picture the way Penn Quarter *used to be*...and to enjoy some of the ambiance of the good old days.

No one is likely to confuse Washington's Chinatown with the one in San Francisco, or those in several other American cities, for that matter. Indeed, over the past several decades, the size and population of Washington's Chinatown have been shrinking drastically. Mexican and Indian restaurants have insinuated themselves upon the Chinese dim sum restaurants normally associated with a Chinatown. There's even an Irish pub there today.

Be that as it may, there's still a distinct Chinese feeling about the place. The local branch of Adams National Bank was designed according to the principles of Feng Shui and Chinese characters appear on the street signs. Import shops and martial arts schools are seen everywhere.

Information
National Theatre: 202/628-6161 or 800/447-7400; Warner Theatre: 202 /628-1818; J Edgar Hoover Federal Bureau of Investigation Building: 202 /324-3447; Ford's Theatre and the Lincoln Museum: 202/347-4833 or 800

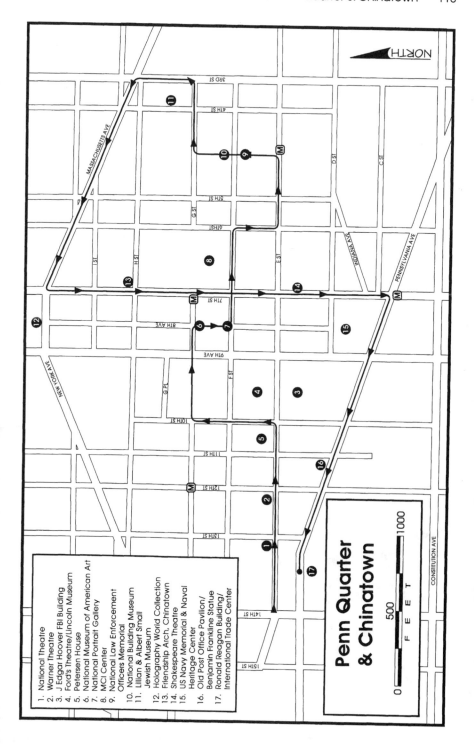

/899-2367, www.fordstheatre.org; the **Petersen House**: 202/426-6924;

National Museum of American Art: 202/357-2700, www.nmaa.si.edu, is open daily from 10 am to 5:30 pm.

National Portrait Gallery: 202/357-1447, 202/357-2700 or 202/357-1729 TDD, www.si.edu. Open daily from 10 am to 5:30 pm. Admission is free.

(NOTE: Both the National Museum of American Art and the National Portrait Gallery were closed in 2000 for a three-year period of renovation.)

National Law Enforcement Officers Memorial: 202/737-3400. The Visitor Center is open daily to 5 pm. The memorial itself is open 24 hours a day.

National Building Museum: 202/272-2448; www.nbm.org. Admission is free.

Lillian & Albert Small Jewish Museum: 202/789-0900. There is no admission fee, although a $2 donation is recommended. The facility is open Sunday through Thursday from 10 am to 4 pm.

Holography World Collection: 202/408-1833. The exhibit is open Tuesday through Sunday from 11 am to 6 pm. A family admission for the 20-minute tour costs $5.

Shakespeare Theatre: 202/393-2700; **US Navy Memorial and Naval Heritage Center**: 202/737-2300 or 800/723-3557, www.lonesailor.org. Admission is free. The Center is open Monday through Saturday from 9:30 am to 5 pm and on Sunday from noon to 4 pm.

The Old Post Office Pavilion: 202/289-4224, www.oldpostofficedc.com. Shopping hours are 10 am to 9 pm Monday through Saturday and noon to 7 pm on Sunday.

Getting there

Convenient Metro stations in this region include the Federal Triangle, the Metro Center, the Gallery Place, and the Judiciary Square stations.

First steps

As you enter the **National Museum of American Art**, you can pick up a map and a calendar of events that will prove not only informative, but interesting and helpful. There also is an information kiosk in the **National Portrait Gallery** to direct you to the things that you would like to see. Every 30 minutes, the **Discovery Channel Theater** presents "Destination DC," the only film in town that provides an informal tour of the capital. Ask for a walking tour map and brochure for the **National Law Enforcement Officers Memorial** at the memorial's Visitor Center, 605 E St NW.

Seasonal highlights

Every Fall, **Ford's Theatre** hosts "A Festival at Ford's," a nationally-televised, celebrity-studded event that is traditionally attended by the president and first lady. Another Washington tradition is a holiday performance of Dickens' *A Christmas Carol*, held at this theatre.

Chinatown provides the setting for Washington's annual Chinese New Year's

Day Celebration and parade (202/638-1041), which is held every February. Between September and July, the **Shakespeare Theatre** stages three Shakespearean plays and two addition, non-Shakespearean plays.

Tours

A guided one-hour tour of the **J Edgar Hoover Federal Bureau of Investigation Building**, E St and 10th St NW leaves the E St entrance every quarter-hour from 9:45 to 11:45 am and from 1:45 to 2:45 pm. The tour begins with a short videotape that describes the priorities of the Bureau and its history.

Free 15-minute talks are given hourly throughout the day at **Ford's Theatre**, site of Abraham Lincoln's assassination. Self-guided tours of the theatre are permitted daily from 9 am to 5 pm except during rehearsals and performances.

Free guided tours of the **National Portrait Gallery** also are offered.

Tickets may be purchased for an hour-long tour of the **MCI Center** locker rooms and press box, which are conducted between 11 am and 4 pm daily.

Appointments for free guided tours of the **National Law Enforcement Officers Memorial** can be arranged at the Visitor Center, 605 E St NW.

Guided one-hour public "Museum and Exhibition Highlights Tours" of the **National Building Museum** are provided at 12:30 pm on weekdays and at 12:30 and 1:30 pm on Saturdays, Sundays and holidays.

Guided tours of the **Lillian & Albert Small Jewish Museum** can be arranged by appointment.

The **Holography World Collection** can be seen *only* on tour.

Guided tours of the **US Navy Memorial and Naval Heritage Center** are given daily at 10 am and 2 pm. Inquire at the front desk.

Self-guided tours of the **Reagan Building and International Trade Center** may be taken from 7 am to 5 pm daily.

Penn Quarter & Chinatown. *To explore this part of the nation's capital, start in Freedom Plaza, located at 14th St and E St NW opposite the Willard Inter-Continental Hotel. The upper terrace of the plaza bears a fountain on one side and an equestrian statue of General Pulaski on the other.* On the north side of the plaza at 1321 Pennsylvania Ave is the **National Theatre**, the closest things to a Broadway-style theatre that Washington has to offer. Hit shows either bound for or fresh from Broadway are presented regularly. The Federal-style National was established in 1835, destroyed three times by fire, and last renovated in 1983 at a cost of $6.5 million. Tickets for the presentations offered in the 1,672-seat theatre run from $20 to $70 each, with discounts available for seniors, students, member of the military, and disabled individuals.

From the National, walk a few doors east to the **Warner Theatre** at 1299 Pennsylvania Ave is the. This Washington classic opened in 1924 as the Earle Theatre, a movie and vaudeville house with a marble-and-golf leaf lobby and an auditorium festooned with gold-leaf ceilings and magnificent chandeliers. After a $10 million restoration in 1992, the theatre has featured Broadway productions, comedy, dance, films, and musical concerts on a year-round basis. Its 2,000 seats typically sell for $20 to $60 per ticket.

Leave the theatre and walk east to 10th St NW. Occupying the entire block between 9th St and 10th St on the south side of the street is the building that houses the FBI. Named for the first director of the FBI, the **J Edgar Hoover Federal Bureau of Investigation Building** receives more than half a million visitors each year. Hoover served as director of the FBI from its founding in 1908 to the time of his death and served through the terms of eight consecutive presidents. The FBI building, festooned with flags, is open weekdays from 8:45 am to 4:15 pm. Once inside, visitors must undergo a security check.

Exhibits portray the careers of such famous criminals as Al Capone, Ma Barker, John Dillinger, Bonnie and Clyde, and "Pretty Boy" Floyd. Visitors get an inside look at the FBI's crime laboratories, see various espionage devices of display, see evidence presented during the prosecution of numerous famous crimes, see more than 5,000 weapons on display (no two of which are alike), see where 187 million fingerprints are kept on file, and witness a live-ammunition firearms demonstration presented by a special agent.Visitors also see the US Crime Clock, which graphically ticks off the numbers and the frequency of various violent crimes as they occur across America, and the Drug Enforcement Agency's world map, which shows the routes favored by the carriers of illicit drugs throughout the world.

Return to E St and retrace your steps to the corner (10th St NW). Head north along 10th St for half a block. **Ford's Theatre** and the **Lincoln Museum** are located at 511 10th St NW, the building in which Abraham Lincoln was fatally wounded. Just five days after Lee's surrender to Grant at Appomattox, ending the Civil War, Lincoln and his wife were attending a presentation of Tom Taylor's comedy *Our American Cousin* in this theatre. Shortly after 10 pm, during the second scene of the third act John Wilkes Booth, a famous actor of the day, crept into the Lincolns' box, shot the president, and jumped from the box onto the stage shouting "Sic semper tyrannis" (Thus ever to tyrants). Booth broke his left leg while making the leap, but managed to mount his horse in the back alley and ride off.

Ford's Theatre, built in 1853, was immediately closed by order of the

Secretary of War, Edwin M Stanton, and for years was used as an office and as an Army Medical Museum by the War Department. In 1893, 22 clerks were killed when three floors of the building collapsed, and the building remained in disuse until the 1960s, when it was restored to appear precisely as it did on the night of Lincoln's assassination.

In the basement of the theatre is the Lincoln Museum, which is open daily from 9 am to 5 pm. More than 400 items are on display, including the Derringer pistol that John Wilkes Booth used to assassinate Lincoln, Booth's diary, the clothes Lincoln wore on the night of his assassination, a Lincoln life mask, and plaster casts of Lincoln's hands. Audiovisual displays describe Lincoln's early life, political experiences, and presidential years, and there is a bookstore.

Across the street, at 516 10th St NW, is the **Petersen House,** to which Abraham Lincoln was carried after he was shot and in which he died the following day. Furnished with period pieces, the house has the appearance of a museum of the period. Built in 1849, it was the home of William Petersen, a tailor. The tiny first-floor bedroom to which Lincoln was taken contained a bed so small that the President had to be laid diagonally across it. Visitors can see the original blood-stained pillow on which his head rested. In the front parlor, Mary Todd Lincoln and her son Robert spent the night waiting for word of the president's condition. In the back parlor, Secretary Stanton held a cabinet meeting, began to question witnesses, and eventually announced at the time of Lincoln's death that he "now belongs to the ages." As it did on April 15, 1865, the house clock always reads 7:22 pm, the time when Lincoln died.

Twelve years after Lincoln's death, the house was sold to Louis Schade, who published a newspaper, *The Washington Sentinel,* in the basement. In 1896, the house was purchased by the government for $30,000. Today, it is maintained by the National Park Service. The house is open daily from 9 am to 5 pm, and there is no admission fee.

Leaving the Petersen House, turn left (north), walk to G St and turn right (east). At 8th St and E St NW is the old Patent Office Building, the third oldest government building in Washington. The building now houses two important art galleries.

Secretary of State Thomas Jefferson created the Patent Office in 1790 and is said to have personally inspected each application that was submitted. The original building, a Greek Revival design with porticoes that replicate those of the Parthenon in Athens, was created by William Parker Elliott, but was destroyed by fire in 1836. When the building was reopened in 1867, it was the largest building in the entire country.

During the Civil War, the Patent Office building served as a hospital and mortuary. Clara Barton took care of patients there, and Walt Whitman read poetry to them as they recuperated. it was the site of Lincoln's second inaugural ball and has been the temporary headquarters for the Department of the Interior and the Civil Service Commission. It was slated for destruction in the 1950s, but instead was turned over to the Smithsonian Institution and reopened in 1968 after an extensive renovation.

One of the two art museums now housed in the old Patent Office Building is the **National Museum of American Art**, which is entered from G St. The statue of a cowboy decorates the front steps. Inside, 1,000 of the museum's 37,500 works are on display. Established in 1976, the museum is the largest of the Smithsonian's art museums and houses the country's oldest federal art collection. Founded in 1829, the collection actually predates the founding of the Smithsonian.

Covering two centuries, the museum's artworks are arranged chronologically and include the most comprehensive collection of 20th-century Latin American art in the country. The second floor exhibits the work of such mid- to late-19th-century artists as Winslow Homer, Mary Cassatt, Albert Pinkham Ryder, and John Singer Sargent. On the third floor is the Lincoln Gallery, in which Abraham Lincoln celebrated his second inaugural in 1865 beneath the vaulted ceilings and amid the marble columns where 20th-century masters can now be seen.

In the southern half of the old Patent Office Building is the **National Portrait Gallery**, which is entered off F St NW. Opened in 1968, the museum is affiliated with the Smithsonian Institution. It surrounds a lovely courtyard that features twin cast-iron fountains and a number of beautiful sculptures. To the right and left of the main entrance are galleries that contain special exhibits, but with the exception of the Presidential portraits, which are displayed in the Hall of Presidents on the second floor, no portrait may become apart of the museum's permanent collection until the subject has been dead for at least 20 years. Among the works included in the permanent collection are Gilbert Stuart's *Lansdowne* portrait of George Washington, Stuart's portrait of Thomas Jefferson, several Jo Davidson sculptures including a Buddha-like figure of Gertrude Stein, a portrait of Mary Cassatt by Edgar Degas, and portraits or bronzes of such diverse dignitaries as Pocahontas, Davy Crockett, Daniel Boone, Ernest Hemingway, Babe Ruth, Casey Stengel, Samuel FB Morse, Washington Irving, Ralph Waldo Emerson, Nathaniel Hawthorne, Henry Wadsworth Longfellow, Albert Einstein, Martin Luther King Jr, Walt

Disney, and Helen Keller.

On the mezzanine, the Civil War is depicted in a series of portraits, including one of the last photographs ever taken of Abraham Lincoln. The Great Hall on the third floor is done in the American Victorian Renaissance style. Along with the assorted paintings, sculptures and photographs, the museum also displays an interesting collection of *Time* magazine covers...and there is a museum shop.

Exit the museum onto F St and turn left. The first intersection is 7th St NW. From here on south to Pennsylvania Ave, there is a succession of art galleries and other places of cultural interest, 10 of which voluntarily extend their evening hours on the third Thursday of every month to better serve the needs of tourists. On the east side of 7th St stands the mammoth MCI Center.

Home of the NBA's Washington Wizards, the WNBA's Washington Mystics, the NHL's Washington Capitals, and the Georgetown Hoyas, the 20,000-seat **MCI Center** at 601 F St NW is more than a sports arena. It also contains shops, a restaurant, and an interactive sports gallery. The MCI National Sports Gallery (202/661-5133) is located on the third floor of the building inside the F St lobby. This is the home of the American Sportscasters Assn Hall of Fame. Here too are such sports-related items as a Honus Wagner baseball card valued at $700,000, Muhammad Ali's robe, and the Bullets' 1978 NBA championship trophy. Interactive and video games allow you to go one-on-one with a virtual NBA star.

Also in the MCI Center is the **Discovery Channel Store: Destination Washington, DC** (202/639-0908), which has interactive exhibits such as a "Dinosaur Dig," where visitors can participate in a simulated excavation for fossils; animal habitats such as a giant any colony to explore; and the cockpit of a B-25 bomber.

Exit the MCI Center onto F St NW and turn left. At the corner of 6th St NW, turn right and walk to the next corner (E St). At 605 E St NW is the Visitor Center for the **National Law Enforcement Officers Memorial**. Check out the gift shop, and if you have children, ask for a free children's activity packet. Interactive video displays let you see the picture of every law enforcement officer who has ever been killed in the line of duty and read a brief biography of that individual.

Now walk a block and one-half East along E St to Judiciary Square, in which the actual memorial can be found. Four bronze lions by Washington sculptor Raymond Kaskey, each weighing 2,500 lbs, guard the entrance to the three-acre landscaped garden, which are bordered by two tree-lined "pathways of remembrance." The park-like setting also contains an 80-foot reflecting pool, plush carpets of grass, 60,000 ornamental plants, and 128 trees. Its blue-gray marble walls display the names of each of the 14,500 federal, state and local law enforcement officers who have been killed in the line of duty since 1794 when US Marshall Robert Forsyth was gunned down. Nearly 90 women officers are among those whose names are inscribed on the walls, and an average of one officer is killed in the line of duty every other day, so the memorial expands annually as new names are added each May. In early April, 14,000 orange and yellow daffodils beautify the walkways.

Across F St from Judiciary Square is the Old Pension Building, which now houses the National Building Museum. In 1887, almost 1.5 million bricks were used to build the US Pension Building at 401 F St NW, designed by Civil War Quartermaster General Montgomery C Meigs. Now, the building contains the **National Building Museum.**The site of 14 Presidential inaugural balls, the Great Hall measures 316 x 115 feet and has a ceiling 15 stories high. Of an impressive Italian Renaissance design, the hall contains a central fountain and eight Corinthian columns 75 feet high, 8 feet in diameter and 25 feet in circumference—the largest interior columns in the world. In all, there are 72 Doric columns on the ground floor of the building and 72 Ionic columns on the second floor, plus 234 busts by American sculptor Gretta Bader that occupy niches high above the center court.

The museum contains photographs, blueprints, eight model buildings, and a number of audiovisual presentations highlighting American achievements in architecture, urban planning, design, construction, engineering, and preservation. There is a museum shop on the ground floor of the building. Museum hours are Monday through Saturday from 10 am to 4 pm and Sunday from noon to 4 pm.

Exit onto G St and turn right. Where the street ends at 3rd St NW stands the Jewish Historical Society of Greater Washington. Inside the oldest Jewish synagogue building in Washington (1876), the Jewish Historical Society building at 701 3rd St NW houses the **Lillian & Albert Small Jewish Museum.** The building also houses a restored sanctuary. The Small Museum contains a permanent exhibit that depicts the history of the Jewish community in Washington.

Leaving the building, take a right on 3rd St and walk to Massachusetts Ave. Turn left and go about five blocks to Mt Vernon Square. In the south lobby of the Tech World Plaza, 800 K St NW, is the **Holography World Collection.** The collection includes holograms (three-dimensional figures) from throughout Asia, Europe and North American, including one of the largest holograms ever created. Operated by the Art, Science & Technology Institute, the exhibit is open Tuesday through Sunday from 11 am to 6 pm. A family admission for the 20-minute tour costs $5.

When you leave Mt Vernon Square, go south on 7th St for two blocks to H St NW, where you will see the entrance to Washington's Chinatown, a small community that extends between G St and H St from 6th St to 8th St NW. There, you will find most of Washington's Chinese restaurants and shops. Just east of the intersection at 7th St and H St NW stands the colorful **Friendship Arch**, once described as a symphony of red and gold dragons. The arch symbolizes the ties between Washington and its sister city, Beijing, China.

Near here is the **Shakespeare Theatre**, 450 7th St NW, located in the historic Landsburgh Building. This 449-seat theatre opened in March 1992 after the performing company realized that it needed greater capacity than was available in the Smithsonian's Folger Shakespeare Library, where they had performed for two decades. Tickets for their performances range in price from $13.50 to $49.50. Standing-room tickets are available for $10 two hours before each sold-out performance. Discounts are provided for seniors (20%) and students (50% one hour before the curtain.

Continue heading south on 7th St until you reach Pennsylvania Ave. On your left at that intersection stands a plaza containing a memorial to the US Navy.

The **US Navy Memorial and Naval Heritage Center**, 701 Pennsylvania Ave NW, www.lonesailor.org, was authorized by Congress in 1980. Interactive video kiosks provide information about naval ships, aircraft, and history. A sculpture depicts a Navy family celebrating a homecoming. The Navy Memorial Log Room contains a computerized record of all past and present Navy personnel, while the Presidents Room honors the six American Presidents who once served in the Navy and the two who served as Secretary of the Navy. A library, open from 10 am to 4 pm weekdays, contains hundreds of books and periodicals. The Ship's Store gift shop is open Monday through Saturday from 9:30 am to 5 pm.

The **Arleigh and Roberta Burke Theater** features a 35-minute wide-screen 70 Surroundsound film called *At Sea* which lets the audience experience the adventure of going to sea on a Naval ship. The film is shown at 10 am, noon, 2 pm and 4 pm from Monday through Saturday and at 11 am, 1 pm, and 3 pm on Sunday. Admission is free to those in uniform but costs $3.75 otherwise, except for seniors and students ($3).

At the outdoor memorial, there is a 10-foot circular plaza bearing the world's largest map, a concrete creation surrounded by flag masts, cascading fountains, and tiered waterfalls salted with waters from each of the seven seas. A statue, *The Lone Sailor*, watches over the map. Two sculptured walls nearby are adorned with 22 bronze bas-reliefs that commemorate naval history and related US maritime services.

Go northwest along Pennsylvania Ave past the J Edgar Hoover FBI Building and cross the street at 11th St NW. **The Old Post Office Pavilion** at 1100 Pennsylvania Ave NW, sits on the Federal Triangle. A former post office erected in 1899, the building was twice scheduled for demolition, but eventually was preserved as a multi-purpose facility that today includes 43 shops, offices, restaurants, and a food court. After a six-year renovation, the building reopened in May 1984 with a Romanesque Revival interior and a 196-foot skylight roof. European-style cart vendors hawk their wares throughout the corridors, and daily day-long entertainment is provided on the lower level.

The 10th floor houses the 10 Congress Bells, each five feet in diameter and weighing from 600 to 3,000 lbs. Replicas of the ones in Westminster Abbey, the bells were presented to the United States by Great Britain in recognition of the American Bicentennial. A full peal honors the opening and closing of Congress, special state occasions, and national holidays. The building's 315-foot clock tower is the second highest point in Washington and affords some magnificent views of the city.

Step outside the building onto 12th St. In front of the Old Post Office Pavilion stands the **Benjamin Franklin Statue**, a tribute to the printer, writer, scientist, patriot, diplomat—and infamous rake—who not only presented us with *Poor Richard's Almanac*, the discovery of electricity, and a pivotal role in the formation of our country, but an illegitimate son, William, who grew up to become the Governor of New Jersey.

Back on Pennsylvania Ave, remain headed in a northwesterly direction. Ahead of you, blocked by the imposing US Treasury Building, is the White House. At 1300 Pennsylvania Ave NW is the **Reagan Building and International Trade Center**, the city's newest landmark building. Designed by James Ingo Freed, the 3.1-million-sq-ft building is the second largest government building ever built (only the Pentagon is larger). It completes the Federal Triangle of government buildings, and houses a 65,000-sq ft conference center, an 11,500-sq-ft exhibition hall, a 625-seat amphitheater equipped with the latest in high-tech capabilities and surrounded by 20 meeting rooms, a 7,900-sq-ft ballroom, a 125-foot glass atrium with an elegant stone staircase, a food court, and a gift shop. On display in the atrium are a number of artworks and a piece of the Berlin Wall.

Continue northwest along Pennsylvania Ave to the Freedom Plaza, where your tour of the Washington downtown, Penn Quarter and Chinatown began.

Lodging

Just six blocks from the White House or Union Station and two blocks from the MCI Arena, the **Renaissance Washington DC Hotel** ($$$, 202/898-9000 or 800/HOTELS-1; www.renaissancehotels.com) at 999 9th St NW, is favored by many people who visit Washington on business. It is large (800 rooms), has a 60-foot swimming pool and an exercise room, and provides guests with a complimentary continental breakfast. The **Florentine Restaurant** serves an outstanding dinner from a menu built around a combination of Mediterranean-style dishes and regional American favorites. The Chinese rock garden and the **Plaza Gourmet** cafe (open 7:30 am to 5 pm) are excellent outdoor venues during the Summer.

Those who enjoy a smaller (340 rooms) or more historic venue will enjoy the **Hotel Washington** ($$$, 202/638-5900 or 800/424-9540) at 515 15th St NW, just one block from the White House. The hotel has been fully restored and renovated.

The **Carlton Hotel** ($$$, 202/638-2626 or 800/562-5661; www.itt sheraton.com), 923 16th St NW, is located just two blocks from the White House and contains 187 rooms, including 14 suites. Guests receive a complimentary morning paper, there is a fitness center and a fine restaurant, and valet parking is provided.

Another fine hotel, also just two blocks from the White House, is the **Capital Hilton** ($$$, 202/393-1000 or 800/HILTONS), 16th St and K St NW, which has 544 rooms and 36 suites and serves a complimentary continental breakfast.

The **Madison** ($$-$$$, 202/862-1600 or 800/424-8577), 1177 15th St NW, offers 353 rooms, with 35 suites, and a fitness center, while the **Westin Washington, DC City Center** ($$$. 202/429-1700 or 800/847-8232; www. westin.com), 1400 M St NW, offers 400 rooms, 13 suites, and your choice of a continental breakfast or free parking.

Other close-in hotels include **Governor's House Hotel** ($$, 202/296-2100 or 800/821-4367; www.governorshousewdc.com), 1615 Rhode Island Ave NW; **Holiday Inn Downtown** ($$$, 202/737-1200), 1155 14th St NW; **Marriott at Metro Center** ($$-$$$, 202/737-2200 or 800/9290), 775 12th St NW; **Grand Hyatt Washington** ($$$, 202/582-1234 or 800/233-1234; www.hyatt.com), 1000 H St NW; **Morrison-Clark Historic Inn & Restaurant** ($$-$$$, 202/898-1200 or 800/332-7898), 1015 L St NW; **Henley Park Hotel** ($$, 202/638-5200 or 800/222-8474), 926 Massachusetts Ave NW; and the **Days Inn Premiere Convention Center** ($$, 202/842-1020), 1201 K St NW.

In the colorful Chinatown area, try the **Red Roof Downtown** ($$, 202 /289-5959 or 800/843-7663) at 500 H St NW, which has 197 rooms, a restaurant (open daily from 6:30 am to 2 pm and from 5:30 to 10 pm), an exercise room, a sauna, and a self-serve laundry. The MCI Arena and a Metro station are just a block-and-a-half away and the convention center is just four blocks away.

Arts & culture

The **National Theatre** at 1321 Pennsylvania Ave is the oldest continuously-operating theatre in Washington. In addition to a full program of current theatre, the National offers free public-service programs on Saturday mornings at 9:30 and 11 am from October through April (202/783-3370) including a children's theater complete with puppets, clowns, magicians, singers, and dancers. Monday night programs often showcase local groups and individual performers, and free films are shown throughout the Summer.

Ford's Theatre now offers contemporary productions more or less year-around from Tuesday through Sunday at 7:30 pm. Matinees are offered on Thursdays at 1 pm, Saturdays at 2 pm, and Sundays at 3 pm. The box office is open Saturday and Sunday from noon to showtime and from 10 am to curtain-time on show days. Tickets run from $27 to $40, with discounts available for families, seniors, and students. Discounts also are offered with matinees and "day of" evening shows.

The National Portrait Gallery has an on-going series of free workshops for families with children between the ages of 9 and 16 (202/357-2729), but pre-registration is required.

In addition to a number of sporting events, the **MCI Center** offers a variety of entertaining and cultural events throughout the year.

The Great Hall at the **National Building Museum** is the site of an on-going Concert Series as well as an on-going series of exhibitions and programs, including family programs and workshops, some of which attract the participation of 12,000 children a year. A film series is conducted at lunch time.

The 1,200-seat open-air amphitheater at the **US Navy Memorial and Naval Heritage Center** is the site of numerous free band concerts. The Navy band and the bands of other military units perform on Tuesdays at 8 pm from Memorial Day through Labor Day. Some 50 mid-day concerts also are presented by high school bands from throughout the country during the spring and early summer. Other special events include the Blessing of the Fleet Festival each spring, a wreath-laying ceremony at 1 pm on Veteran's Day in November, and Family Holiday Caroling in December.

By riding a glass elevator to the bell-ringing chamber in the **Old Post Office Pavilion** on Thursdays between 7 and 9 pm, the public can attend a practice session of the playing of the Congress Bells. Free tours of the tower (202/606-8691) are given daily from 8:45 to 10:45 pm, although the tower is closed from 6:30 to 10 pm on Thursdays for bell-ringing practice. Meet the guide in the lower lobby near the 12th St entrance. The elevator to the 12th floor observation deck is *not* the same elevator as that which goes to the bell-ringing area.

Food & drink

In the Tower Building near the McPherson Square Metro station is **DC Coast** ($$, 202/216-5988), 1401 K St NW, which provides contemporary American cooking in a newly-restored Art Deco building with dramatic high ceilings. Seafood, meat, poultry, and game grace the menu, and valet parking is available after 5:30 pm. Lunch is served on weekdays; dinner Monday through Saturday.

Done up in a western motif, the **Red Sage** ($$, 202/638-4444), 605 14th St NW, has a downstairs grill decorated in orange and turquoise, plus a casual upstairs cafe. Around the corner is the **Red Sage Market**, a good spot to catch a quick sandwich or a breakfast pastry on the run.

Cafe Mozart ($$-$$$, 202/347-5732), 1331 H St NW, provides a European flair by providing German and Austrian fare such as shnitzel, sauerbraten, and spaetzle. The full-service deli is open daily until 10 pm for breakfast, lunch and dinner. But if your taste runs more to Italian foods, you can try **Cafe Luigino** ($$-$$$, 202/371-0595), 1100 New York Ave NW, which serves Italian dishes ranging from pizza and spinach-filled ravioli to venison, wild boar, and ostrich...with a delightful outdoor patio and free parking to further stimulate your interest.

Photographs of 3,000 Washington power brokers, politicians and celebrities line the walls of the **Occidental Grill** ($$, 202/783-1475), 1475 Pennsylvania Ave, a local favorite since 1906 where regional American cuisine is served amid wood-paneled walls and deep-cushioned booths. Lunch and dinner are available Monday through Saturday from 11:30 am to 11 pm and on Sunday from noon to 9:30 pm.

Down the street at 801 Pennsylvania Ave is the **Peasant Restaurant & Bar** ($$, 202/638-2140), presenting a plush interior highlighted by potted palms, brass chandeliers, and French silhouette portraits. Tables on the Navy Memorial Plaza are available during nice weather. Lunch is served from 11 am to 3 pm on weekdays only; dinner, beginning at 5:30 pm from Monday through Saturday and beginning at 5 pm on Sunday.

An exotic treat is **Jaleo** ($$, 202/628-7949) at 480 7th St NW, a Spanish regional/tapas restaurant housed in the Civil War-era Landsburgh Building. On the wall hangs a large mural of a flamenco dancer based on John Singer Sargent's *Jaleo*, from which the restaurant chose its name. Lunch is served Monday through Saturday from 11:30 am to 2:30 pm; a limited tapas menu from 2:30 to 5:30 pm. Dinner is served nightly from 5:30 pm.

As one would expect, Chinatown is full of interesting places to eat, including **Golden Palace Restaurant** ($-$$, 202/783-1225) at 720 7th St NW; **Hunan Chinatown** ($-$$, 202/783-5858) at 624 H St NW; and **Tony Cheng's Mongolian Restaurant** ($-$$, 202/842-8669) at 619 H St NW.

At the National Museum of American Art, the **Patent Pending Cafe** (202/357-2700) occupies a hallway between the museum and its neighbor, the National Portrait Gallery. The cafe is open daily from 10 am to 3 pm and offers an excellent salad bar (34 cents per ounce) plus sandwiches ($2.75 to $3.75). Courtyard dining is available, weather permitting, but no credit cards or reservations are accepted.

The **Velocity Grill** (202/347-7780) inside the MCI Center serves lunch and dinner on two levels of the building. Its lounge overlooks the Wizards' practice court, and offers 12 different beers from no fewer than 120 taps.

Nightlife

The **Hard Rock Cafe** (202/737-7625), 999 E St NW, serves up rock and roll daily until 2 am, while the **Comedy Cafe** (202/638-5653), 1520 K St NW, presents top comedians from Wednesday through Saturday.

A sports and entertainment-themed restaurant, **Velocity Grill**, 601 F St NW, serves buffalo wings, sandwiches, and 120 popular beers and microbrews while a number of video screens deliver an uninterrupted variety of cable-produced programming. Customers also can get a view of the Wizards' professional basketball practice court. The grill contains one of the largest textured glass floors in the country, a 3-story glass staircase, and a glass-framed atrium. It is open for lunch, dinner, and late-night enjoyment.

One of the liveliest clubs in town is **Coco Loco** (202/289-2626), located at 810 7th St NW in Chinatown. Late tapas and a mixed grill dinner are available Thursday through Saturday night, and dancing (occasionally to the music of a live band) is offered until 2 am on Thursday and 3 am on Friday and Saturday. A sexy floorshow featuring Brazilian exhibition dancers is staged at 11 pm on Fridays and Saturdays, ending with a conga line and a limbo contest, complete with laser lights and special effects. There is a $5 to $10 cover and valet parking costs an additional $4.

Across from the Old Post Office at 1101 Pennsylvania Ave NW is the popular **Planet Hollywood** (202/783-7827). A part of the well-known national chain of nightspots, it contains a life-size model of the Terminator and maintains the inevitable (and expensive) gift shop.

Events

Each June, the **Shakespeare Theatre Co** offers admission-free Summer Shakespearean productions (Shakespeare Free for All) in the Carter Barron Amphitheatre in Rock Creek Park, 16th St and Colorado Ave NW. Every September, there is an open house in the company's home theatre (450 7th St NW) that shows what transpires backstage at a theatre.

Foggy Bottom

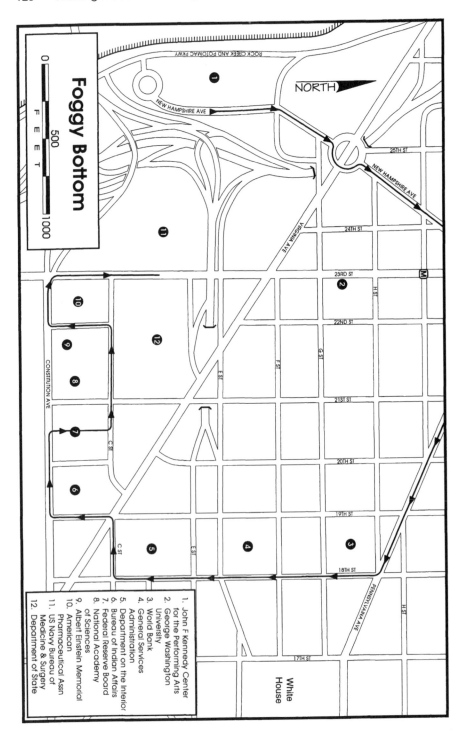

Foggy Bottom

0 500 1000
FEET

NORTH

1. John F Kennedy Center for the Performing Arts
2. George Washington University
3. World Bank
4. General Services Administration
5. Department on the Interior
6. Bureau of Indian Affairs
7. Federal Reserve Board
8. National Academy of Sciences
9. Albert Einstein Memorial
10. American Pharmaceutical Assn
11. US Navy Bureau of Medicine & Surgery
12. Department of State

ROCK CREEK AND POTOMAC PKWY

NEW HAMPSHIRE AVE

NEW HAMPSHIRE AVE

25TH ST

24TH ST

23RD ST

22ND ST

21ST ST

20TH ST

19TH ST

18TH ST

17TH ST

VIRGINIA AVE

PENNSYLVANIA AVE

CONSTITUTION AVE

C ST

E ST

F ST

G ST

H ST

White House

Foggy Bottom

As we have previously pointed out, Washington was originally laid out along the edge of a swamp along the banks of the Potomac River. Here the early clipper ships came to dock, and here the city's first industrial center was developed. Here too Jacob Funk acquired a little property, divided it into 287 lots, and created a tiny community that he called Hamburgh. Others began to call it Funkstown.

Gradually, the marshland was filled in, and the area began to develop and grow. Still, during the hot Summer months, it remained a hot steamy marshland, infested with malaria-bearing mosquitoes. The residents began to refer to it by a new name: Foggy Bottom.

Today, the area north of Potomac Park and south of K St between 17th St and 25th St NW is full of government buildings and colorful row houses, many of which date from the early 1800s. A shopping center at 2000 Pennsylvania Ave provides the residents with the restaurants and stores that they desire, and there are Metro stops at 23rd St and at I St NW.

Information

John F Kennedy Center for the Performing Arts: 202/467-4600 or 800/444-1324, www.kennedy-center.org. The building is open daily from 10 am to midnight.

Getting there

The tour begins at the Kennedy Center. If you have a car, park in the lot at the south end of the building. If you are traveling by Metro, get off at the Foggy Bottom-George Washington University (GWU) exit and take the free shuttle that operates every 15 minutes from 9:45 am to midnight Monday through Saturday and from noon to 8 pm on Sundays and holidays.

First steps

The Plaza Level of the John F Kennedy Center for the Performing Arts has an information desk where you can pick up a free map of the building, a ticket office where visitors can purchase tickets for any of the programs held in the Center, and a gift shop, all of which are located on the Hall of States. The Level A Motor Lobby also has a gift shop.

Seasonal Highlights

The annual televised "Kennedy Center Honors" is staged in the Opera House of the John F Kennedy Center for the Performing Arts.

Tours

Free 50-minute guided tours are offered daily from 10 am to 1 pm at the **John F Kennedy Center for the Performing Arts** except on Christmas. The tours begin on Level A. A free open house is held there every September.

Foggy Bottom. *The best place from which to start a walking tour of this section is the John F Kennedy Center for the Performing Arts.* A presidential memorial, national performing arts center, and education resource for the performing arts, the **John F Kennedy Center for the Performing Arts** sits on Rock Creek Pkwy beside the Potomac River, just south of the Watergate complex. Occupying 17 acres, the $73 million building was opened in 1971. All of the marble used in the building—3,700 tons of it—was donated by Italy. The 18 crystal chandeliers in the Grand Foyer were a gift from Sweden. The Terrace Theater was a gift from Japan.

The building has two levels, the lower Plaza Level and the upper Roof Terrace Level. Located on the Plaza Level, the outdoor River Terrace faces the Potomac River and provides some lovely views of the waterfront. Inside, the building's Grand Foyer is one of the world's largest rooms, measuring 40 feet wide, 60 feet high, and 630 feet long—longer than the Washington Monument is tall. Lighted by 18 Orrefors crystal chandeliers, each one weighing a ton, the Grand Foyer provides free pre-performance entertainment as well as food and beverage service before each performance and during each intermission. The Grand Foyer also doubles as the reception area for all three of the theaters on the building's main level. A Robert Berks bust of President John F Kennedy sits facing the Opera House, which occupies the center of the building.

To accommodate the foot traffic, the Plaza Level has two magnificent hallways, each running east and west. The Hall of States displays the flags of the 50 United States arranged in the same order as that in which the states entered the Union, as well as the flags of the various US Territories and the District of Columbia. The Hall of Nations displays the flags of nations that are diplomatically recognized by the United States, all arranged in alphabetical order.

There are six theaters within the Kennedy Center and of the six, four are located on the Plaza Level. The largest is the 2,450-seat Concert Hall, home of the National Symphony Orchestra. Next largest is the 2,300-seat Opera House, a combination musical theater, opera house, and ballet venue, brilliantly illuminated by a spectacular Lobmeyr chandelier. Next in size is the 1,100-seat Eisenhower Theater, which also features theater, opera, dance, and finally the 250-seat American Film Institute theatre.

On the upper Roof Terrace level, there are two outdoor terraces, the East (facing toward the city) and the West (looking out over the Potomac). This level also provides two lovely hallways, the North Roof Gallery and the South Roof Gallery, both running in the same direction as the hallways below, and two additional theaters. The 500-seat Terrace Theater was a Bicentennial gift from Japan in which chamber music, recitals, family theater productions, dance programs, and occasional theatrical productions are held. The 350-seat Theater Lab is used for experimental works and family theater productions.

Also on the Roof Terrace Level is the Education Resource Center and three restaurants. The Education Resource Center hosts numerous workshops, lectures, discussions, seminars, and classes concerning the performing arts and is open Tuesday through Saturday from noon to 8 pm.

International works of art and artifacts are on display throughout the building

As you leave the JFK Center, head northeast along New Hampshire Ave, cross Juarez Circle (at the intersection of New Hampshire Ave and Virginia Ave), and cross through a portion of the George Washington University campus to Washington Circle (at the intersection of New Hampshire Ave and Pennsylvania Ave). Between G St and K St from 20th St to 24th St NW, is the campus of **George Washington University,** a private institution founded in 1821. Originally known as Columbian College, it became Columbian University in 1873 and adopted its present name in 1904. The university consists of eight schools and colleges.

Travel southeast on Pennsylvania Ave toward the White House until you come to 18th St NW. Occupying an entire block on the southwest side of this intersection is the World Bank. Actually, the institution headquartered at 1818 H St NW is popularly called the **World Bank** but is more correctly known as the International Bank for Reconstruction & Development (IBRD). Affiliated with the UN, the organization's purpose is to provide loans and technical assistance for the development of projects within the UN's member countries. It has three affiliates that include the International Development Assn (IDA), the International Finance Corp (IFC), and the Multilateral Investment Guarantee Agency (MIGA). The World Bank is run by a Board of Governors, made up of representatives from all of the member countries. A group of 21 executive directors approves all of the loans.

The recent expenditure of $315 million for renovations to the headquarters building has been the subject of severe criticism.

Turn south on 18th St and follow it to F St NW, where you will find the General Services Administration building, which occupies another entire block from E St to F St between 18th St and 19th St NW. It is the job of the **General Services Administration** to manage all of the government's property and records. Established in 1949, the organization now employs over 14,000 people.

Continuing south on 18th St NW, pass Rawlins Park, cross E St, and walk past another huge government building on your right, the headquarters of the Department of the Interior. Created in 1849, the **Department of the Interior**, 1849 C St NW, occupies an entire city block from C St to E St between 18th St and 19th St NW. Charged with managing the government's many internal affairs, such as the US Fish & Wildlife Service, the National Park Service, the Bureau of Indian Affairs, and the Bureau of Land Management, the Department of the Interior employs nearly 71,000 people.

Past secretaries of the Department include Harold Ickes, Stewart Udall, and Albert Fall, the infamous secretary who became involved in the Teapot Dome oil scandal during the administration of President Warren G Harding.

From the Interior Building, turn right (west) on C St and walk one block. At 1849 C St NW is the **Bureau of Indian Affairs**, the agency that bears the responsibility of caring for the interests of our Native American population, including the Eskimos. Created by the War Department in 1824, the Bureau became a part of the Department of the Interior in 1849. Its 14,500 employees, primarily Native Americans, manage 12 area offices throughout the country.

Return to the three-way intersection of C St, Virginia Ave and 19th St NW. Turn right (south) and go one block to Constitution Ave. Turn right once more, go past the back side of the Bureau of Indian Affairs Building, and cross 20th St NW. On Constitution Ave between 20th St and 21st St NW is the **Federal Reserve Board**, the government's central bank. Established in 1913, the bank now operates a network of 12 District Reserve Banks and 24 branch banks throughout the country. Its seven-member board is appointed to a 14-year term by the president and approved by the Senate. The chairman and vice chairman are appointed to four-year terms by the president.

Exit the building onto C St on the opposite side of the building from where you entered. Turn left and walk across 21st St NW. At 2100 C St NW is the

National Academy of Sciences (202/334-2436), which occupies the entire block between 21st St and 22nd St NW. Created by an act of Congress in 1863, the Academy has the responsibility to investigate and report on an endless variety of scientific matters at the request of the federal government. Open to the public between 9 am and 5 pm on weekdays, the building features a particularly ornate Great Hall.

Returning to C St, turn left, walk to the first intersection, and turn left again, going one block to Constitution Ave, which forms the northern boundary of West Potomac Park. On the northeast corner of 22nd St and Constitution Ave, in the gardens of the National Academy of Sciences, sits the **Albert Einstein Memorial.** The statue shows Einstein in a sitting position, which entices countless children daily to climb up and have their pictures taken seated in Einstein's lap.

Continuing west on Constitution Ave, across 22nd St NW, will take you to the American Institute of Pharmacy, the headquarters of the American Pharmaceutical Assn. Founded in 1852, the **American Pharmaceutical Assn (APhA)** (202/628-4410), 2215 Constitution Ave NW, will be celebrating its Sesquicentennial in 2002. Designed by John Russell Pope and dedicated in 1934, the headquarters building occupies the entire block between 22nd St and 23rd St NW and is the only building on Constitution Ave that is not occupied by some office of the federal government. An annex was added to the building in 1960. The staff serves the needs of the APhA's 50,000 members nationwide.

Continue heading west on Constitution Ave to the next intersection (23rd St NW) and turn right. Across the street is a multi-building complex that houses the US Navy's Bureau of Medicine & Surgery. The **US Navy Bureau of Medicine & Surgery,** 2300 E St NW, serves the medical needs of the 700,000 men and women on active duty with the United States Navy plus 2.6 million of their family members and retired Navy personnel.

On the east side of 23rd St NW, across from the Navy complex, is another huge government building that extends from 21st St to 23rd St between C St and E St NW. The **Department of State,** 2201 C St NW, www.state.gov /html, is arguably the most powerful arm of the federal government beyond the US Congress, the Supreme Court, and the White House itself. It is the component of our federal government that is charged with establishing and maintaining America's relationships with other countries throughout the world. Past Secretaries of State have included such prominent individuals as John Quincy Adams, James Buchanan, John C Calhoun, Henry Clay, Charles Evans Hughes, Cordell Hull, Thomas Jefferson, Henry Kissinger, James Madison, George C Marshall, John

Marshall, James Monroe, Edmund Muskie, William Seward (who was responsible for bringing Alaska into the Union), Martin Van Buren, Cyrus Vance, and Daniel Webster.

Lodging

To garner the ohs and ahs of your friends back home, stay in the **Watergate Hotel** ($$$-$$$$, 202/965-2300 or 800/225-5843), 2650 Virginia Ave NW—if you can afford it. The location is excellent, the surrounding area contains some of Washington's most exclusive restaurants, the balconies overlook the Potomac River, there is a health club plus an indoor pool and a sauna, and the people-watching can be spectacular. The Potomac Lounge serves a British-style afternoon tea from Tuesday through Saturday and hosts special early-evening events on a regular basis. Complimentary services include a shoe shine, a daily newspaper, and a weekday-morning ride downtown in a limousine. Relatively small (it contains just 85 suites and 60 junior suites), the hotel is but one part of an enormous complex that includes both residential apartments and business offices. Monica Lewinski once lived there, but the complex is best remembered as the site of a notorious break-in at the headquarters of the Democratic National Committee in 1972. G Gordon Liddy, general counsel to President Richard M Nixon's Council to Reelect the President (CREEP), went to prison for his role in that scandal, along with two dozen of his associates. Nixon himself was forced to resign in 1974.

Virtually across the street from the Watergate is **Howard Johnson's Premiere** ($$, 202/965-2700 or 800/654-2000; www.premieredc.com), 2601 Virginia Ave NW. Containing 192 rooms, the hotel has recently undergone a $3.5 million renovation. Amenities include the America's Best Restaurant, a business center, secure underground parking, a large L-shaped rooftop pool, a fitness center, and a coin-operated laundry.

Another excellent choice while visiting Foggy Bottom is the **State Plaza Hotel** ($$, 202/861-8200 or 800/424-2859), 2117 E St NW, which is set in a tree-lined neighborhood and offers 225 suites with full kitchens. The rooms cover eight floors (a north and a south tower connected by a garage) and the hotel has a small fitness center, garage parking, two rooftop sun decks, and the Garden Cafe. Amenities include a complimentary continental breakfast, a daily copy of the *Washington Post*, and a shoe shine.

The **Doubletree Guest Suites—New Hampshire Ave** ($$$, 202/785-2000 or 800/222-TREE), 801 New Hampshire Ave NW, is just one block from the Metro, provides valet parking, has a small rooftop pool, and serves a continental breakfast on the weekends.

Formerly the Inn at Foggy Bottom, an apartment building turned into a hotel in 1968, the eight-story **George Washington University Inn** ($$, 202/337-6620 or 800/426-4455; www.gwuinn.com), 824 New Hampshire Ave NW, was purchased by the university in 1994 and renovated. It now contains 95 European-style suites with kitchenettes, plus the Zuki Moon Restaurant, which is designed like a Japanese tea garden.

The **Hotel Lombard** ($$$$, 202/828-2600 or 800/424-5486), 2019 Pennsylvania Ave NW, also is located in the university neighborhood. The 11-story building has a fashionable walnut-lined lobby and contains 87 rooms and 38 suites. Guests receive weekday delivery of *The Washington Post*, twice-a-day maid service, and a complimentary shoe shine.

Arts & culture

Numerous free concerts and programs are held in the Grand Foyer of the **John F Kennedy Center for the Performing Arts**. Off this foyer are three of the Center's six theatres. Between them, the six theatres present programs that include concerts, film classics, theatre, opera, dance, chamber music, recitals, family theatre productions, and theatrical workshops.

The 1,500-seat Lisner Auditorium (202/994-1500), located on the corner of 21st St and H St NW on the campus of **George Washington University**, hosts a variety of musical programs each season.

Food & drink

Located near the Kennedy Center in The River Inn, **Foggy Bottom Cafe** ($$, 202/338-8707), 924 25th St NW, serves Continental cuisine for breakfast, lunch, and dinner from 7 am to 10 pm daily. The premiere Watergate restaurant, **Aquarelle** ($$$$, 202/298-4455 or 800/424-2736), 2650 Virginia Ave NW, also serves breakfast, lunch, and dinner daily as well as a Sunday brunch. **Kinkead's** ($$, 202/296-7700), 2000 Pennsylvania Ave NW, occupies a Foggy Bottom townhouse, where "modern American" food is available at lunch, dinner, and a Sunday brunch. Piano entertainment is available six nights a week in the casual cafe/bar downstairs.

Cajun food can be found at **Lulu's New Orleans Cafe** ($, 202/861-5858), 1217 22nd St NW, which serves lunch Monday through Saturday, dinner daily, and a brunch on Sunday. For French food, try **Provence** ($$$, 202/296-1166), 2401 Pennsylvania Ave NW, for lunch on weekdays and dinner from Monday through Saturday. A jacket and tie are suggested.

Fans of Italian food should explore the four-star, jacket-and-tie **Galileo Restaurant** ($$$, 202/293-7191), 1110 21st St NW, serving lunch on weekdays and dinner daily; **Primi Piatti** ($$, 202/223-3600), 2013 I St NW; **Ristorante i Ricchi** ($$$, 202/835-0459), 1220 19th St NW, fax 202/872-1220, which serves lunch on weekdays from 11:30 am to 2 pm and dinner from 5:30 to 10 pm on weekdays and 5:30 to 10:30 pm on Saturdays; or **Goldoni** ($$$, 202/452-0875), 1113 23rd St NW, fax 202/452-0875, where lunch is served from 11:30 am to 2 pm on weekdays and dinner is served from 5:30 to 10 pm Monday through Thursday, 5 to 10:30m on Friday and Saturday, and 5 to 10 pm on Sunday.

Meat-and-potatoes folks might like **Blackie's House of Beef** ($-$$, 202

/333-1100), 1217 22nd St NW, which serves lunch on weekdays and dinner daily. Dancing is offered nightly in Blackie's Deja Vu. An alternate choice would be the coat-and-tie **Prime Rib** ($$$, 202/466-8811), 2020 K St NW, which serves lunch on weekdays and dinner from Monday through Saturday

The **Roof Terrace Restaurant** (202/416-8555) in the Kennedy Center overlooks the river and provides dinner on the evenings when performances are given as well as a Sunday brunch. The adjacent Hors D'Oeuverie serves cocktails and light fare, while the Encore Cafe, at the opposite end of the hall, serves casual fare daily.

Nightlife
Foggy Bottom Pub (202/338-3000), 2142 L St NW, which is a popular hangout for students from George Washington University and Howard University, has an outdoor cafe, an upstairs restaurant, and a downstairs bar. Free appetizers are served on Friday nights, and on Saturdays guests pay $10 for all the beer or wine they can drink from 8 pm to midnight.

Darts, dancing and beer are the attractions at **Black Rooster Pub** (202 /659-4431), 1919 L St NW, another neighborhood hangout that is open only on weekdays.

For live piano music, visit **West End Cafe** (202/293-5390), One Washington Circle NW, while billiards and live music can be enjoyed at the **Washington Brewing Co** (202/965-2739), 1875 I St NW, Washington's largest brew-pub. Daily tours of the latter's brewhouse also are available.

Events
The American Film Institute theatre at the **John F Kennedy Center for the Performing Arts** presents screen classics on a daily basis and hosts various film festivals and movie premieres throughout the year.

Georgetown

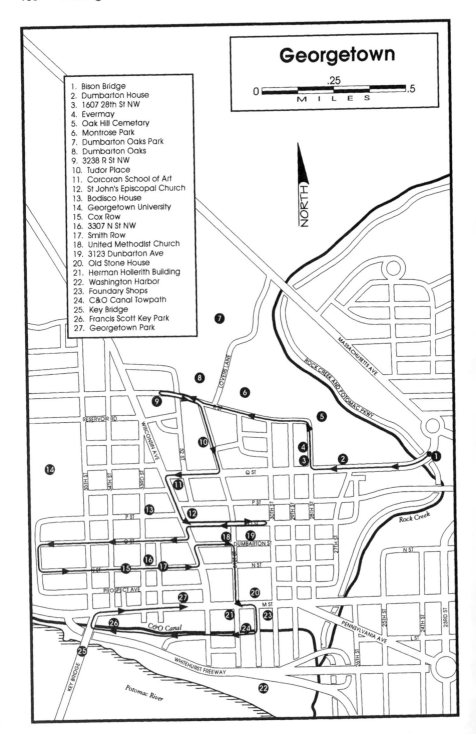

Georgetown

1. Bison Bridge
2. Dumbarton House
3. 1607 28th St NW
4. Evermay
5. Oak Hill Cemetary
6. Montrose Park
7. Dumbarton Oaks Park
8. Dumbarton Oaks
9. 3238 R St NW
10. Tudor Place
11. Corcoran School of Art
12. St John's Episcopal Church
13. Bodisco House
14. Georgetown University
15. Cox Row
16. 3307 N St NW
17. Smith Row
18. United Methodist Church
19. 3123 Dunbarton Ave
20. Old Stone House
21. Herman Hollerith Building
22. Washington Harbor
23. Foundary Shops
24. C&O Canal Towpath
25. Key Bridge
26. Francis Scott Key Park
27. Georgetown Park

Georgetown

Arguably Washington's most popular residential-business community, Georgetown sits just northwest of Foggy Bottom on the far side of Rock Creek Park. Once occupied by a native village called Tohoga, the area is believed to have been seen in 1608 by the first white man to reach the region, none other than Capt John Smith. It became part of the province of Maryland in 1700 and was established as a British colony in 1751. In other words, it predated the city of Washington by nearly half a century.

Pioneers founded the town of George on a 60-acre site and named it for the King of England. As a thriving Colonial port, it handled the shipment of crops from the farms in western Maryland to Europe and soon became a bustling tobacco port. Incorporated into the District of Columbia in 1878, it was annexed to the city of Washington in 1895 and designated a National Monument in 1967.

During the Civil War, Georgetown was a strategic location on the Underground Railroad, and many of the area's restored Colonial-era homes actually were used as slave quarters during the years before Emancipation.

Today, Washington's oldest neighborhood is a community of Georgian, Federal and Greek Revival houses, set on quiet, tree-lined, brick- and cobble-stoned streets. It is a charming, historic area with specialty stores, nightclubs, and intriguing restaurants. It is the center of Washington's trendy shops and nightlife.

Information

The Georgetown Information Center (202/653-5844 or 202/653-5190) at 1057 Thomas Jefferson St NW is open from Wednesday through Sunday between April and November. Tickets for barge rides on the C&O Canal, offered from April through September, can be purchased here. Free maps also are available.

Maps of Oak Hill Cemetery may be purchased at the cemetery's gatehouse.

Getting there

The Metro underground doesn't yet serve Georgetown (DuPont Circle is the closest stop), so you'll have to arrive by car, cab, foot, bike, or bus. There's plenty of on-street parking as well as several public lots and decks.

Seasonal highlights

A Garden Day is held at Tudor Place each Fall. Candlelight Evenings are offered during the Christmas season.

A candlelight tour of the Old Stone House also is conducted around

Christmastime.

Every April there is a 12-mi hike along the **C&O Canal** in honor of William O Douglas' historic crusade to keep the canal from being filled in during the 1950s.

Tours

Mary Kay Ricks, a freelance writer (301/588-8999), leads a 90-minute, $12 walking tour of the historic district every Saturday and Thursday at 10:30 am and walks through upper Georgetown during the month of May.

Another writer, Ian Pottker (301/762-3049), author of *Celebrity Washington*, leads a $15 two-hour Celebrity Tour past notable residences, watering holes, and movie locations on Thursdays, Fridays and Saturdays at 10 am. Pottker's tours begin at the Barnes a & Noble bookstore on M St NW.

Guided 40-minute tours of **Dumbarton House** are conducted from 10:15 am to 12:15 pm Tuesday through Saturday for a $3 fee. The house is closed during August, on Thanksgiving, and from December 24 to January 2.

Tudor Place can be toured only with a guide. The 45-minute guided tours are available at 10 and 11:30 am and at 1 and 2:30 pm from Tuesday through Friday and hourly from 10 am to 3 pm on Saturday. Visitors may tour the gardens on their own between 10 am and 4 pm Monday through Saturday except during the months of April, May, September, and October, when the gardens are open for self-guided tours only on Sunday afternoons. A map is provided. A donation of $5 for adults is suggested for the guided house tour, $2 for a self-guided garden tour.

Tours of **Georgetown University** (202/687-5055) also are available, as are free self-guided tours of the **Old Stone House**.

Float trips aboard the mule-drawn barge *Georgetown* are offered on the C&O Canal on a seasonal basis (202/653-5844 or 301/299-3613). The tours are led by Park Service rangers in period dress, and leave the Georgetown waterfront from Wednesday through Sunday between mid-April and early November. Tickets cost $5 for adults and $3.50 for children under 12 or seniors over 62.

Georgetown. *Start your walking tour of Georgetown on Q St NW, just south of Sheridan Circle, where the road crosses Rock Creek. Head in a westerly direction.* Q St crosses Rock Creek over the **Bison Bridge** (actually the Dumbarton Bridge), which was built in 1914. The bridge, designed by sculptor A Phimister Proctor, is colorfully decorated with four lifesize bronze statues of bison, while the sides of the bridge are ornamented with busts of Native Americans.

Follow Q St west for a block and one-half. At 2715 Q St NW is the **Dumbarton House** (202/337-2288), which dates from about 1800. Originally called Bellevue, the house was moved 100 yards to its present location in 1915 to accommodate the construction of a nearby bridge.

One of the house's first owners was Joseph Nourse, the first Registrar of the US Treasury. The man who designed the Washington Monument, architect Robert Mills, boarded with the Nourse family. Fleeing from the burning White House in 1812, Dolley Madison stopped here for a spot of tea before taking a ferry to safety in nearby Virginia. The building is now the headquarters for the Colonial Dames of America, which restored the house.

The Federal-style mansion, tucked behind a long brick wall, contains a magnificent collection of 18th- and 19th-Century American furniture, silver, textiles, ceramics, and art, and is listed on the National Register of Historic Places. Benjamin Henry Latrobe, who contributed to the design of the White House and the US Capitol, designed the entrance portico. A graceful stairway leads to a lovely landing, backlighted by an arched Palladian window.

Hepplewhite, Sheraton, Chippendale, and Louis XVI furnishings are displayed throughout, and many of the rooms have exquisite moldings. A magnificent George III mahogany breakfront bookcase contains an entire set of the 1797 Encyclopedia Britannica, and visitors can see historic letters and documents signed by George Washington, Thomas Jefferson, and James and Dolley Madison on display. A painting by Charles Willson Peale hangs above a late-18th Century sideboard in the dining room.

Continue heading west on Q St to 28th St NW and turn right. Senator Edward Kennedy occupied **1607 28th St NW** in the 1960s.

At 1623 28th St NW is **Evermay**, an elegant 1800s Georgian manor house, a private residence that is not open to the public, although it does offer occasional garden tours in season. The house was built between 1792 and 1794 by Samuel Davidson, a Scotsman who formerly owned some of the property now occupied by the White House and Lafayette Square.

One block north of Q St, 28th St NW and R St meet to form a right angle. **Oak Hill Cemetery** , 3001 R St NW, flanks both the North and East sides of the intersection. The cemetery occupies 25 acres that are bordered by Rock Creek Park on the north and Montrose Park on the west. The burial place, landscaped in a Victorian manner, was founded in 1850 by William Wilson Corcoran, founder of the Corcoran Gallery of Art. Corcoran, who is buried here, purchased the property from George Corbin Washington, a great-nephew of George Washington. James Renwick, architect of the Smithsonian "Castle" as well as New York's St Patrick's Cathedral and Grace Church, designed the iron enclosure and the Gothic-style stone chapel that stands inside.

Interred in the cemetery are Edwin Stanton, Abraham Lincoln's

Secretary of War; John Howard Payne, composer of *Home Sweet Home*; and Dean Acheson, Secretary of State under Harry Truman. No photography is allowed. The cemetery is open on weekdays between 10 am and 4 pm.

Across from the cemetery at 2920 R St NW is a beautiful home with a lovely, sweeping front drive. This is the home of Katherine Graham, publisher of the powerful *Washington Post* newspaper.

East of the cemetery at R St at Avon Pl NW is **Montrose Park** (202/282-1063), a free, heavily-wooded park that is open to the public from dawn to dusk without a fee. Plan ahead and you can take along a picnic lunch to be eaten here. Lover's Lane, a cobblestoned path that ran all the way to Baltimore during the 18th century, marks the western edge of Montrose Park. Strolling North along it will lead you to the lovely wooded **Dumbarton Oaks Park** (202/282-1063), which is open daily from 8 am to dusk. The 27-acre park once was a portion of the Dumbarton Oaks property, located immediately to the south of the park.

Having explored the parks, return to R St and turn right (west) to the next intersection (32nd St NW). Turn right once more. **Dumbarton Oaks** (202/343-3200), 1703 32nd St NW, is an 1801 Federal-style mansion surrounded by 10 acres of formal gardens. The gardens, modeled upon the magnificent gardens of Europe, may be entered off R St. They include wisteria-covered arbors, herbaceous borders, an Orangery, a Rose Garden with 1,000 rose bushes, and groves of cherry trees and magnolias, laced with winding brick paths set upon many different levels.

During the 1920s, Dumbarton Oaks was the residence of Robert and Mildred Bliss, who then donated the house to Harvard University, Robert's alma mater, in 1940. Now a museum, library, and research center for studies in Byzantine arts and history, pre-Columbian arts and history, and landscape architecture, the building is most widely known for the two international conferences that were held there in 1944 to lay the foundation upon which the United Nations was later formed. Those meetings were held in the Music Room, which has a beamed, painted 16th-century French-style ceiling and contains antique furniture, a large 16th-century stone fireplace, an 18th-century parquet floor, and El Greco's painting *The Visitation*.

Two wings were added to the building in 1963, one to house the Bliss collection of Pre-Columbia artworks and one to hold Mrs Bliss' collection of rare books on landscape gardening.

The Pre-Columbian museum was designed by Philip Johnson. The Olmec jade and serpentine figures, Mayan relief panels, textiles from 900

BC to the Spanish Conquest, funerary pottery, and sculptures of Aztec gods and goddesses that it contains are displayed in chronological order in eight glass pavilions that have floors of marble and oak.

The museum's Byzantine collection includes illuminated manuscripts, a 13th-century icon of St Peter, mosaics, ivory carvings, a 4th-century sarcophagus, and numerous pieces of jewelry. The museum is open from 2 to 5 pm Tuesday through Sunday except on holidays. A library containing more than 100,000 volumes is open Tuesday through Saturday from 2 to 5 pm and closed on Mondays. The yard behind the property wanders down to the nearby Rock Creek ravine.

Continue west along R St. At 3238 R St NW is an early 19th-century Adams-style brick building with a Doric-colonnaded portico. One of the early residents was Henry Wager Halleck, a Union army general who enraged his neighbors (many of them Confederate sympathizers) by quartering soldiers in the house, using R St as a drill field, and having a bugler sound reveille and taps at dawn and dusk each day. The home was later used as a Summer White House by President Ulysses S Grant.

Now backtrack one block along R St to 31st St NW and turn right. **Tudor Place** (202/965-0400), 1644 31st St NW, a Neoclassical 1816 mansion with five acres of gardens, occupies the entire city block. The centerpiece is a Palladian-style manor house designed by Dr William Thornton, the first architect of the US Capitol and the creator of The Octagon.

The house was purchased by Martha Parke Custis Peter, a grand-daughter of Martha Washington, using a legacy she had received from her step-grandfather George in 1805. The son of a Scottish tobacco and shipping magnate, Mrs Peter's husband Thomas was the mayor of Georgetown, and the couple's descendants lived in the house until 1984. When the last owner, Armistead Peter III, died, the house was left to the Tudor Place Foundation and opened to the public.

Henry Clay, Daniel Webster, and John Calhoun visited Tudor Place. From the dining room window, Martha Peter and Anna Maria Thornton, the wife of the architect, watched the burning of Washington during the War of 1812. The Marquis de Lafayette attended a reception here in 1824, and Robert E Lee, a close friend of the family, spent his last night in Washington prior to the Civil War in an upstairs bedroom.

The home's circular domed portico was designed by Dr William Thornton, and many of the furnishings were either inherited or purchased at auction from the Mount Vernon estate of George and Martha Washington. On display is a letter from George Washington to his wife on having received command of the Revolutionary Army, June

18, 1775. No cameras are allowed inside.

Go south on 31st St to Q St NW, turn right to Wisconsin Ave, and then turn left (south). The **Corcoran School of Art**, 1680 Wisconsin Ave NW, is the Georgetown branch of the only professional school of art and design in Washington. The school was founded in 1890.

Take Wisconsin Ave south for two blocks to O St and turn left (east). Partially designed by Dr William Thornton, **St John's Episcopal Church**, 3240 O St NW, was built in 1809. Thomas Jefferson was a parishioner.

Thomas and Martha Peter, residents of Tudor Place, also were parishioners, as was Dolley Madison. Francis Scott Key once served as a vestryman here. The parish office will open the church for you. Notice particularly the one Tiffany stained glass window that is inside the church. *Return to Wisconsin Ave and turn left (south) to O St. Then turn right (west) and make your way to 33rd St NW.* The Federal-style **Bodisco House** at 3322 O St was built in 1815 and was the home of Robert E Lee's mother. During the 1850s, the building housed a Russian diplomatic mission.

Continue west along O St to 37th St NW. **Georgetown University** was founded in 1789 by John Carroll, a friend of both George Washington and Benjamin Franklin and the cousin of a person from Maryland who signed the Declaration of Independence. It is Washington's oldest university and the nation's first Catholic institution of higher learning. After the Civil War, the school colors were changed to blue and gray to honor the students who were slain on both sides.

The modern rectangular building on the hill houses students and administrative offices. The building with twin spires is the Healy Building, named for Father Patrick Healy, a Jesuit priest who was the first African-American to receive a doctorate and to serve as the president of a predominantly white American university (1873-82).

President Bill Clinton graduated from Georgetown in 1968.

Follow 37th St NW south for one block to N St, then turn left (east). **Cox Row**, 3327-39 N St, includes five handsome Federal houses built in 1817. They are named for owner/builder John Cox, who was mayor of Georgetown for 20 years. Cox himself occupied the corner house (#3339) and in 1824 Lafayette was a house guest at #3337. The brick townhouse at **3307 N St NW** was purchased by John and Jackie Kennedy shortly after the birth of their daughter Caroline, while Kennedy still served as a United States Senator. The family lived in the house from 1957 to 1961, when they moved into the White House.

Smith Row, 3255-63 N St, is a string of Federal rowhouses whose exteriors remain much as they were when they were built in 1815 by brothers Walter and Clement Smith as speculative housing. Architectural features include column-framed freestanding porticoes, elliptical fanlights, oval interiors, circular and freestanding stairs, delicate moldings, and slim proportions throughout.

The 3000 block of N St NW, another elegant row of townhouses, dates from 1795. Jacqueline Kennedy lived briefly at 3017 N St NW after the death of President Kennedy.

At Wisconsin Ave, turn left, then take a right onto Dumbarton Ave. The Romanesque Revival **United Methodist Church** at 3133 Dumbarton Ave dates from 1849 and served as an infirmary during the Civil War. Walt Whitman worked with the soldiers hospitalized there.

3123 Dumbarton Ave is an exquisite building dating from 1810. The house is said to harbor a ghost.

Continue east on Dumbarton Ave to 31st St, turn right (south), and go to M St. The **Herman Hollerith Building** at 31st St and M St NW, was owned by the man who invented the punched-card tabulating machine, forerunner of our modern computers. While working for the Census Bureau in 1911, Hollerith sold his company to the firm that would later become IBM.

Turn east onto M St. The **Old Stone House** (202/426-6851 or 202/426-0125 TDD), 3051 M St NW, was built in 1765 by Pennsylvania-born cabinetmaker Christopher Layman. Layman used the ground floor for a workshop and kept pigs outside on the grounds. The rear of the house and the second story were added later. The area's only pre-Revolutionary War building, the house stands on one of the first 80 lots surveyed in 1751, making it the oldest house in Washington.

Bounded by a white picket fence, the house contains four small rooms decorated in the style of the period. From the early 1880s until 1950, the house served as a residence, a gun shop, a clockmaker's shop, a tailor shop, and a haberdashery. Operated by the National Park Service since 1950, its terraced grounds feature lovely 18th-century English flower gardens, where the public is allowed to picnic. The building is open from 8 am to 4:30 pm Wednesday through Sunday.

Occasionally, Park Service personnel will demonstrate how to cook over an open fireplace, how to do spinning, and how to make pomander balls (a mixture of aromatic materials, thought to ward off illnesses, that once were commonly carried in perforated bags or boxes).

Across the street from the Old Stone House is Thomas Jefferson St, so named because Jefferson once resided there. Adjacent to it at Wisconsin Ave and Grace St is **Washington Harbor**, which features a boardwalk promenade, a fountained courtyard, and waterfront dining.

A complex of galleries, shops, restaurants, movie theatres, and galleries, the **Foundary Shops** at 1055 Thomas Jefferson St NW are housed in a converted foundary beside the C&O Canal.

The **C&O Canal and Towpath** (202/472-4376) also can be entered off Thomas Jefferson St. Although the canal was first envisioned by George Washington, construction didn't begin until 1828, when President John Quincy Adams personally turned the first spadeful of dirt. Opened for traffic in 1831, the canal brought in manufactured goods from the east and returned to the ports of the Atlantic Seaboard with coal from the west, to be exported to Europe and used to fuel the factories along the industrial tidewater.

As a means of transport, the canal was very important in its time. From towpaths that paralleled the canal, mules pulled barges along the waterway. While four horses could normally transport a one-ton load 12 to 18 miles in a day, the canal towpath allowed the same four horses to move 100 tons a distance of 24 miles in the same period of time—thereby allowing its users to move nearly 400 times the payload.

Paralleling the Potomac River, the C&O Canal linked Georgetown with Cumberland, Maryland in the 1850s, but it was almost immediately rendered obsolete by the completion of the B&O Railroad, which could move goods even farther and faster than the mule-drawn barges. In 1924, extensive flooding caused some major damage to the system, putting an end to its already-dwindling use. The canal and towpath began to deteriorate, and by 1954, plans were under way to fill it in and create a scenic parkway along the route. One of the most vocal advocates for the change was the *Washington Post*, but William O Douglas, Chief Justice of the Supreme Court and a noted advocate of outdoor life, challenged the *Post*'s pro-development writers to join him in walking the entire 185-mile length of the canal. The *Post* then reversed its position and the canal was saved. (As you enter the towpath, look for a bust of Justice Douglas on your right.)

The C&O Canal was designated a national monument in 1960 and became a National Historical Park in 1971 and is equally popular with joggers, picnickers, and cyclists. At Swain's Lock, 16 miles outside of Georgetown, camping areas also become available, along with picnic tables and barbecue grills.

Follow C&O Canal towpath west for about five blocks until you reach a bridge, decorated with a colorful railing and lampposts, that leads to Rosslyn, VA on the other side of the Potomac. The **Key Bridge** was named for Francis

Scott Key, a native son and local lawyer. Key watched the British bombard Fort McHenry in Baltimore harbor during the War of 1812, and the event was so stirring, Key was moved to write a song, set to the tune of an old drinking song, *To Anacreon in Heaven*. Key's *The Star Spangled Banner* became our national anthem in 1931.

Nearby, at 34th St and M St NW, is **Francis Scott Key Park**, a circular colonnaded brick plaza behind a rose garden. In the center of the plaza is a bronze bust of Francis Scott Key (1799-1843), capped by a flag with 15 stars and stripes, just like the one that inspired Key to write the national anthem in 1814. These are commonly called the **Francis Scott Key Memorial** and the **Star Spangled Banner Monument**. Between 1803 and 1833, Key's home and law office stood about 100 yards West of this park, which is open daily from dawn to dusk.

Across from **1111 34th St NW** is a brick landing which bears a marker that indicates the spot from which Revolutionary War General George Washington and French Army Commander-in-Chief Jean-Baptiste Rochambeau crossed the Potomac in 1781 en route to Yorktown.

Walk east along M St. At 3222 M St NW stands **Georgetown Park** (202/342-8190, www.gtpark.com). Built in the 1800s, this four-story building once was a tobacco warehouse designed in the Victorian style. Later, it housed horse-drawn omnibuses, and later still, as a facility to service electric street cars and trolleys. In the 1960s, the building housed a "situation room" equipped to establish the country's first hotline to Moscow. Now a multilevel shopping center, the upscale mall contains more than 120 shops, restaurants, and a food court, plus the Georgetown Park Museum, which displays thousands of artifacts found when the building was being excavated. The museum is open daily.

Of equal importance in a town that suffers from an acute shortage of parking space, the building houses a parking garage, accessed at Wisconsin Ave and M St.

Either take one of the numbered streets north for six blocks to Q St and turn right (east) to return to the Bison Bridge from which you began your tour of Georgetown OR follow M St east to Rock Creek Park and stroll northward through that beautiful park to the Bison Bridge.

Lodging

The **Four Seasons Hotel** ($$$-$$$$, 202/342-0444 or 800/332-3442; www.fourseasons.com), 2800 Pennsylvania Ave, is Washington's only AAA 5-diamond hotel. It overlooks Rock Creek Park and the C&O Canal, has 258 rooms and 59 suites, and with its twice-daily room service, spa and indoor pool, is a favorite among the movie stars who occasionally visit the city. The Seasons restaurant serves an afternoon tea daily and stages a Sunday jazz brunch between 10:30 am and 2 pm.

Also overlooking the C&O Canal, the **Latham Hotel** ($$$, 202/726-5000 or 800/368-5922), 3000 M St NW, has 143 rooms and 9 suites, a pool, and the upscale Citronelle restaurant (202/625-2150), which has just undergone a $2 million renovation, while **Georgetown Dutch Inn** ($$$, 202/337-0900 or 800/388-2410), 1075 Thomas Jefferson St NW, is a small, recently-renovated European-style hotel that offers 47 apartment-like suites and provides a health club and a complimentary continental breakfast, but no on-site restaurant.

Georgetown Suites ($$, 202/298-7800 or 800/348-7203; www.georgetown-suites.com), 1111 30th St NW, offers 214 suites with kitchenette, coin-operated laundry, a complimentary continental breakfast, a morning newspaper, and a health club facility. Its namesake facility, **Georgetown Suites - Harbor** ($$, 202/298-1600 or 800/348-7203), 1000 29th St NW, sits across from the Washington Harbor, is about the same size and offers visitors the same amenities.

The **Georgetown University Conference Center** ($$, 202/687-3200 or 800/228-9290), 3800 Reservoir Rd NW, is owned by the university but managed by Marriott. Its 146 rooms and five suites occupy 104 sequestered acres of the campus, and its food and beverage facilities include a sports bar, a cafeteria, and a cafe.

On restaurant-rich Wisconsin Ave, the **Georgetown Inn** ($$$-$$$$, 202/333-8900 or 800/424-2979; www.georgetowninn.com), 1310 Wisconsin Ave NW, has 86 rooms with 10 suites, provides valet parking, has a fit center, and furnishes its guests with a daily newspaper.

Arts & culture
Concerts are held in the garden of the **Old Stone House** during the Summer.

Food & drink
Noted throughout the Washington area for its restaurants, many of Georgetown's finest can be found along M St and along Wisconsin Ave.

For atmosphere, look into the 1789 Restaurant ($$-$$$, 202/965-1789), 1226 36th St NW, located in a lovely residential area. Housed in a Federal-period townhouse, the award-winning restaurant has the feeling of a traditional country inn. There are four distinctively decorated dining rooms and complimentary valet parking. The restaurant is open Sunday through Thursday from 6 to 10 pm and on Fridays to 11 pm.

For seafood, **The Sea Catch** ($$, 202/337-8855), 1054 31st St NW, is a good choice. Located in a restored 156-year-old building that once was a warehouse, the restaurant offers seating beside the C&O Canal on an awninged wooden deck or seating indoors, which has rich wood paneling, two fireplaces, a 31-foot white marble raw bar, and rough-hewn stone walls. Lunch is served Monday through Saturday from noon to 3 pm, and dinner from 5:30 to 10:30 pm. **Tony and Joe's**

Seafood Place ($$, 202/944-4545), 3000 K St NW, would make another excellent choice. Fresh fish is flown in daily, and there are lovely views of the Potomac, of Washington Harbor, and of the Kennedy Center. Lunch, dinner, and Sunday brunch are served daily, either indoors or out.

Got a taste for German? Try **Old Europe** ($$$, 202/333-7600), 2434 Wisconsin Ave NW, where the waitresses wear authentic Bavarian costumes. Family-owned for 50 years, the restaurant hosts numerous festivals, including Oktoberfest and an Asparagus Festival, among others. Live piano music is furnished five nights a week.

For Italian food, there's the **Riverside Grille** ($, 202/342-3535), 3050 K St NW, at Washington Harbor, which provides indoor and outdoor seating for lunch and dinner daily. **Paolo's** ($$, 202/333-7353), 1303 Wisconsin Ave NW, serves "California-style" Italian cuisine, has a peach-tinted Italian marble floor and an open-air patio, and serves a Sunday jazz brunch. **Luciano's Cafe** ($$, 202 /342-1888), 1219 Wisconsin Ave NW, a real neighborhood find located above Il Radicchio, is open Monday through Friday from 8:30 am to 8:30 pm and Saturday from 11 am to 8:30 pm. **Cafe Milano** ($$, 202/333-6183), 3251 Prospect St NW, specializes in Northern Italian.

When it comes to French cuisine, it's hard to top **La Chaumiere** ($$$, 202/338-1784), 2813 M st NW, across the street from the Four Seasons Hotel, where lunch is served on weekdays and dinner is served every day but Sunday. The restaurant has the atmosphere of a French country inn, with a massive free-standing central stone fireplace that helps to warm the place during the winter. A favorite of Washington's "old guard," it has been included among the city's 100 Best for more than 20 years in a row. Down the street, **Bistro Francais** ($$-$$$, 202/338-3830), 3124-28 M St NW, has two parts, a cafe and a more formal dining room. Open until 3 am Sunday through Thursday and until 4 am on Friday and Saturday, the bistro offers a champagne brunch on Saturdays and Sundays. **Cafe La Ruche** ($$-$$$, 202/965-2684) at 1039 31st St NW is Georgetown's oldest French restaurant. Open daily, it serves brunch on Saturdays and Sundays and has a seasonal outdoor patio.

Good places to try Asian fare include **Busara** ($$, 202/337-2340), 2340 Wisconsin Ave NW, a Thai restaurant that serves lunch, dinner and a weekend brunch. The garden patio is open from spring through autumn. **Bangkok Bistro** ($$, 202/337-2424), 3251 Prospect St NW, also serves Thai. It is open daily and offers valet parking after 6 pm. **Vietnam Georgetown** ($$, 202/337-4536), 30th St and M St NW, has been in Georgetown for a quarter-century. Garden dining is available seasonally. For Ethiopian dishes, go to **Zed's** ($-$$, 202/333-4710), 3318 M St NW, which is open for lunch and dinner daily between 11 am and 11 pm. The tri-level restaurant, voted one of city's 50 Very Best and 50 Best Bargains restaurants, is decorated with Ethiopian artifacts, presented in a cozy, candlelit environment. **Aditi** ($$, 202/625-6825), 3299 M St NW, can provide you with

Tandouri, vegetarian and curry specialties, while **Japan Inn** ($$, 202/337-3400), 1715 Wisconsin Ave NW, and **Hisago** ($$, 202/944-4200) are the places to go for Japanese.

Nightlife

Billy Martin's Tavern (202/333-7370), 1264 Wisconsin Ave NW, is the oldest family-owned restaurant in Washington. Resembling an old-world pub, it serves breakfast, lunch, and dinner daily, and a brunch on Saturdays and Sundays. President Clinton used to eat here when he was a student at Georgetown University.

Mr. Smith's of Georgetown (202/333-3104), 3104 M St NW, provides a nightly piano bar and honors the great bands every Friday and Saturday night, while **Alamo Grill** (202/342-2000), 1063 31st St NW, features music and dancing with its Tex-Mex food.

Calling itself "the nation's oldest continuing jazz supper club," **Blues Alley** (202/337-4141) in the rear of 1073 Wisconsin Ave NW, also provides nightly music. Featured artists have included Nancy Wilson, Charlie Byrd, Branford Marsalis, and Maynard Ferguson as well as local jazz and blues acts. Featuring New Orleans creole cuisine, dinner is served from 6 pm and there are shows at 8 and 10 pm.

The Tombs ($-$$, 202/337-6668), 1226 36th St NW (at Prospect St), is a popular college hangout located below the upscale 1789 Restaurant in a converted 19th-century house. Innlike with low ceilings, brick floors and a working fireplace, The Tombs is open weekdays from 11:30 am, Saturdays from 11 am, and Sundays from 9 am. A Sunday brunch is offered between 9 am and 2 pm. This is another spot that President Clinton once haunted during his college years. Another local tradition is the **Tiki Bar**, located on the patio of the Third Edition restaurant (202/333-3700) at 1218 Wisconsin Ave NW. Decorated like a tropical paradise, it has a thatched roof and a Hawaiian Bar, and dancing is available upstairs on Georgetown's largest dance floor, where a DJ spins top-40 hits from Wednesday through Saturday.

For a different form of entertainment, the **Key Theatre** (202/333-5100), 1222 Wisconsin Ave NW, presents first-run releases of foreign and American independent films including documentaries and animation.

Events

The gardens at **Dumbarton Oaks** are open daily between April and October from 2 to 6 pm, when the admission fee is $3 ($2 for seniors and children under 12). The rest of the year, the gardens are open from 2 to 5 pm and there is no admission fee.

If you should visit the area around Dumbarton Oaks on a Sunday, continue walking north on 32nd St as you leave Dumbarton Oaks. At S St, the two streets form a right angle. Turn left (west) onto S St and go one block to Wisconsin Ave, where a Sunday flea market is held every Sunday throughout the year.

Embassy Row

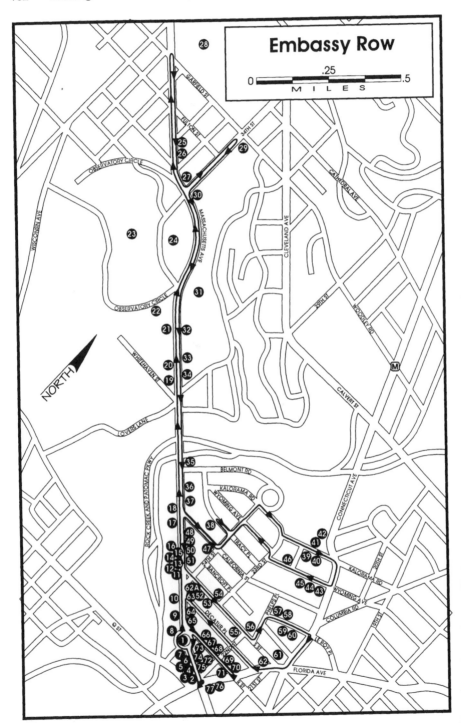

1. Sheridan Circle
2. Residence of the Luxembourg Ambassador
3. Emabssy of Turkey
4. Emabssy of the Republic of Togo
5. Emabssy of Sudan
6. Emabssy of the Commonwealth of the Bahamas
7. Emabssy of Ireland
8. Emabssy of Burkina Faso
9. Emabssy of (South) Korea
10. Emabssy of Madagascar
11. Emabssy of Paraguay
12. Residence of the United Arab Emirates Ambassaador
13. Emabssy of Republic of Malawi
14. Emabssy of Cote d'Ivoire
15. Mexican mission to the Organization of American States
16. Emabssy of (North) Korea
17. Embassy of Japan
18. Embassy of India
19. Emabssy of Brazil
20. Emabssy of Bolivia
21. Emabssy of the United Kingdom
22. Emabssy of New Zealand
23. US Naval Observatory
24. Residence of the Vice President
25. Embassy of the Republic of Kazakhstan
26. Emabssy of Cape Verde
27. Emabssy of Norway
28. Washington National Cathedral
29. Embassy of Belgium
30. Emabssy of Finland
31. Normanstone Parkway
32. Kahlil Gibran Memorial Garden
33. Embassy of South Africa
34. Former Iranian embassy
35. Islamic Center
36. Emabssy of Belize
37. Emabssy of Lesotha
38. Emabssy of Guyana
39. Emabssy of Ethiopia
40. Emabssy of Algeria
41. Emabssy of Portugal
42. Emabssy of China
43. Emabssy of Senegal
44. Emabssy of Barbados
45. Emabssy of Sri Lanka
46. Emabssy of Syria
47. Emabssy of Yugoslavia
48. Residence of the Venezuelan Ambassador
49. Emabssy of the Republic of the Marshall Islands
50. Emabssy of Zambia
51. Emabssy of Malaysia
52. Woodrow Wilson House
53. Textile Museum
54. Emabssy of Myanmar
55. Emabssy of Laos
56. Emabssy of Costa Rica
57. Emabssy of Nepal
58. Emabssy of Mauritania
59. Emabssy of Colombia
60. Emabssy of Guinea
61. Emabssy of Moldova
62. Emabssy of Albania
62A. Emabssy of Croatia
63. Emabssy of Cameroon
64. Emabssy of Pakistan
65. Emabssy of Haiti
66. Emabssy of Kenya
67. Emabssy of Armenia
68. Emabssy of Angola
69. Emabssy of the Dominican Republic
70. Emabssy of Tanzania
71. Emabssy of Niger
72. Emabssy of Mali
73. Emabssy of Guatemala
74. Emabssy of Greece
75. Emabssy of the Central Aftican Republic
76. Emabssy of Bulgaria
77. Emabssy of Estonia

Embassy Row

Sightseeing along Washington's Embassy Row means dealing with an embarassment of riches. Most of the city's 170 foreign embassies and chancelleries are found on a two-mile region stretching roughly between Scott and Observatory Circles along Massachusetts Ave NW and its cross-streets.

During the first quarter of the 20th century, this was Washington's most exclusive address. Many of today's embassies are housed in mansions that were built by some of Washington's most illustrious and socially elite families in the years between 1900 and the First World War. Many were designed in a Beaux Arts style made fashionable by the elegant apartment houses that were built in Paris around the turn of the century.

Although their primary function is the conduct of official business, many embassies will admit visitors and even provide a guided tour *if they are contacted in advance*. Each spring, many of the embassies open their doors to the public as part of a benefit for the Davis Memorial Goodwill. Most embassies are easily identified by plaques out front and/or by the flags of their nations that fly overhead.

Information
The **Republic of (South) Korea** maintains an Information Center at 2370 Massachusetts Ave NW.

Getting there
Metrobus travels the entire length of Massachusetts Ave.

Seasonal highlights
A Preservation Garden Party is held at the **Woodrow Wilson House** each May.

Tours
Free 90-minute tours of the **US Naval Observatory** are offered every Monday evening on a first-come, first-served basis. The tours begin at 7:30 pm between November and March and at 8:30 pm between April and October.

Tours of the **Islamic Center** can be arranged between 10 am and 5 pm Saturday through Thursday and on Friday between 10 am and noon and 3 and 5 pm. Donations are accepted. (NOTE: Female visitors must be covered except for their hands, face and feet. No shorts or short skirts are allowed.)

A guided 45-minute tour of the **Woodrow Wilson House**, a National Trust Historic Site, is offered, as is a 25-minute film about the President. Admission is $5, $2.50 for students.

Tours of the **Textile Museum** are available for an admission fee of $5.

Embassy Row. *Start your tour one block southeast of Sheridan Circle at a place where 22nd St, Q St, and Florida Ave NW converge. Take the left (south) side of Massachusetts Ave and begin walking in a northwesterly direction.*

At 2200 Massachusetts Ave NW, you will see the residence of the **Luxembourg** ambassador, a limestone Louis XV-style building with a lovely rock garden in front. A Grand Duchy with a half-million population, the little European nation of Luxembourg (999 sq mi) is smaller than Rhode Island.

Next door, at #2202, is the **Turkish** embassy, which uses the building as an office for its Military Attache, and at #2208 sits the embassy of the **Republic of Togo.** Located west of Ghana on the southern coast of West Africa, Togo is an agricultural nation whose chief crops are coffee and cocoa.

The embassy of **Sudan,** the largest country in Africa, is located at 2210 Massachusetts Ave NW. The **Commonwealth of the Bahamas,** a favorite vacation spot for many Americans, has an embassy at #2220, and the embassy of **Ireland** occupies a limestone Louis XVI-style building at #2234.

As you reach Sheridan Circle, walk around the circle in a clockwise direction. **Sheridan Circle** is named for Gen Philip Sheridan, a Civil War hero. It bears an equestrian statue of the general created by Guzon Borglum, the sculptor who created the presidents' faces on Mount Rushmore. Midway around the circle, at 2340 Massachusetts Ave NW, is the embassy of **Burkina Faso,** a virtually unknown nation in western Africa south of the Sahara that was known as Upper Volta until 1984. A poor country, Burkina Faso has a literacy rate of just 19% and the life expectancy of its people is just 42.5 years for men and 42.1 years for women.

Once past Sheridan Circle, continue walking northwest along Massachusettes Ave. The embassy of the **Republic of (South) Korea** is at 2320 Massachusetts Ave NW and maintains an Information Center next door at #2370.

At 2374 Massachusetts Ave NW is the embassy of **Madagascar,** a Texas-sized island off the East coast of Africa. Then at 2400 Massachusetts Ave NW comes the embassy of **Paraguay,** a South American country with a population of 6 million people, followed by the residence of the ambassador from the **United Arab Emirates** at #2406 and the embassy of the **Republic of Malawi** at #2408. Malawi is a nation of 10 million people located in Southeast Africa, where it is surrounded by Zambia on the west, Mozambique on the south and east, and Tanzania on the north.

Cote d'Ivoire (Ivory Coast) occupies the next two buildings, maintaining a consulate at 2412 Massachusetts Ave NW and an embassy at #2424. At #2440, **Mexico** houses its mission to the Organization of American States, and at #2450, the embassy for **North Korea** occupies the former home of the Canadian ambassador.

Move on to the 2500 block of Massachusetts Ave NW. There, behind a white fence at 2520 Massachusetts Ave NW, is the embassy of **Japan**. The embassy occupies the former residence of the Japanese ambassador. At #2536, with elephant statuary guarding the entrance, is an annex to the embassy of **India**.

Now take the Charles C Glover Bridge across Rock Creek, pass Whitehaven St NW, and move into the 3000 block of Massachusetts Ave. Resembling a 15th-century Roman palace, the residence of the Brazilian ambassador is a three-story building sitting behind an enormous hedge at 3000 Massachusetts Ave NW. Next door, at #3006, is the embassy of **Brazil**, which resembles a glass box sitting atop a columned concrete slab.

The embassy for the South American country of **Bolivia** is at 3014 Massachusetts Ave NW.

As you approach the embassy of the **United Kingdom** at 3100 Massachusetts Ave NW, you will see the statue of a familiar figure, former Prime Minister **Winston Churchill**, with one hand raised in the familiar symbol of V for victory and the other hand holding his ever-present cigar. On the embassy grounds, south of the school building-like embassy, notice the ambassador's residence, which sits on the embassy grounds. The embassy itself, the largest British embassy in the world, is fronted by a traditional red British telephone booth. Queen Elizabeth II personally laid the cornerstone for the embassy in 1957.

Observatory Circle Dr will intersect Massachusetts Ave as you approach the US Naval Observatory. Take a sharp left and walk one block. At 37 Observatory Circle NW sits the embassy for the island-nation of **New Zealand**.

Return to Massachusetts Ave and turn left. Behind the guarded gate and up the hill is the **US Naval Observatory** (202/762-1467). Established in 1830 as the Depot of Charts & Instruments, a title it bore until 1844, the observatory was moved to this location from Foggy Bottom in 1893.

From the north entrance to the Observatory near 34th St NW, you can see the **Vice President's Mansion**, a white house flying the American flag.

Continue along Massachusetts Ave past Edmunds St and walk one more block to 35th St NW. Cross to the north side of Massachusetts Ave and begin to retrace your steps toward Sheridan Circle. Another virtually unknown country, the **Republic of Kazakhstan** has an embassy at 3421 Massachusetts Ave NW. A nation of 17 million people, Kazakhstan, once a part of the USSR, is located in central Asia South of Russia.

The **Cape Verde** embassy is at 3415 Massachusetts Ave NW. A group of 10 volcanic islands in the Atlantic Ocean off the western tip of Africa, Cape Verde gained its independence from Portugal in 1975.

Pass 34th Pl and take a short left at the next street (34th St NW). On the left-hand side of the street, at 2720 34th St NW, you will find the embassy of **Norway.**

Go north along 34th St for two more blocks, where you will be able to see the grounds of Washington National Cathedral occupying the northwest corner of 34th and Garfield Sts NW. (The National Cathedral will be discussed during a later tour covering Upper Northwest Washington.) On the southeast corner of that intersection, at 3330 Garfield St NW, sits the embassy of **Belgium**, a European kingdom just slightly larger (11,800 sq mi) than the state of Vermont.

Backtrack south along 34th St for two blocks and turn left onto Massachusetts Ave. At #3301 is the modern metal-and-glass embassy of **Finland**, a Scandinavian country of 5 million bordered by Norway, Sweden and Russia. Inside, should you be able to enter the embassy to see it, is a graceful, curved staircase that leads to a central atrium with an enormous window/wall that provides a gorgeous view of the neighboring grounds.

Pass Normanstone Parkway, a large park-like area. **Kahlil Gibran Memorial Garden**, 3100 Massachusetts Ave NW, occupies two acres adjacent to the parkway and opposite the British embassy. Surrounded by a circular wall, the garden opened in May 1991 to honor a Lebanese-born mystical poet/philosopher who spent much of his time in the United States and died in New York City in 1931. Reached via a small bridge, the garden contains a fountain and benches that are inscribed with quotations from some of Gibran's writings plus a bronze bust of Gibran created by Washington sculptor Gordon Kray.

The embassy of **South Africa** is at 3051 Massachusetts Ave NW, built in 1965 on the site of the old Dutch-style embassy. The building with a turquoise dome and decoratively-screened windows at #3005 is the former **Iranian** embassy.

Ahead of you is the Glover Bridge across Rock Creek. Cross it and continue walking south along Massachusetts Ave. At #2551 is the **Islamic**

Center (202/332-8343), an institution of Muslim worship, education, and culture opened in 1957. Angled to face in the direction of Mecca, the building has a rotunda with 24 attractive stained glass windows. There is a 160-foot minaret, mosaic inscriptions in Arabic quoting verses from the Holy Koran, and a library of works about Islam. The building contains intricate tilework (a gift from Turkey), marble columns, Persian rugs (a gift from Iran), and a huge brass chandelier (a gift from Egypt).

Follow Massachusetts Ave across Belmont Rd. At #2535 is the embassy of **Belize**, formerly known as British Honduras. Located on the East coast of Central America south of Mexico, Belize has a population (225,000) roughly equal to that of Raleigh, NC.

The small brick house at #2511 contains the embassy of **Lesotha**, once called Basutoland. An 11,720-sq mi kingdom of two million people, Lesotha is completely surrounded by the Republic of South Africa.

At California St, turn left and walk one block to 24th St NW. Turn left and walk one block to Tracy Pl, then turn left once more. At 2490 Tracy Pl NW is the embassy of **Guyana**, a "co-operative republic" on the north coast of South America with a population of 706,000 people, roughly equal to that of Baltimore.

Go back to 24th St and turn left. Walk two blocks to Kalorama Rd and turn right. Just past Thornton St on your right, at 2134 Kalorama Rd NW, is the embassy of **Ethiopia**, a 437,794-sq mi East African country best known for the export of coffee. At 2118 Kalorama Rd NW is the embassy of **Algeria**, a Sunni Muslim nation of 30 million people.

On the west side of the street, The embassy of **Portugal** sits at 2125 Kalorama Rd NW on the corner of Belmont Rd.

Head north on Belmont Rd for one short block. The embassy of **China** will be on your left at 2300 Connecticut Ave NW. In a country roughly equal to the United States in size, the Chinese population of 1.2 billion people is roughly four times as large as ours.

Follow Belmont Rd to the first intersection, take a sharp right, and then walk South along Connecticut Ave for one block to Wyoming Ave. Turn right onto Wyoming Ave. On the left-hand side of the street, at 2112 Wyoming Ave NW, is the embassy of **Senegal**, a nation roughly the size of Nebraska that is located on the west coast of Africa. At #2144 is the embassy of **Barbados**, an island-nation that occupies 166 sq mi in the Atlantic Ocean—the farthest East of the islands that comprise the West Indies. The **Sri Lanka** embassy at #2148 represents a "Democratic Socialist Republic" in the Indian Ocean southeast of India known in ancient times as Taprobane (copper-colored). The embassy of the Arabic republic of **Syria** is at 2215 Wyoming Ave NW.

Continue along Wyoming Ave to 24th St NW and take a left. Then walk south to California St and make a right. At 2410 California St NW is the embassy of **Yugoslavia**, a Slavic nation about the size of Indiana.

Continue walking in a westerly direction along California St for one more block and you will be back to Massachusetts Ave. Turn left, staying on the east side of the street. At 2443 Massachusetts Ave NW, enclosed by a black wrought-iron fence, is the residence of the ambassador from **Venezuela**. At #2433 is the embassy of the **Republic of the Marshall Islands**, a nation of 60,000 people that occupies an area of 70 sq mi in the North Pacific that acquired its independence in 1991. The embassy of **Zambia**, formerly known as Northern Rhodesia, is at #2419, and the embassy of **Malaysia**, a nation formed in 1969 at the southeastern tip of Asia, is at #2401.

At S St NW, turn left. On the south side of the street is the **Woodrow Wilson House** (202/387-4062, www.nthp.org/main/sites/wilson house.htm), 2340 S St NW. Occupying a brick 3-floor Georgian Revival townhouse built in 1915, this is the only presidential museum in the nation's capital.

Wilson moved to this house in 1921 after leading the nation through WW I, thus becoming the only President to reside in Washington after completing his term of office.

Wilson lived here with his second wife Edith until his death in 1924. Edith, 16 years the president's junior, continued living in the house until her death in 1961. Visitors can glimpse into the life of an educator, scholar, world statesman, president of Princeton University, governor of New Jersey, and 28th president of the United States. The house is full of trophies, souvenirs, and keepsakes, including its original furnishings. Visitors can see a typical kitchen of the 1920s, including one of first electric refrigerators, and President Wilson's ground-floor office (often referred to as the "dugout"). They also can see Wilson's portrait hooked into a rug, his portrait depicted by 2,000 soldiers in formation, and his portrait carved on a walrus tusk. The house is open between 10 am and 4 pm Tuesday through Sunday, and there is a museum shop.

Near the Wilson House at 2320 S St NW is the **Textile Museum** (202/667-0441), founded in 1925 by George Hewitt Myers, heir to the Bristol-Myers fortune, and his wife. Myers founded the Merganthaler Linotype firm and the YE Booker & Co investment firm, and his son-in-law, Hans Kinders, founded the National Symphony Orhcestra. In this house, the family entertained such famous personalities as Tallulah

Bankhead, the Alfred Lunts, and Cornelia Otis Skinner. There are exhibits from a collection of more than 15,000 textiles and 1,800 Oriental carpets housed in two red-brick Georgian residences. The Myers home (#2310) was designed by John Russell Pope and built in 1913. An adjoining house (#2320) was designed by Washington architect Waddy B Wood, who also designed the Wilson house. A Textile Learning Center has two galleries that are devoted to weaving techniques, textile makers, and their cultures. The Arthur D Jenkins Library contains more than 13,000 books and periodicals on the subject. A unique gift shop carries such unusual items as silk scarves from India, Kilim pillows, Bolivian ruapas, and Bokhara crepe silk ties. The museum's hours are 10 am to 5 pm Monday through Saturday and 1 to 5 pm on Sunday. Library hours are 10 am to 2 pm Wednesday through Saturday or by appointment.

Continue walking east along S St. At the next intersection (23rd St NW), look at the building on the northwest corner. At 2300 S St NW is the embassy of **Myanmar**, formerly known as Burma. With an area of 261,228 sq mi, Myanmar is approximately the size of Texas.

At 2222 S St NW is the embassy of **Laos**, a Communist country located on the Indochina Peninsula of southeast Asia whose best-known export item is opium. Across the street at #2114 is the embassy of the South American nation of **Costa Rica**.

From the Costa Rican embassy, walk south along 22nd St NW. Highlighted by a lion's head fountain, the brick, granite and concrete stairway known as the **Spanish Steps** was built in 1912. Graceful and curving, the steps are bordered with flowers and shaded by overhanging trees.

Now return to the Costa Rican embassy on the corner of S St, cross the road, make a short right turn, and almost immediately take a left turn into Phelps St. At the second intersection, turn right onto Leroy Pl. Along the north side of the street at 2131 Leroy Pl NW is the embassy of **Nepal**, a 56,827-sq-mi kingdom that straddles the Himalaya Mountains. Nepal officially abolished polygamy, child marriage, and the practice of the caste system in 1963. At #2129 is the embassy of the northwest African nation of **Mauritania**, while on the south side of the street at #2118 is the embassy of the South American country of **Colombia** and at #2112 is the embassy of the West African nation of **Guinea**.

At the corner (Connecticut Ave), take a right and head south. Go two blocks and turn right onto Florida St. On your right, facing onto S St is the embassy of **Moldova**, a small (13,012 sq mi) nation in eastern Europe that once was a part of Romania. Independent since 1994, Moldova now occupies the building that formerly served as the Romanian embassy. On a triangular lot across the street is the embassy of **Albania**, an equally small nation located on the coast of the Adriatic Sea in southeastern Europe.

Continue to walk south along Florida St to Decatur Pl, then turn right (west) and walk to Massachusetts Ave. Turn left on Massachusetts Ave. At 2343 Massachusetts Ave NW is the embassy of **Croatia**, a nation located on the Balkan Peninsula in southeastern Europe. Just past that, at #2349, is the embassy of **Cameroon**, a 183,569-sq-mi nation about the size of California. At #2315 is the **Pakistan** embassy, which represents a 307,374-sq-mi nation in the west part of South Asia where the literacy rate is just 38%. On the next corner, at #2311, opposite Sheridan Circle, is the embassy of **Haiti**, a Caribbean country whose population of 7 million is roughly equal to that of New York City. Christopher Columbus visited Haiti on his historic journey in 1492.

Turn left (east) onto R St and down the left-hand (north) side of the street. At 2249 R St NW is the embassy of **Kenya**, an East African nation on the Indian Ocean that is about the size of Maryland. Next door is the embassy of **Armenia**, a nation about the size of Massachusetts. And beyond that, on the northwest corner of R St and 22nd St NW, is the embassy of **Angola**, a nation of 10 million people that is located on the Atlantic coast of southwestern Africa. Across the street, on the northeastern corner, is the embassy of the West Indian nation of **The Dominican Republic**. At 2139 R St NW is the embassy of **Tanzania**. The nation, which has a population of 28.5 million people and a land area of 364,000 sq mi, resulted from the 1964 union of the former Tanganyika and Zanzibar.

Cross the street and retrace your steps, following the south side of R St. On the southwest corner of 22nd St is the embassy of **Niger**, a small country in the interior of northern Africa, and past that the embassy of **Mali**, an equally small country in the interior of western Africa. At 2220 R St NW is the embassy of the Central American country of **Guatemala**.

Return to Sheridan Circle, take a left and go south on Massachusetts Ave. At 2221 Massachusetts Ave NW is the embassy of **Greece**, and at #2211, the Greek consular office.

At the next intersection, look left (north) into 22nd St NW. At 1618 22nd St NW is the embassy for the **Central African Republic**. Across the street at #1621 is the **Bulgarian** embassy.

Continuing southward on Massachusetts Ave, you come to the embassy of **Estonia**, a nation of 1.4 million people on the Baltic Sea in eastern Europe.

Continue walking southeast along Massachusetts Ave to Q St, where you first started your tour of Embassy Row.

A number of additional embassies are clustered around DuPont Circle. You can read about them in the section that follows.

Lodging

Accommodations and restaurants in this upscale part of town are few...and expensive. You might try the **Washington Courtyard by Marriott** ($$-$$$, 202/332-9300 or 800/842-4211) at 1900 Connecticut Ave NW, for its European elegance, or the **Embassy Row Hotel** ($$$, 202/265-1600 or 800424-2400) at 2015 Massachusetts Ave NW, which offers 193 rooms, 33 suites, a fitness center, a rooftop pool, and a complimentary continental breakfast. The latter also has a nice restaurant, the International Marketplace.

Other than those, your best bet is the pricey **Hotel Sofitel** ($$$$, 202 /797-2000 or 800/424-2464) at 1914 Connecticut Ave NW where there are 144 rooms including 30 suites, a restaurant, a bar, a business center, valet parking, and a health club.

Food & drink

Perhaps the best choice is one of the hotel dining rooms. One, the **Bistro Twenty Fifteen** ($$, 202/265-1600 or 800/424-2400) at the Embassy Row Hotel, 2015 Massachusetts Ave NW, which serves American cuisine for breakfast, lunch and dinner daily. Another is the **Jockey Club** ($$$, 202/293-2100 or 800/241-3333) at the Ritz-Carlton Hotel, 2100 Massachusetts Ave NW, a recently renovated restaurant that favors food with a French accent. The latter is known as a place where Washington insiders go to "power dine" and a jacket-and-tie are recommended.

Around the Circles: Du Pont, Scott, Thomas & Logan

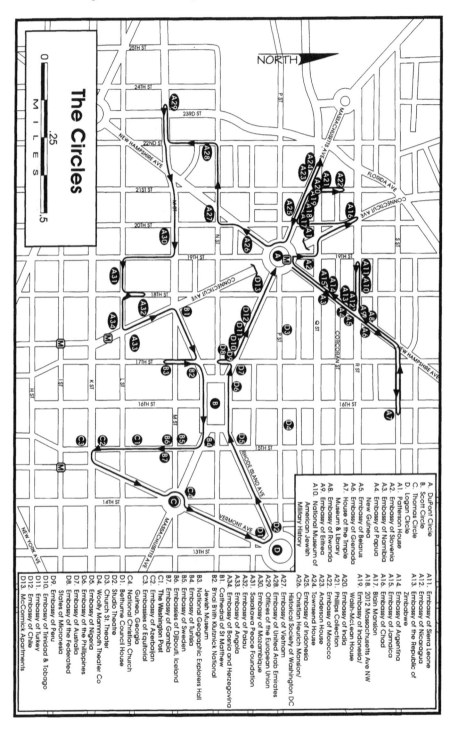

The Circles

0 — .25 — .5
MILES

NORTH

A. DuPont Circle
B. Scott Circle
C. Thomas Circle
D. Logan Circle
A1. Patterson House
A2. Embassy of Slovenia
A3. Embassy of Namibia
A4. Embassy of Papua New Guinea
A5. Embassy of Grenada
A6. Embassy of Belarus
A7. House of the Temple Museum & Library
A8. Embassy of Rwanda
A9. Embassy of Eritrea
A10. National Museum of American Jewish Military History
A11. Embassy of Sierra Leone
A12. Embassy of Nicaragua
A13. Embassy of the Republic of Zimbabwe
A14. Embassy of Argentina
A15. Embassy of Jamaica
A16. Embassy of Chad
A17. Blain Mansion
A18. 2012 Massachusetts Ave NW
A19. Embassy of Indonesia/ Walsh-McLean House
A20. Embassy of India
A21. Phillips Collection
A22. Embassy of Morocco
A23. Anderson House
A24. Townsend House
A25. Embassy of Indonesia
A26. Embassy of Bosnia and Herzegovina
A27. Embassy of Angola
A28. Embassy of Palau
A29. Saakawa Peace Foundation
A30. Embassy of Mozambique
A31. Offices of the European Union
A32. Embassy of Tunisia
A33. National Geographic Explorers Hall
A34. Embassy of Gambia

A26. Embassy of Morocco
A27. Embassy of Vietnam
A28. Embassy of United Arab Emirates

B. Scott Circle
B1. Cathedral of St Matthew
B2. B'nai B'rith Klutznick National Jewish Museum
B3. National Geographic Explorers Hall
B4. Embassy of Tunisia
B5. Embassy of Sweden
B6. Embassies of Djibouti, Iceland
B7. Embassy of Gambia

C. Thomas Circle
C1. The Washington Post
C2. Embassy of Azerbaijan
C3. Embassies of Equatorial Guinea, Georgia
C4. National Christian Church

D. Logan Circle
D1. Bethune Council House
D2. Studio Theatre
D3. Church St. Theater
D4. Woolly Mammoth Theater Co
D5. Embassy of Nigeria
D6. Embassy of the Phillipines
D7. Embassy of Australia
D8. Embassy of the Federated States of Micronesia
D9. Embassy of Peru
D10. Embassy of Trinidad & Tobago
D11. Embassy of Turkey
D12. Embassy of Chile
D13. McCormick Apartments

Around the Circles

Originally called Pacific Circle, DuPont Circle was renamed in 1884 in honor of Rear Admiral Samuel Francis du Pont, a Civil War hero and the grandson of Pierre Samuel du Pont de Nemours, the French economist who became a powerful figure in American industry and banking. In 1861, Admiral du Pont directed the Union victory at Port Royal, SC, and for a time, a statue of him stood in the park, but in 1921 the du Pont family had the statue of their relative replaced by the present marble fountain.

In the late 1800s and well into the 1900s, DuPont Circle was Washington's most fashionable residential area. Magnificent mansions, many of them now used as embassies by foreign nations, graced the streets. Today, the Circle is the Washington version of Greenwich Village as well as the center of the District's gay bar scene.

Massachusetts Ave, New Hampshire Ave and Connecticut Ave all intersect at DuPont Circle, Washington's largest circular park. Containing a central marble fountain surrounded by traditional wooden park benches often occupied by people engaged in open-air chess games, the park provides the centerpiece for an area replete with shops, historic townhouses, fascinating ethnic restaurants, all-night bookstores, coffee shops, art galleries, and small museums. The art galleries focus generally on the contemporary American artists, particularly the Washington-area artists.

Getting there

The underground Metro has a station at Du Pont Circle. By Metrobus, take the Glover Park-Du Pont Circle Line.

First steps

A free copy of *Dupont-Kalorama Museum Walk* can be obtained by sending a stamped, self-addressed #10 envelope to The Textile Museum, 2320 S St NW, Washington, DC 20008, or by stopping at the museum (202/667-0441) when you are in Washington.

On entering the **Phillips Collection**, get a copy of *A Child's Adventure into the Artist's World of Color*, a wonderful introduction to the world of art, especially for children.

Seasonal highlights

From September through May, a program of classical music is offered at the **Phillips Collection** every Sunday at 5 pm.

The US Air Force Chamber Players perform in concert at the **Anderson House** on the second and fourth Tuesdays of each month between October and May. On most Tuesdays between October and April, free films are shown in the **National Geographic Explorers Hall** at noon.

The **B'nai B'rith Klutznick National Jewish Museum** sponsors family events throughout the year, including an Annual Run for Art, a family Hanukkah celebration in December, and a family fun day on December 25.

Tours

Free 20-minute guided tours of the **Patterson House** are offered on Monday, Wednesday and Friday between 9:30 and 11:30 am.

Free guided 2-hour tours of the **House of the Temple Museum and Library** are conducted on weekdays from 8 am to 2 pm and on Saturdays by appointment. Guided tours of the **National Museum of American Jewish Military History** also are available.

The Historical Society of Washington, DC encourages both guided and self-guided tours of the **Christian Heurich Mansion**. Self-guided tours may be taken between 10 am and 4 pm Wednesday through Saturday. Guided tours, which can be scheduled by appointment, cover three floors of the mansion.

Guided tours of the **Cathedral of St Matthew** are given between 2:30 and 4:30 pm on Sundays.

Guided tours of the **B'nai B'rith Klutznick National Jewish Museum** can be provided by appointment.

The *Washington Post* conducts tours of the newsroom, composing room, and press room on Mondays at 10 and 11 am and at 1, 2 and 3 pm.

DuPont Circle. *Start your tour on the northeast side of DuPont Circle.* At 15 DuPont Circle is the **Patterson House** (202/483-9200), built in 1903 for Cissy Patterson, socialite owner of the *Washington Times-Herald*. The house was designed by architect Stanford White, a central figure in the scandalous New York *Girl on the Red Velvet Swing* murder case. In 1927, President and Mrs Calvin Coolidge were house guests while the White House was being renovated. Coolidge received and honored aviator Charles Lindbergh here upon Lindbergh's return from Europe after having made the world's first transAtlantic solo flight. When Patterson died in 1948, she willed the house to the American Red Cross, and in 1951 that organization sold it to the Washington Club, an exclusive private women's group.

East of the DuPont Plaza Hotel, turn onto New Hampshire Ave NW. Behind the hotel at 1525 New Hampshire Ave NW is the embassy of **Slovenia**, a republic in southeastern Europe that is somewhat smaller than the state of Vermont and has a population of some two million people.

Walk northeast along New Hampshire Ave, staying on the east (right-hand) side of the street. Just after you pass Q St NW, you will see the embassy of **Namibia**, a nation on the Atlantic coast of South Africa, at 1605 New Hampshire Ave NW, followed by the embassy of **Papua New Guinea**, an independent state encompassing the east half of the island of New Guinea plus 600 nearby islands off southeastern Asia, at 1615 New Hampshire Ave NW. At #1619, on the southeast corner of R St, is the embassy of **Belarus** which occupies 80,153 sq mi in eastern Europe. Located near Poland, Latvia, and Lithuania, Belarus became independent when the USSR disbanded in 1991. On the North side of R St at #1701 is the embassy for the 133-sq mi island nation of **Grenada**, located in the Caribbean Sea 90 miles North of Venezuela. Grenada came to most people's attention when violence erupted there in 1983, prompting President Ronald Reagan to send in some American troops.

Continue along New Hampshire Ave to S St NW, turn right (east), and walk to 16th St NW. At 1733 16th St NW is the **House of the Temple Museum and Library** (202/232-3579), which houses the Supreme Council of the 33rd degree of the Ancient and Accepted Scottish Rite of Freemasonry, Southern Jurisdiction, USA. Modeled upon the tomb of Mausolus at Halicarnassus (now Bodrum) in Asia Minor, the library contains an extensive collection of works on Masonic issues and related matters. Memorabilia and works by and about the Scottish poet Robert Burns also are on display, as are some of the personal belongings of the late FBI chief J Edgar Hoover.

Now return west along S St to New Hampshire Ave, cross to the west side of the street, and head back toward DuPont Circle, this time walking on the west side of the street. Just past Riggs Pl, at 1714 New Hampshire Ave NW, is the embassy of **Rwanda**, a republic on the east coast of Africa. Just south of there is the embassy of another east African country, **Eritrea**, which is located on the southwestern coast of the Red Sea. Eritrea once was a part of the Ethiopian kingdom of Aksum and has only been an independent nation since 1993.

At the next intersection, turn right and head west along R St NW. Passing 18th St NW, you will see the **National Museum of American Jewish Military History** (202/265-6280) at 1811 R St NW. This unusual facility contains artifacts, photographs, and memorabilia depicting Jewish men and women in the US armed forces. Operated under the auspices of the Jewish War Veterans of the USA, it presents special changing exhibits on two levels, and is open from 9 am to 5 pm on weekdays and from 1 to 5 pm on Sundays. Admission is free, but voluntary contributions are suggested. On the next corner, facing onto 19th St, is the embassy of **Sierra Leone**, 1701 19th St NW, a republic of 4.9 million people located on the west coast of Africa.

If you are interested in touring art galleries, there are many of them along R St NW between 20th St and 22nd St NW, just a few blocks ahead of you. If not...*turn around and return east along R St for a block and one-half until you reach New Hampshire Ave. Then take a right.* On a triangular lot at 1627 New Hampshire Ave NW is the embassy of **Nicaragua**, the Central American country slightly larger than Ohio that maintains 4.4 million population. Past Corcoran St, at 1608 New Hampshire Ave NW, the embassy of **Republic of Zimbabwe** tends to the diplomatic needs of that South African nation, and at #1600 is the embassy of **Argentina**, the second largest country in South America. A popular vacation spot for many Americans, the West Indian nation of **Jamaica** maintains an embassy at 1520 New Hampshire Ave NW.

Walk counter-clockwise around DuPont Circle to Connecticut Ave and turn right. At R St, cross Connecticut Ave to the west side. On the southwest corner of the intersection at 2002 R St NW is the embassy of **Chad**, a 500,000 sq mi nation in central Africa.

Turn left onto 20th St and go south to Massachusetts Ave. On the corner at 2000 Massachusetts Ave NW is the red brick **Blain Mansion**, built in 1881 by James Gillespie "Slippery Jim" Blain, congressman, senator, Speaker of the House, Secretary of State under Presidents James Garfield and William Henry Harrison, and four-time unsuccessful candidate for the Presidency (1876-1892). In 1901, George Westinghouse, inventor and founder of Westinghouse Electric, bought the house and lived there until his death in 1914.

Next door, at 2012 Massachusetts Ave NW, is a five-story 1898 brick-and-sandstone mansion built in the Georgian/Italian Renaissance Revival style. In 1904, the house was bought by Samuel Spencer, one-time partner of financier JP Morgan and the first president of the Southern Railroad. Renovated in 1988, the building has housed the national headquarters for the Business & Professional Women's Clubs and its sister foundation since 1957. Bricks honoring many of the clubs' members can be seen out front.

At 2020 Massachusetts Ave NW, the embassy of **Indonesia** occupies the one-time **Walsh-McLean House**, a mansion with an interesting history. Built in 1903 by Thomas Walsh, an Irish immigrant who struck it rich in the Colorado goldfields and amassed a $43 million fortune. In 1908, Walsh's daughter Evalyn married Edward McLean, son of the family that owned the *Washington Post*. Two years later, the McLean's inherited the house, where they lived between 1912 and 1916. Evalyn was the last private owner of the ill-fated Hope Diamond, now on exhibit in the National Museum of National History. The McLeans entertained lavishly, hosting Adm George Dewey, Alice Roosevelt (daughter of old TR), and many others. In the process, however, the McLeans managed to squander both of their fortunes, and in 1951 sold their house to the government of Indonesia.

The 60-room Walsh-McLean mansion/embassy is now open to the public. It has a mansard roof and an entrance where the stylish Ionic columns are flanked by statues of Bali, an Indonesian god who is said to attract good fortune while repulsing evil. Inside, there is a three-story entrance hall, a stained-glass skylight, and a carved mahogany grand staircase. The Garuda Room contains an enormous wood organ.

At 2107 Massachusetts Ave NW is the embassy of **India**, a republic of one billion population, which makes it the world's most populous country. The lobby is often used for art exhibits, and the ground-floor reading room is full of books, magazines and newspapers. Photographs of various Indian leaders, including the Gandhis, decorate the walls. The embassy is open to the public on weekdays from 9:30 am to 6 pm.

At the next intersection (21st St NW) is the **Phillips Collection** (202/387-2151), the nation's oldest museum of modern art. Duncan Phillips, heir to the Jones & Laughlin steel fortune, and his wife Marjorie dedicated their lives to building the collection as a memorial to Phillips' father and brother. The 1897 Georgian Revival mansion has carpeted rooms with oak paneling and leaded- and stained-glass windows. Opened to the public in 1921, the collection includes over 2,500 works, including paintings by van Gogh, O'Keefe, Marin, Degas, Monet, Manet, Cezanne, Bonnard, Braque, Daumier, Dove, El Greco, Matisse, Miro, Picasso, Ingres, Delacroix, Corot, Constable, Courbet, Giorgione, Chardin, Rothko, Hopper, Kandinsky, Klee, and Rouault. To many, the pride of the collection is Renoir's *Luncheon of the Boating Party*.

The museum is open between 10 am and 5 pm from Tuesday through Saturday and between noon and 7 pm on Sunday. Admission is $6.50 for adults and $3.25 for students with an ID. There is a museum shop and a cafe on the lower level that serves light fare between 10:45 am and 4:30 pm Tuesday through Saturday and between noon and 4:30 pm on Sunday.

North of the museum, the embassy of **Morocco** occupies a white brick building with a tower at 1601 21st St NW. A kingdom of 30.4 million people on the northwest coast of Africa, Morocco is probably best known for the classic movie which was named after one of its major cities, Casablanca. The movie starred Humphrey Bogart and Ingrid Bergman. Indeed, many are surprised to learn that Rabat, not Casablanca, is the capital of Morocco.

Return south to Massachusetts Ave. Just to your right and across the street is the **Anderson House** (202/785-2040), 2118 Massachusetts Ave NW, a limestone Italianate mansion fronted by two arches and a portico with Corinthian columns.

The mansion was built between 1902 and 1905 as the winter home of Ambassador Larz Anderson III and his heiress wife Isabel. Anderson, a career diplomat, was America's ambassador to Japan in 1912 and 1913. Isabel inherited $17 million from her grandfather, shipping magnate William Fletcher Weld. Recently renovated, the 50-room Beaux Arts mansion is now a library and a museum for Anderson's collection of international art treasures and Revolutionary War objects, which include Belgian tapestries woven for Louis XIII, 18th-century Louis XV chairs from Versailles, 18th-century Flemish silk tapestries, Revolutionary War swords worn by various famous commanders, a Meissen clock and candelabra, 16th-century Spanish wood carvings, Ming Dynasty jade trees, and a Japanese samurai sword with a carved ivory scabbard.

After Anderson died in 1937, the mansion became the headquarters of the Society of the Cincinnati, an organization founded in 1783 and named for Cincinnatus, a Roman farmer, patriot and military hero. George Washington was the first president of the organization, which was dedicated to the descendants of army officers who fought in the Revolutionary War. Anderson's great-grandfather was one of the founders of the Society, and a mural in the Key Room upstairs shows his great-grandfather looking on while Lafayette receives his certificate of membership into the Society. The Society of the Cincinnati is America's oldest patriotic organization.

The museum is open from 1 to 4 pm, Tuesday through Saturday, free of charge. The library is open only by appointment.

At 2121 Massachusetts Ave is the **Townsend House**, a French Renaissance mansion, the central section of which was built in 1873. In 1898, the house was acquired by Mary Scott Townsend, heiress to the Pennsylvania Railroad fortune, and her husband Richard, who was president of the Erie & Pittsburgh Railroad. The Townsends built a new house around the original one because, as rumor has it, a gypsy once warned Mrs Townsend that she was destined to die "under a new roof."

The Townsends' daughter Mathilde married Sumner Welles, who served in the administration of President Franklin Delano Roosevelt, and the Roosevelts stayed in this house for several weeks prior to moving into the White House.

In 1950, the building became the headquarters of the exclusive Cosmos Club, a private club founded in 1878 whose members describe themselves as "individuals of distinction, character, and sociability." Those members have included three US Presidents, 29 Nobel Prize winners, and 50 Pulitzer Prize winners, among them Sinclair Lewis, Henry Kissinger, William Allen White, Walter Lippmann, and Helen Hayes. The building is not open to the public.

Turn right (southeast) onto Massachusetts Ave, heading toward DuPont Circle. At 2020 Massachusetts Ave NW is the embassy of **Indonesia**, a southeast Asian archipelago along the Equator.

At the Circle, turn right onto New Hampshire Ave. In the first block at 1307 New Hampshire Ave NW is the **Christian Heurich Mansion**, now the headquarters of the **Historical Society of Washington, DC** (202 /785-2068, www.hswdc.org), founded in 1894. In 1892, the four-story, 31-room brownstone-and-brick house was built in the Romanesque Revival style by Washington brewer Christian Heurich. The basement contains a *bierstube* (beerhall) with murals that include popular old-time drinking mottoes. Heurich's grandson Gary revived the business in 1986 and now sells Foggy Bottom Ale throughout the Washington area.

The interior of the mansion has a Victorian flavor and includes 17 onyx-faced fireplaces. Constructed of poured concrete, it is the city's first fireproof building. The foyer has a mosaic floor and exhibits a magnificent coat of armor. In back is a brick patio and a lovely Victorian garden.
The Historical Society, which occupies offices on the second and third floors, maintains two galleries that feature changing exhibits. The museum is open between 10 am and 4 pm Tuesday through Saturday. The library is open for research from 10 am to 4 pm on Wednesday, Friday and Saturday. There is an on-site gift shop. The Washingtonian Bookstore is on premises, and the garden is open to the public between 10 am and 4 pm on weekdays. Admission costs $3 for adults and children over 12 and $1.50 for seniors and students.

At 20th St NW, head south and walk past N St. At 1233 20th St NW is the embassy of **Vietnam**, the Socialist republic in which 47,369 American soldiers lost their lives during a war waged during the late 1960s and early 1970s.

Backtrack north on 20th St to the first intersection (N St) and turn left. At

22nd St, turn left for one short block to Ward Pl and turn left again. The embassy of the **United Arab Emirates**, an oil-producing country on the South shore of the Persian Gulf will be on your left. The nation, which gained its independence in 1971, was formed by the union of seven "Trucial Sheikdoms."

Return to 22nd St, take a left, and continue south to M St. Then turn right. On the northwest corner of 23rd St NW and M St is the office of the **European Union**, until 1994 known as the European Community. This organization represents the interests of three separate yet important bodies, the European Economic Community (Common Market), the European Coal & Steel Community, and the European Atomic Energy Community.

Turn east on M St. At #1990 is the embassy of **Mozambique**, a republic on the southeast coast of Africa.

Walk to the next intersection (19th St NW) and turn right. Go one block to L St and turn left. The **Sasakawa Peace Foundation** (202/296-6694), 1819 L St NW, features contemporary Japanese art and is open from 10 am to 6 pm on weekdays and from 10 am to 4 pm on the third Saturday of each month. There is a similar facility in the city of Tokyo.

At 18th St, turn left. In the first block, on the east side of the street, the embassy of **Palau** occupies Suite 407 of the building at 2000 L St NW. Consisting of 26 islands and more than 300 separate islets, the nation of Palau covers an area of 188 sq mi in the Pacific Ocean 530 miles southeast of the Philippines. The **Chilean** government houses its delegation to the Organization of American States (OAS) in the same building.

Backtrack to L St. Turn left. In the first block is the embassy of **Angola**, 1819 L St, a republic located on the Atlantic coast of southwestern Africa.

Cross the street. Just east of Connecticut Ave, the embassy of **Bosnia & Herzegovina** is located on the north side of the street in Suite 760 of the building at 1707 L St NW. A 19,741 sq mi nation of 2.6 million people, this country has been prominent in the news recently due to the problems involving Kosovo.

Scott Circle. Actually a circle within a square, Scott Circle is where Massachusetts Ave and Rhode Island Ave form a cross. In addition, 16th St NW and N St bisect the circle heading north-south and east-west, respectively.

Walk northwest along Connecticut Ave to Rhode Island Ave and turn right.

On the north side of the street is the **Cathedral of St Matthew**

(202/347-3215), 1725 Rhode Island Ave NW, seat of the Archbishop of Washington. Designed in Renaissance style, the church was established in 1840 and moved to its present location in 1893. President John F Kennedy was buried from here in 1963, and Pope John Paul II celebrated Mass here in 1979. There are eye-catching frescoes and mosaics throughout the church. The white marble altar and the baptismal font are gifts from India. The church is open daily from 7 am to 6:30 pm.

Past 17th St NW on the South side of the street is the **B'nai B'rith Klutznick National Jewish Museum** (202/857-6583), 1640 Rhode Island Ave. Part art museum, part history museum, and part ethnographic museum, the building offers changing exhibits, monthly lectures, concerts, films, and family programs. The national headquarters of B'nai B'rith, it reflects 4,000 years of Jewish history, culture and tradition. Artworks include paintings, drawings, lithographs, woodcuts, photographs, and sculptures. Recently added to the facility is the National Jewish American Sports Hall of Fame. Outdoors, there is a lovely sculpture garden.

The museum is open between 10 am and 5 pm every day but Saturday and admission is free. A museum shop (202/857-6608) is available until half an hour prior to closing.

From the Jewish museum, return to 17th St NW and go south to the next intersection. On the southeast corner of 17th St and M St stands the **National Geographic Explorers Hall** (202/857-7588, www.national-geographic.com). An interactive geography science center, the first floor of the building includes such attractions as a 3.9 billion-year-old moon rock, the egg of an extinct half-ton "elephant bird" *(Aepyornis maximus)* from Madagascar, an Olmec stone head from Mexico that dates from 32 BC, and equipment used on the expedition of Adm Robert E Perry, the first man to reach the North Pole.

In Geographica, on the north side of the hall, you can touch a tornado, find out what the inside of the earth is like, explore the Martian landscape, or study the origin of humankind. In Earth Station One, a 72-seat amphitheater centered on an 11-ft sphere, you can simulate orbital flight. The museum has many interactive videos, you can a look into a video microscope, and you can see excerpts from some of the Society's many years of magnificent TV specials in the National Geographic Television Room.

The museum is open Monday through Saturday, plus holidays (except Christmas), between 9 am and 5 pm and on Sundays between 10 am and 5 pm.

Take 17th St north to Rhode Island Ave, turn right and walk one short block to Scott Circle. Walk east along the south side of Scott Circle to 15th St NW and turn right. On the northwest corner of 15th St and Massachusetts Ave, is the embassy of **Tunisia** at 1515 Massachusetts Ave NW. A republic of 10 million people on the North coast of Africa, Tunisia was the site of ancient Carthage and a former Barbary state. It attained independence in 1956.

On the corner of 15th St and M St at 1501 M St NW is the embassy of **Sweden**, a Scandinavian kingdom that is a member of the European Union. On the southwest corner, the embassy of **Djibouti**, a largely-Muslim nation on the East coast of Africa, occupies Suite 515 in the building at 1156 15th St NW, while the embassy of **Iceland** occupies Suite 1200. A volcanic 40,000-sq mi island republic, Iceland boasts of having the world's oldest Parliament.

Across the street, the embassy of **Gambia**, a nation on the Atlantic coast near the western tip of Africa, occupies Suite 1000 of the building at 1155 15th St NW.

At 1150 15th St NW are the offices of the daily *Washington Post* newspaper (202/334-7969). Years ago, when the newspaper sponsored a music competition for the public, John Philip Sousa was asked to compose a march for the awards ceremony. For writing *The Washington Post March*, Sousa earned the grand sum of $35.

Thomas Circle. Thomas Circle sits at the conjunction of four streets: M St NW, running east and west; 14th St NW, running north and south; Massachusetts Ave NW, running from the northwest to the southeast; and Vermont Ave NW, running from the southwest to the northeast.

Keep walking south along 15th St NW. On the northwest corner of 15th St and K St (927 15th St NW) is the embassy of **Azerbaijan**, a 33,400-sq mi republic in southwest Asia that once was a part of the Roman Empire. Across the street, in a building at 1511 K St, the embassy of **Equitorial Guinea**, a nation that includes Bioko Island off the coast of west Africa as well as the mainland enclave of Rio Muni, occupies Suite 405; and the embassy of **Georgia**, a nation on the east coast of the Black Sea in southwest Asia, occupies Suite 424.

Turn left onto K St, go one short block, and turn left into Vermont Ave. Walk two blocks to Thomas Circle. On the northwest side of the circle, between Massachusetts Ave and 14th St NW, is the **National Christian Church**.

Logan Circle. Logan Circle sits at the junction of 13th St NW, running north and south, and P St, running east and west. Vermont Ave passes through on an angle, heading from the southwest to the northeast. It is an area of beautifully restored Victorian and Edwardian mansions and is one of the city's foremost theatrical centers.

Follow Vermont Ave northeast for two blocks. At 1318 Vermont Ave NW is the **Mary McLeod Bethune Council House** (202/673-2402). This is Ms Bethune's former home, a Victorian townhouse she acquired after President Franklin Roosevelt invited her to Washington in 1935 to become a special advisor on minority affairs in Washington.

An African-American educator and activist, Bethune was born in 1875, the 15th of 17 children of former slaves. She founded a girls' school in 1904 that has evolved into today's Bethune-Cookman College in Daytona Beach, FL. In 1935, she founded the National Council of Negro Women, which was headquartered in this house from 1943 to 1966. A half-hour video that details her life and her accomplishments is available for viewing on request.

Two levels of the Bethune house are open to the public. On the entry level, a red-carpeted living room is adorned with a crystal chandelier and a replica of the baby grand piano that Bethune once played. Photographs of various members of the National Council of Negro Women are on display as well. Up the carved wooden staircase, tourists may visit Bethune's bedroom and two other rooms in which more pictures are on display, along with some antique furniture.

Continue along Vermont Ave to P St. **Studio Theatre** (202/332-3300), 1333 P St NW, has served Washington theatre-goers for more than 20 seasons. The 200-seat theater underwent a $4.5 million renovation in 1997, at which time a new theatre, the **Milton**, was added. Tickets average $20-$30, but discounts are provided for seniors and students. The on-site **Secondstage**, is a 50-seat loft located on the third floor where emerging artists, directors, and actors can showcase their work. Street parking is available and a paid lot is located on P St between 14th St and 15th St NW.

Two other popular theaters are located on Church St, which is located directly east of DuPont Circle between 14th St and 18th St NW. The **Church St Theater** (202/265-3748) is at 1742 Church St NW and the **Woolly Mammoth Theater Co** (202/234-6130) is at 1401 Church St NW. *Take a sharp left onto Rhode Island Ave and head southwest toward Scott Circle. At Rhode Island and 15th St NW, pass the Holiday Inn Central and turn right.*

At 1333 16th St NW is the embassy of **Nigeria**, a strife-torn nation on the southern coast of West Africa.

Walk west along the North side of Scott Circle. At 1600 Massachusetts Ave NW is the embassy of the **Philippines**, cluster of 7,100 islands off the southeast coast of Asia. Visited by Magellan in 1521 and used as a major command center by Gen Douglas MacArthur during World War II, the country most recently has been known for the political abuses of Ferdinand Marcos and his wife Imelda.

At 1601 Massachusetts Ave NW is the embassy of **Australia**, an island-continent roughly the size of the United States but with only 18.5 million people, spread primarily along Australia's East and West coasts.

At 17th St NW, turn left (south) and walk one short block to N St. Then take a right. Not far beyond the corner, on the right-hand side of the street at 1725 N St NW, is the embassy for the **Federated States of Micronesia**, a cluster of 607 small islands in the western Pacific.

Return to 17th St, turn left and walk the short block back to Massachusetts Ave. Turn left and follow the south side of the street toward DuPont Circle, just two blocks away. The embassy of **Peru**, a South American nation located between the Andes Mountains and the Pacific Ocean, is at 1700 Massachusetts Ave NW. At #1708 is the embassy of **Trinidad & Tobago**, an island-nation originally sighted by Christopher Columbus in 1498 off the East coast of Venezuela, and at #1714 is the embassy of **Turkey**, center of the Byzantine Empire for more than 1,000 years. At 1732 Massachusetts Ave NW is the embassy of the republic of **Chile**, located on the west coast of South America.

Just before you reach DuPont Circle, you will encounter the enormous **McCormick Apartment** complex (202/673-4000), built in 1917, in which the typical apartment unit contains 11,000 sq ft of space and the ceilings are 14 feet high. Today, the building serves as the headquarters for the **National Trust for Historic Preservation**.

Return to the point where you originally started touring the Washington circles.

Lodging

All of America's best-known hotel chains can be found in this highly-desirable part of town. Take your pick between **Best Western New Hampshire Suites Hotel** ($$-$$$, 202/457-0565 or 800/762-3777), 1121 New Hampshire Ave NW; **Clarion Hampshire** ($$$, 202/246-7600 or 800/368-5691), 1310 New Hampshire Ave NW; **Doubletree Hotel Park Terrace** ($$$, 202/23-7000), 1515 Rhode Island Ave NW; **Embassy Suites Hotel Downtown** ($$$, 202/857-3388 or 800/EMBASSY), 1250

22nd St NW; **Holiday Inn Central** ($$$, 202/483-2000 or 800/248-0016), 1501 Rhode Island Ave NW; **Howard Johnson Plaza & Suites** ($$$, 202/462-7777 or 800/5690), 1430 Rhode Island Ave NW; **Park Hyatt Washington** ($$$-$$$$, 202/789-1234 or 800/233-1234), 24th St and M St; **Radisson Barcelo** ($$$-$$$$, 202/293-3100 or 800/333-3333), 2121 P St NW; **Sheraton City Center** ($$$-$$$$, 202/775-0800 or 800/771-9042), 1143 New Hampshire Ave NW; **Washington Marriott** ($$$, 202/872-1500), 1221 22nd St NW; and **Westin Washington Hotel** ($$$, 202/424-0100), 2350 M St NW.

Less well-advertised, but very popular hotels in the region include the 415-room **ANA Hotel Washington** ($$$, 202/429-2400 or 800/262-4683) at 2401 M St NW; the all-suite, 151-unit **One Washington Circle Hotel** ($$$, 202/872-1680 or 800/424-9671) at One Washington Circle, which includes the popular West End Cafe that offers a Sunday champagne brunch and provides a pianist between Tuesday and Saturday in its Piano Room; our personal favorite, the **Renaissance Mayflower** ($$$-$$$$, 202/347-3000 or 800/HOTELS-1) at 1127 Connecticut Ave NW; and the small, but well-located **Jefferson Hotel** ($$$, 202/347-2200 or 800/368-5966) at 1200 16th St NW, which hosts traditional afternoon teas and a Sunday brunch.

Alternate possibilities include several exceptional bed-and-breakfast facilities. The six-room **DuPont at the Circle** ($$$, 202/408-8308) is just half a block from the Metro in a Victorian townhouse at 1606 19th St NW, where it offers large rooms with high ceilings and in-room fireplaces, marble bathrooms with Jacuzzis, a complimentary continental breakfast, and a free daily newspaper. The four-room **Simpkins B&B** ($$$-$$$, 202/387-1308) at 1601 19th St NW occupies a restored, air-conditioned 1888 Victorian townhouse, while the 46-room **Windsor Inn** ($$$, 202/667-0300 or 800/423-9111), enormous by B&B standards is at 1842 16th St NW.

If you don't choose to stay there, at least try to tour the **Mansion on O St** ($$$$, 202/496-2000, www.erols.com/mansion), 2020 O St NW. Located on a residential block, the popular and trendy B&B, frequent host to movie stars and other dignitaries, consists of three townhouses that have been combined. It was designed in 1892 by architect Alan Clark, brother of Champ Clark, who was Speaker of the House during the presidency of Theodore Roosevelt. Costume jewelry, Western cow-horn chairs, lithographs, antique puppets, and a virtual catalog of other items, all available for purchase, are crammed into every nook and cranny of the building, There are secret doors, a mirrored stairway that leads nowhere, 16 fireplaces, and ten kitchenettes. Rooms include the Safari Room; the psychedelic Fifth Dimension Suite; a Midshipman's Room, where the curtains are arranged like signal flags; a Corporation Suite that employs filing cabinets for the bed's headboard and is decorated like an office; and the Log Cabin Room, where a sauna/spa simulates a rain forest, a full kitchen occupies the loft, and a bubbling aquarium sits above the bed.

Arts & culture

The Gamelan Room in the **Walsh-McLean House** is often used for concerts and for *wayang* (shadow puppetry).

The Education Department (202/387-2151) of the **Phillips Collection** provides two programs for families with children between the ages of 6 and 12 which are offered from Tuesday through Sunday: "Art at Home," which requires children to write a story or poem about a particular painting, and "Observation and Imagination," in which children learn to express themselves through a variety of media. Participation must be prearranged. Every Thursday the museum stays open until 8:30 pm and guests can enjoy a program of "Artful Evenings," which consists of live music, gallery talks, and a cash bar for a $5 fee. Family workshops are staged in the museum throughout the year.

A free concert series is offered at the **Anderson House** one Saturday of each month, and guest lecturers often appear in the Grosvenor Auditorium at the **National Geographic Explorers Hall** (202/857-7700).

Food & drink

When it comes to dining, price and variety are limitless in this upscale area. Some of the most popular are the Ethiopian **Red Sea** ($$-202/483-5000), 3416 18th St NW, open daily from 11:30 am to 11:30 pm and voted one of the "Best 50" for more than seven consecutive years; the **La Tomate** ($-$$, 202/667-5505), 1701 Connecticut Ave NW, which occupies an unusual triangular building, offers daily regional and contemporary Italian specials at lunch and dinner, and has a ground-floor bar, sidewalk tables, seasonal patio dining, and an upper deck; and **Du Pont Down Under**, a food court that occupies an old trolley tunnel that ran beneath the circle from the 1940s until 1961.

Nightlife

The **Improv** (202/296-7008), 1140 Connecticut Ave NW, is a well-known Washington comedy club. **Fox and Hounds** (202/232-6307), 1533 17th St NW, has a large patio fronting onto 17th St NW that is packed from Spring through Fall. **Buffalo Billiards** (202/331-7665), 1330 19th St NW, touts 30 pool tables, a snooker table, five dart boards, a restaurant, two bars, a cigar bar, and two outdoor patios. Thursdays are college nights at the **New Vegas Lounge** (202/483-3971), 1415 P St NW, which has a cover charge on weekends and features take-what-you-get entertainment from Tuesday through Sunday.

Gay clubs in the area include the all-male **JRs** (202/328-0090), 1519 17th St NW, open until 2 am from Sunday through Thursday and 3 am on Friday and Saturday, which provides a pool table on the balcony but no food. The three-story **Circle Bar & Tavern** (202/462-5575), 1629 Connecticut Ave NW, features half-price drinks on Tuesdays, a free gift grab bag, and a drag show in the Underground on Sundays. Patronized by both men and women, Circle Bar is open until 2 am from Sunday through Thursday and 3 am on Friday and Saturday.

Events

On the first Friday of each month, most of the art galleries on Du Pont Circle stay open until 8 pm.

The Upper Northwest Side,
The National Zoo,
& Rock Creek Park

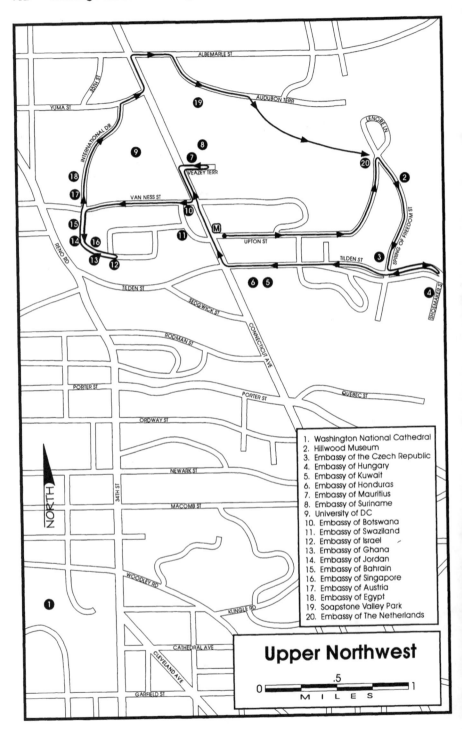

1. Washington National Cathedral
2. Hillwood Museum
3. Embassy of the Czech Republic
4. Embassy of Hungary
5. Embassy of Kuwait
6. Embassy of Honduras
7. Embassy of Mauritius
8. Embassy of Suriname
9. University of DC
10. Embassy of Botswana
11. Embassy of Swaziland
12. Embassy of Israel
13. Embassy of Ghana
14. Embassy of Jordan
15. Embassy of Bahrain
16. Embassy of Singapore
17. Embassy of Austria
18. Embassy of Egypt
19. Soapstone Valley Park
20. Embassy of The Netherlands

Upper Northwest

NORTH

0   .5   1
MILES

The Upper Northwest Side

In the far northwestern quadrant of the District of Columbia, there is a scattering of largely residential communities, some located within the Washington city limits and others without.

Woodley Park and Cathedral Heights, site of the Washington National Cathedral, are located inside the city limits. Cleveland Park, Forest Hills, Barnaby Woods, Pinehurst Circle, Friendship Heights, American University Park, Spring Valley, and The Palisades are outside the city limits, as are Tenleytown, the site of Fort Reno Park, and Foxhall, the site of Mt Vernon College.

In this chapter, we have subdivided this sizeable area into several interesting, manageable, and walkable tours from which you may pick and choose.

Information

Hillwood Museum (202/686-8500), located at 4155 Linnean Ave NW. Reservations are required to visit both the house and the gardens. The gardens are open between 9 am and 5 pm Tuesday through Saturday. The house and grounds are closed on Sunday, on Monday, and during the entire month of February. The museum hosts various seasonal events including a series of lectures.

Getting there

Take the Metro to the Van Ness-UDC station. If you drive, you can park for free at the Hillwood Museum.

Tours

Tours of the **Hillwood Museum** are conducted at 9 am, 10:30 am, noon, 1:30 pm, and 3 pm from Tuesday through Saturday, but only by reservation. Adult admission is $10, but children under 12 and students can get in for $5.

DC's Upper Northwest. *From the Metro station on Connecticut Ave, walk east on Tilden St to Linnean St. Turn left onto Linnean and walk the block and a half to the Hillwood Museum.* The former home of Marjorie Merriweather Post, heir to the Post cereal fortune, is now the **Hillwood Museum**. Ms Post's husband served as the American ambassador to Russia following the Russian Revolution, and her former mansion contains a wealth of art and decorative treasures from Imperialist Russia as well as other 18th- and 19th-century European artworks.

Among the treasures in the Porcelain Room is a china service and glassware originally commissioned by Catherine the Great. The Drawing Room contains tapestries and 18th-century French furniture, and the Icon Room holds gold and silver chalices, various jeweled items created by Carl Faberge, and of course icons.

Carl Faberge's Imperial Easter Eggs are a particular delight.

A log cabin-style structure displays rugs, quillwork, pottery, featherwork headdresses, and other American Indian objects, and a one-room *dacha* (Russian country house) displays decorative Russian art. Reopened in the spring of 2000 after a thorough renovation, the mansion is surrounded by 25 acres of lawn, some glorious gardens, and a greenhouse.

From the Hillwood Museum, walk south along Spring of Freedom Ave. At 3900 Spring of Freedom is the embassy of the **Czech Republic.** The 30,450-sq-mi country, slightly smaller than South Carolina, has a population that is slightly larger than that of Michigan.

At Tilden St, turn left and walk one block to Shoemaker. Turn right. At 3910 Shoemaker is the embassy of **Hungary,** another formerly-Communist central European country.

Return to Tilden St and turn left. At 2940 Tilden is the embassy of **Kuwait,** a country located at the north end of the Persian Gulf, and at 3007 Tilden sits the embassy of the Central American republic of **Honduras.**

At Connecticut Ave, turn right and go three blocks to Vezey Terr. On the northeast corner, at 4301 Connecticut Ave, are two embassies, those of the Islamic republic of **Mauritius,** a 788-sq mi country located in the Indian Ocean 500 miles East of Madagascar, and the Florida-sized nation of **Suriname,** which is located on the northern coast of South America.

Return one block along Connecticut Ave and turn right onto Van Ness St. You are now on the campus of the coeducational **University of The District of Columbia,** the only public institution of higher education in the District of Columbia and the first exclusively-urban land-grant university.

UDC began in 1851 as the Minor Normal School, a "school for colored girls" that specialized in training teachers. In 1873, a similar school, Washington Normal, was founded for the education of white female students. In 1929, both Minor Normal and Washington Normal became four-year teachers' colleges, and in 1955, the two schools merged to form the District of Columbia Teachers College. Eleven years later, two other schools, Federal City College and Washington Technical Institute, were founded, and in 1977, all three institutions joined together to form the University of the District of Columbia. The university has an enrollment of 14,000 and occupies three Washington-area campuses, one at Georgia St and Harvard St, one on Van Ness, and one at Mount Vernon

As you walk onto the campus look, to the south side of the street. At 2400 Van Ness St NW is the embassy of **Botswana,** a South African republic with an area about twice the size of Arizona and a population about half that of Chicago. At 3400 Van Ness is the embassy of **Swaziland,** a kingdom located near the coast of the Indian Ocean in southern Africa.

Continue along Van Ness to International Dr and turn left. On the southwest corner, at 3514 International Dr, is the embassy of **Israel,** Middle-Eastern homeland of the Jews. Next door, at #3512, is the embassy of **Ghana**, a republic situated on the southern coast of west Africa that is best known as the home of UN Secretary General Kofi Annan.

Around the corner, at 3504 International Pl, is the embassy of **Jordan**, a kingdom that represents 4.5 million people in the strife-torn Middle East. The embassy of **Bahrain**, a tiny 268-sq mi nation in the Persian Gulf, occupies the building at #3502, and the embassy of **Singapore** is at #3501. One of the world's largest ports, the Republic of Singapore occupies just 250 sq mi in southeast Asia, consisting of a flat, formerly swampy island and 40 nearby islets. A British colony until 1959, it became a part of Malaysia for a short time, and then became a separate nation in 1985.

Return North along International Dr. Past Van Ness, at #3524 on the West side of the street, is the embassy of **Austria**, a mountainous republic of 8 million people that is located just East of Bavarian Germany. At #3522 is the embassy of **Egypt**, fabled land of Cleopatra, the Pharaohs, and the pyramids.

Follow International Dr off campus to Yuma St and turn left. Go one block and turn right onto 35th St. Go one more block and turn right again onto Albemarle St. Cross Connecticut Ave and turn right onto Audubon Terr. Soapstone Valley Park will be on your right. About one block past 29th St, turn right and walk through the park to Lenore Ln. At Lenore Ln and Upton St is the embassy of the **Netherlands**, a kingdom of 15.5 million people on the North Sea that is best known for supplying the world with Delft china, tulip bulbs, and Gouda cheese. *Hillwood Museum, where you began your tour, is less than a block farther on.*

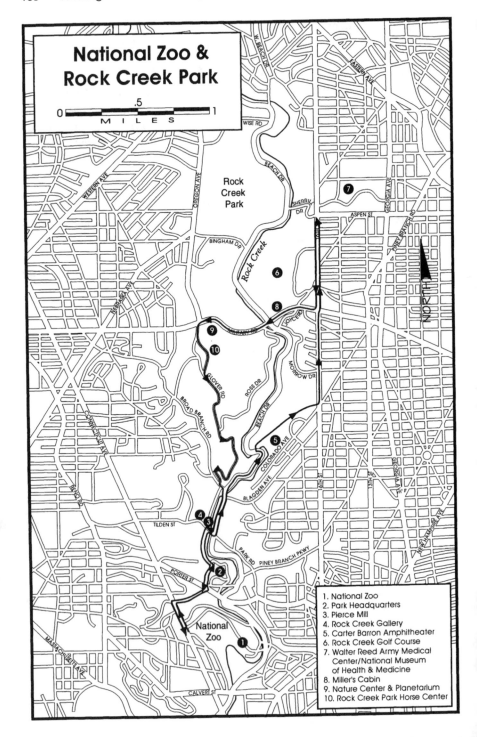

National Zoo &
Rock Creek Park

0 .5 1
MILES

Rock
Creek
Park

WISE RD

N. BEACH DR

EASTERN AVE

BEACH DR

SHERRIL DR

ASPEN ST

Rock Creek

⑦

GEORGIA AVE

PINEY BRANCH RD

BINGHAM DR

⑥

⑧

SPICER RD

MORROW DR

NORTH

MILITARY RD

⑨
⑩

GLOVER RD

ROSS DR

BEACH DR

BROAD BRANCH RD

WESTERN AVE

OREGON AVE

NEBRASKA AVE

CONNECTICUT AVE

RENO RD

⑤

COLORADO AVE

BLAGDEN AVE

16TH ST

13TH ST

GEORGIA AVE

NEW HAMPSHIRE AVE

④③

TILDEN ST

②

PARK RD

PINEY BRANCH PKWY

PORTER ST

MASSACHUSETTS AVE

National
Zoo

①

CALVERT ST

1. National Zoo
2. Park Headquarters
3. Pierce Mill
4. Rock Creek Gallery
5. Carter Barron Amphitheater
6. Rock Creek Golf Course
7. Walter Reed Army Medical
   Center/National Museum
   of Health & Medicine
8. Miller's Cabin
9. Nature Center & Planetarium
10. Rock Creek Park Horse Center

The National Zoo & Rock Creek Park

Woodley Park is a lovely residential area stretching along Connecticut Ave north of Calvert St NW. Presidents Martin Van Buren and Grover Cleveland spent their summers here. It is an area of shaded streets and rolling hills, turn-of-the-century mansions and Art Deco apartment buildings, sidewalk cafes, and the Art Deco Uptown Theater, a showcase for first-run films. At its southeast corner is the National Zoo; Rock Creek Park runs north from there and forms the area's eastern boundary.

A part of the Smithsonian Institution, the National Zoological Park occupies 163 acres and is one of the world's largest zoos. It was established in 1889 "for the advancement of science and the instruction and recreation of the people."

Rock Creek Park, Washington's largest, was purchased by congress in 1890 for its "pleasant valleys and ravines, primeval forests and open fields, its running waters, its rocks clothed with rich ferns and mosses, its repose and tranquility, its light and shade, its ever-varying shrubbery, its beautiful and extensive views,". Its 1,754 wooded acres extend nearly the entire length of the city along rapidly-flowing Rock Creek. The creek is 12 miles long, meandering from the Potomac River to the Maryland border.

The park has been a recreational destination for presidents and less exalted citizens for more than 100 years. Abraham Lincoln took carriage rides here. Theodore Roosevelt came often, frequently with his children, to fish, hike and swim. Woodrow Wilson and his wife enjoyed driving through.

It is an area marked by deep valleys, the hillsides broken by rocky ledges, and it remains predominantly natural. An occasional deer can be spotted in the fields, and there are over 100 different species of trees and shrubs. During the summer, temperatures often are 10 degrees cooler here than in the city. Scattered throughout the park are 30 separate picnic areas, some equipped with grills, available to the public for use by permit (202/673-7646).

The Rock Creek & Potomac Parkway begins at the Lincoln Memorial and winds its way north through the park as far as the zoo. After a short break, it resumes again, this time with a new name, Beach Dr, and continues its northerly run all the way to the Maryland border, providing a convenient sign-posted, 11-mile route for bikers, hikers and joggers. The park also offers access to athletic fields, exercise courses, tennis courts, horse paths, additional hiking trails, and a golf course. Convenient free parking is available throughout the park.

Most of the park's attractions are located north of the zoo, but those who choose to explore the southern end of the park can enjoy its natural wonders as well. From the Lincoln Memorial to the JFK Center, the path parallels the Potomac River. North of Virginia Ave, it runs beneath a concrete "cobweb" of roadways and ramps near downtown Georgetown, but it regains a more pristine atmosphere once it passes M St NW. At P St, the pathway and the river make a turn to the northwest. North of Q St, the mansions lining Embassy Row parallel the pathway to your right, while the Dumbarton House and the historic Oak Hill Cemetery lie to your left. The next bridge carries Massachusetts Ave over the creek and the pathway and river take another turn, this time to the northeast. The Islamic Center is atop the hill on your right immediately past the bridge. Near Cathedral Ave, there is a mile and one-half Perrier parcourse exercise facility with 18 calisthenics stations along the way. You then pass under Connecticut Ave and Calvert Ave, marked by the Duke Ellington Memorial Bridge, and arrive at the south end of the zoo.

Information

The main entrance to the National Zoological Park (202/673-4800, 202/673-4717 or 202/673-4823 TTY) is at 3001 Connecticut Ave NW. Admission is free, and the grounds are open daily from 6 am to 8 pm. The various buildings on the grounds are open daily from 9 am to 6 pm between April 15 and October 15 and from 10 am to 4:30 pm between September 16 and April 30, except for Christmas. If possible, go early in the day, not only to avoid congestion but because the animals tend to be most active and alert at that time of day. And wear comfortable walking shoes because the grounds are quite hilly.

Rock Creek Park Headquarters (202/282-1063) at 3545 Williamsburg Rd NW is open between 7:45 am and 4:15 pm on weekdays.

Getting there

Take the Metro Red Line subway to the Woodley Park-Zoo or the Cleveland Park exits; the L2 or L4 buses, which stop at the Connecticut Ave entrance to the zoo; or the H2 or H4 buses, which stop at the Harvard St entrance to the zoo. If you arrive by car you'll find ample parking at the zoo.

First steps

There is a Visitor Center at the Education Building, just inside the main gate at the National Zoological Park. Pick up a map, find out when the various animals will be fed, and see if any special events have been scheduled during the time you will be on the grounds. Also check to see whether the panda feedings will be conducted indoors or out. Other information centers with brochures, maps, wagons, strollers, and wheelchairs are scattered throughout the park, as are snack bars, ice cream kiosks, and a number of gift shops.

At the **Rock Creek Park** headquarters, you can pick up detailed maps of the park, brochures, and other information. Detailed maps of the park's 20 miles of hiking trails, ranging from easy to strenuous, also are available at the **Rock Creek Nature Center and Planetarium.**

Seasonal highlights

On the first weekend in October, a free Zoo Arts Festival (202/673-4961) is held at the **National Zoological Park**, with workshops and demonstrations by local artists, a wildlife art exhibit and sale, and a kids' "Creation Station."

The **Carter Barron Amphitheater** in Rock Creek Park offers a variety of programs from late June to late August. Each year, generally in June, the Shakespeare Theatre's "Free For All" (202/628-5770) takes place on this stage, usually for a span of two or three weeks on Tuesday-through-Sunday evenings. Free tickets are available on the day of the performance only. In August, the amphitheater hosts the Children's Festival (202/260-6836), which provides music, the performing arts, and hands-on activities free of charge. In September, the DC Blues Festival (202/828-3028) is held here.

Special hikes, activities, and talks geared to children take place at the **Rock Creek Nature Center and Planetarium** every month, including nature films, crafts demonstrations, live animal demonstrations, and a daily mix of lectures, films, and other events.

A stargazing activity, "Exploring the Sky," is held monthly at 8:30 pm from April through May, at 9 pm from June through August, at 8:30 pm in October, and at 7:30 pm in November. Co-sponsored by National Park Service and the National Capital Astronomers, participants meet at Picnic Grove #13, Military and Glover Rds NW. The sessions are free, but participants must have a ticket that can be picked up half an hour in advance.

Rock Creek Park Day (202/426-6829) is held on the Saturday closest to September 25, the park's birthday. Festivities include free children's activities, environmental and recreational exhibits, food, crafts, and music.

Tours

Guided tours of the **National Zoological Park** can be arranged by appointment (202/673-4955). The Bird Resource Center at the rear of the Bird House also provides a guided tour of the room in which birds' eggs incubate and zoo employees tend to the needs of birds in need of medical attention.

Visitors may take self-guided tours of the **National Museum of Health & Medicine** on the grounds of Walter Reed Army Medical Center.

All of the Rock Creek Park guided nature walks and self-guided trails begin and end at the **Rock Creek Nature Center and Planetarium.**

The National Zoo & Rock Creek Park. *Start your tour at the zoo's main entrance at 3001 Connecticut Ave NW.* Enter the Education Building, which contains a Visitor Center, as well as the zoo's largest gift shop and a bookstore. You may wish to postpone shopping here until the end of your visit so you won't have to carry your purchases with you while you wander the grounds.

Outside the Education Building and across a pathway is a flower bed. Inside the flower bed is a sculpture carved from a fallen willow oak to form a stylized totem of animal and human forms. The sculpture was created by a local artist, Steven Weitzman, and designed to honor the many volunteers who work at the zoo and in the field of wildlife conservation. A sign in front of the sculpture lists the zoo's daily events.

In the spring and summer, the zoo's pathways are lined with blooming flowers, always attractive to butterflies and hummingbirds, and beside the Small Mammal House is a cactus garden. Also next to the Education Building is the Cheetah Conservation Station and signs that indicate the presence of baby animals on the premises. From here, you have the option of following either of two numbered pathways, the U-shaped Olmstead Walk or the blue Valley Trail. Olmstead Walk, the main walkway, was named in honor of the zoo's principal designer, Frederick Law Olmstead, who also designed Central Park in New York City and the grounds of the US Capitol.

Begin on the Valley Trail. Cheetahs and zebras will be exhibited on your left, then the tapirs and antelopes. At the Wetlands Exhibit, you can follow a boardwalk over a similar marsh to a point where you can see brown pelicans, herons, and other waterfowl swimming about amid a profusion of water lilies and cattails. Watching the staff feed the white pelicans is a particular delight. The Great Outdoor Flight Cage, a walk-in aviary, is 130 feet in diameter.

Head back along the boardwalk and turn right onto Valley Trail once more. When you reach the Olmstead Trail, turn left. Swans will be the first thing you see, followed by the Australia Pavilion, which occupies the center of the park, and is surrounded by kangaroos, camels, and antelopes. Across the way will be the hippos, rhinos, giraffes, and elephants. Near the rhinos outside the Elephant House is "Uncle Beazley," the replica of a 25 ft-long triceratops. The Elephant House contains pygmy hippos, rhinos, and a variety of interesting exhibits as well as elephants. Elephant demonstrations are conducted daily at 10:30 and 11:30 am.

Opposite the elephants' and giraffes' outdoor habitat is the panda enclosure where the zoo's most famous resident is housed. Hsing-Hsing (pronounced "Shing-Shing") and a companion, Ling-Ling, were a gift from the People's Republic of China in 1972. Ling-Ling died in 1992. Pandas are found only in the bamboo forests on the mountains of central China and fewer than 1,000 of them are believed to still exist. Hsing-Hsing's habitat at the zoo consists of two big, interconnected play yards, and his daily feedings at 11 am and 3 pm are among the zoo's most popular attractions.

Walk down the hill on Olmstead Walk. The Great Apes House is inhabited by gorillas and orangutans. It adjoins another building, called the Think Tank, to which it is connected by an overhead passage rigged with cables suspended 45 feet above the main path. Orangutans move freely between the two buildings, propelling themselves rapidly along the cables. If you can ignore the possibility of having an orangutan unexpectedly "drop in" for a visit, the Think Tank helps you to explore the ways in which animals think. Visitors can view orangutans and monkeys using tools, sending and receiving messages, employing social strategies, and showing other signs of their innate cleverness.

Exit out the other side of the Ape House. Your next destination will be the Reptile Discovery Center, which showcases a mixture of critters ranging from 12- to 15-foot Burmese pythons to African softshell turtles, Cuban crocodiles, rhinoceros iguanas, snakes, turtles, and tortoises. Also found in the Center are a number of hands-on exhibits. Perhaps the major attraction, however, is the Komodo dragon, the world's largest lizard. Sixty Komodo dragons have been born at the National Zoo thus far.

As you exit the Discovery Center, turn left toward the gift shop and then left again at the zoo signs across the path. This is where you will find the circular moated enclosures of the ever-popular lions and tigers.

Walk around the circular enclosure, exiting where you came in, and then turn left. In an area called the American Prairie, cuddly little prairie dogs can be found atop a small earth mound, happily munching on carrots, sweet potatoes, and corn. If you...and the prairie dogs...both have children, you'll have a tough time prying them apart.

At the bottom of the hill is the Mane Restaurant, a pleasant, plant-filled cafeteria with picnic tables outside. It's a nice place to get refreshed and take a rest before you move on.

Take the semicircular path opposite the Mane Restaurant (look for marker #22). The Bat Cave brings back memories of Count Dracula. In a cavern that was built into the hillside, live bats fly around, hang from the ceiling, or feast on strings of cantaloupe, watermelon, and bananas that have been suspended from the roof.

Return to the Mane Restaurant and take the Valley Trail. The Invertebrate Exhibit at the National Zoo is the only one in the country to house both terrestrial and aquatic species. Here, you will see starfish, sponges, giant crabs, anemones, insects, octopuses, and coral. The exhibit is open Tuesday through Sunday year-around.

Across the way is Amazonia and the Amazonia Science Gallery. Amazonia opened in 1992 and simulates a tropical river and rain forest. Glass enclosures contain a sampling of the animals, fish, and birds that can be found in the Amazon region. Some of the freshwater fish are 7 feet long. The futuristic building sits beneath a 50-foot glass dome and contains 358 species of plants, orchids and vines, hummingbirds, monkeys, frogs, dozens of animals and tropical birds, and enormous naturalistic aquariums that are designed to simulate deep river pools. Water cascades over rocks into quiet river pools, and there are a number of interactive displays on hand. Exhibits include a typical Amazon villager's hut and a child's canoe, along with murals that depict the Amazon delta.

In the Amazonia Science Gallery, visitors can watch Smithsonian scientists at work. Visitors are allowed to analyze their own voices and compare them to actual animal vocalizations. One exhibit strives to recreate a tropical biology field station that belongs to an eccentric scientist named Dr Brasil.

Continue climbing in an up-hill direction. You will pass the rare South America spectacled bears and come to a pool full of seals and sea lions. A sea lion training demonstration is given daily at 11:30 am. Upstairs, the pool is bordered by a trellised walkway.

If you wish, you can retrace your steps to a small bridge that you passed just prior to reaching Amazonia. Crossing the bridge and turning right onto the first asphalt path you find will take you into the neighboring Rock Creek Park, which is described in detail below.

In all, the National Zoological Park contains more than 5,000 animals of 500 separate species. The GeoSphere provides visual images that illustrate the earth's geophysical process. The Pollinarium, a part of the zoo's BioPark exhibit, employs a 6-foot model of a sage flower and a 4-foot honeybee to demonstrate plant reproduction, and there is an acrylic-enclosed beehive that is large enough for a person to enter and observe the bees' activities. In the ZOOlab, children between the ages of three and seven can handle animal bones, skins, nests, and feathers; hear tape recordings of animal sounds; and ask questions of the highly-trained docents.

Leave the zoo through the main entrance and return to Connecticut Ave. Walk north to Klingle Rd and turn right. At Porter St, take a left and watch for Williamsburg Rd, entering from your right. Turn onto Williamsburg. (NOTE: For the benefit of pedestrians and bicyclists, Beach Dr is closed to automobile traffic from just South of Military Rd at Joyce Rd to Broad Branch Rd on Saturday, Sunday and holidays.) At 3545 Williamsburg Rd NW is the **Rock Creek Park Headquarters** (202/282-1063). The headquarters is open between 7:45 am and 4:15 pm on weekdays.

Go north from the headquarters building to Tilden St NW and turn right to cross Rock Creek. Near Beach and Tilden you will find **Pierce Mill** (202/426-6908), a genuine water-powered 19th-century grist mill built by Isaac Pierce to grind grain into flour and meal. The restored stone building is no longer operating, unfortunately, but self-guided tours are allowed from 9 am to 5 pm between Wednesday and Sunday. Pierce's old carriage house is now the **Rock Creek Gallery** (202/244-2482), where works of local artists are displayed between 11 am and 4:30 pm from Thursday to Sunday. The Gallery is closed on holidays and throughout the month of August. Just east of Pierce Mill off Park Rd, there are six clay tennis courts. Fees depend upon the court surface (elsewhere in the park are non-clay courts) and the length of play.

Follow Beach Dr north along Rock Creek for roughly one mile. After taking a footbridge across Rock Creek, head due east across the park. At 16th St NW and Colorado Ave is the 4,250-seat **Carter Barron Amphitheater** (202/619-7222 weekdays or 202/426-6837 weekends). Adjacent to the amphitheater is the **Family Tree of Life Statue,** a 15-foot red oak totem by Dennis Stoy Jr that represents an African-American family.

East of the amphitheater at the intersection of Colorado Ave and 16th St NW is a parking lot. Just past the parking lot and the adjacent picnic area, Morrow Dr exits the park onto 16th St. Take a left to the next intersection (Kennedy St). At Kennedy St and 16th St NW, look for a Perrier parcourse with four exercise stations and more than two dozen tennis courts, 15 soft-surface courts and 10 hard-surface courts, five of which are enclosed for indoor play between October and May. The tennis courts must be reserved *in person* at Guest Services (202/722-5949).

Roughly half a mile farther north along 16th St NW, Rittenhouse St enters the park from the east and curves its way to the golf course. The 18-hole **Rock Creek Golf Course** (202/882-7332) is open from dawn to dusk year-around except on Christmas. There is a clubhouse and clubs, lockers, and carts are available for rent.

North of the golf course along 16th St NW is a picnic area. From the east, Aspen St joins 16th St, changing its name to Sherrill Dr as it enters Rock Creek Park. On the northeast corner of 16th St and Aspen St NW is the huge **Walter Reed Army Medical Center.** In Building 54 of this massive complex is the **National Museum of Health & Medicine** (202/782-2200, www.natmedmuse.afip.org). Opened to the public during the Civil War in 1862, the museum displays interesting, sometimes bizarre, exhibits including a smoker's lung, the bullet that killed Abraham Lincoln, Incan skulls that indicate the use of surgery long before Columbus visited the Americas, Paul Revere's dental tools, and a kidney stone. You can ask a computer to count your heartbeats since the day you were born, learn that you breathe 20,000 times each day, learn that a square inch of skin contains three feet of blood vessels, and see that it's possible to tie a bone into a knot. You can touch a brain and try on a garment that makes you experience some of the discomforts of being pregnant. The museum contains one of the world's most extensive microscope collections and models of some of history's earliest medical instruments. There is an AIDS exhibit theater and a video that explains HIV.

The museum is open between 10 am and 5:30 pm daily except on Christmas. Admission is free, but you will be asked for a drivers license or other picture ID when you enter. (NOTE: weekend and evening visitors must enter the grounds via the Georgia Ave and Elder St gate.)

Return to 16th St NW and turn south. At Military Rd, take a right and cross to the west side of the park. Just north of Military Rd on Beach Dr is **Miller's Cabin** (202/426-6829), the log studio of eccentric, High Sierra poet Joaquin Miller, who lived here at one time. During the summer, poetry readings and workshops are held in this cabin.

Continue walking west on Military Rd until you reach Oregon Ave, which enters from the right. Nearby stand the remains of Fort De Russy, one of a circle of 68 forts that defended the city during the Civil War. Other such forts include Fort Reno and Fort Bayard.

Opposite the entrance to Oregon St is the beginning of Glover Rd. Go south on Glover. **Rock Creek Nature Center and Planetarium** (202/426-6829) at 5200 Glover Rd NW is open year-around between 9 am and 5 pm Wednesday through Sunday, except for holidays.

The Center also maintains environmental exhibits and wildlife displays, has a hands-on nature "discovery room," and conducts nature talks. There is an observation deck and an auditorium.

Near the Nature Center on Glover Rd is the **Rock Creek Park Horse**

Center (202/362-0117), where visitors can rent a horse or take lessons. Trail rides are conducted at 3 pm from Tuesday through Thursday, at noon on Saturday, and at noon, 1:30 pm and 3 pm on Sunday.

Continue south on Glover Rd until you come to Broad Branch Rd. Turn left and walk a short distance until you're back on Beach Dr. Turn right and walk and retrace your route back to Connecticut Ave and the entrance to the National Zoo.

Lodging

Located near the National Zoo at 2660 Woodley Rd NW, Washington's largest hotel, the 1,239-room **Sheraton Washington** ($$-$$$, 202/328-2000 or 800/325-3535, www.sheraton.com), sits in a park-like setting, has an on-site Metro station and two self-parking garages, and offers an outdoor pool, a fitness center, a business center, restaurants, and a post office. A close competitor is the **Omni Shoreham Hotel** ($$$$, 202/234-0700 or 800/334-6664), 2500 Calvert St NW, which has 836 rooms, is within walking distance of the zoo, and has a prime location adjacent to Rock Creek. The Omni is just one block from the Metro, provides both indoor and outdoor parking, and features an outdoor pool, tennis courts, and a fitness center.

Washington Hilton & Towers ($$$$, 202/483-3000 or 800/HILTONS), 1919 Connecticut Ave NW, stands at the corner of T St NW. The 1,041-room hotel features 82 suites, a mahogany-paneled grill, the sports-themed McClellan's lounge, the Capital Court lobby lounge and piano bar, a health club, a heated outdoor pool, three lighted tennis courts, a jogging path, shops, a business center, and an ATM with foreign-currency capability. Less expensive is the **Windsor Park Hotel** ($$-$$$, 202/483-7700 or 800/247-3064), 2116 Kalorama Rd NW, located in a quiet neighborhood just off Connecticut Ave.

B&B fans should look into **Kalorama Guest House** ($-$$, 202/667-6369), 1854 Mintwood Pl NW. Located between 19th St and Columbia Rd at Kalorama Park, the B&B has 31 rooms...12 with private baths. The original six-bedroom Victorian townhouse proved to be so popular that it gradually grew to include four other houses on Mintwood Pl and two on Cathedral Ave NW. There is a garden with umbrella-tables, a parlor with a fireplace, and a guest laundry. None of the rooms has a telephone, but some of the buildings prohibit smoking.

Arts & culture

The **Washington National Cathedral** Choir sings at 4 pm on Monday, Tuesday, and Wednesday during the school year. Organ demonstrations are given at 12:45 pm on Wednesday and organ recitals at 5 pm on Sunday after the regular services have been concluded. The 53-bell carillon is played at 12:30 pm on Saturday.

Food & drink

Around Woodley Park and the zoo, the Tex-Mex **Cactus Cantina** ($-$$, 202/686-7222) at 3300 Wisconsin Ave NW is just one block north of the Washington National Cathedral and houses the city's only American Indian & Cowboy Museum. At 2331 Calvert St NW, **Washington Park Gourmet** ($$, 202/462-5566) is open from 8 am to 8 pm on weekdays and from 8 am to 7 pm on weekends, while the nearby **New Heights Restaurant** at 2317 Calvert St NW ($$, 202/234-4110) serves "New American" cuisine and offers a great view of Rock Creek Park.

Near the zoo, two restaurants are **Animal Crackers** ($, 202/667-0503), a self-service restaurant across from the zoo entrance at 3000 Connecticut Ave, which has outdoor seating in season and is open at 7:30 am on weekdays and 8 am on weekends, and **Petitto's** ($-$$, 202/667-5350), an Italian restaurant at 2633 Connecticut Ave across from the Metro station that occupies a turn-of-the-century townhouse with working fireplaces in each dining area, provides umbrella tables on the street during warm weather, and is open for lunch from 11:30 am to 2:30 pm on weekdays.

Nightlife

The **Oxford Tavern** (202/232-4225) at 3000 Connecticut Ave across from the zoo, is a colorful neighborhood pub with seasonal outdoor seating. Popularly known as the Zoo Bar, it features live music on Tuesday and Saturday and a DJ with recorded music on Friday. Another nearby musical attraction is the **City Blues Cafe** at 2651 Connecticut Ave NW (202/232-2300), which features live performances nightly in a Victorian house-turned-nightclub. Lunch and dinner are served daily, and the walls are covered with life-size paintings of musical personalities such as Dizzy Gillespie and Ella Fitzgerald. A more relaxed hangout might be the **Aroma** at 3417 Connecticut Ave NW, a cigar bar with free board games.

Just four blocks from Rock Creek Park's Carter Barron Amphitheater, **Twins Lounge** (202/882-2523), 5516 Colorado Ave NW, provides live jazz music every night. On weeknights, local artists are featured; Wednesday is an open mike night; out-of-town acts are featured on weekends; and there's a jam session on Sunday night. The restaurant serves Italian, Ethiopian, and Caribbean food. On weeknights there is a $7 minimum, and on weekends there is a variable cover charge plus a $10 minimum.

One of the more popular attractions after dark is the **Marquee Cabaret**, an art deco club in the Omni-Sheraton Hotel. Political satirist Mark Russell performed here for 20 years, and name talent is still featured.

Events

Numerous special events are scheduled at the **Washington National Cathedral**. These include calligraphy workshops and jazz, folk, and classical concerts. The Medieval Workshop for Families (202/537-2934), held between 10 am and 2 pm on

Saturdays and overseen by docents, features arts and crafts projects in which gargoyles can be modeled out of clay and participants can carve a chunk of Indiana limestone or make a small stained-glass window. Participation is on a first-come basis and there is a $2 fee to participate.

Free planetarium shows for adults and children are given at the **Rock Creek Nature Center and Planetarium** on weekends and on Wednesday afternoons at 3:45 pm.

Sidetrip—Washington National Cathedral

North and west of downtown, north of Georgetown, and west of the linear Rock Creek Park, a large part of the city is devoted to sprawling residential areas, college campuses, and one of the world's largest churches, the Washington National Cathedral. A tour through the area provides a pleasant respite from the congestion and confusion of the inner city.

Information

Washington National Cathedral (202/537-6200 or 202/537-6211 TDD). The cathedral is open daily from 10 am to 4 pm. Services are conducted throughout the week. They are held at 7:30 am, noon, 2:30 pm and 4 pm from Monday through Saturday, and at 8, 9 and 11 am and 4 and 6:30 pm on Sunday.

Getting there

The Cathedral is at the junction of Massachusetts Ave and Wisconsin Ave. The area is served by the Metrobus (#32, #34 or #36 South on Wisconsin Ave). To get there by underground Metro, one must ride to the Tenleytown exit and then walk for about 20 minutes to reach the church.

First Steps

As you enter the Cathedral, pick up an illustrated guide in the building's Museum Shop.

Seasonal highlights

Folk guitar masses are held in the Cathedral at 10 am on Sundays from September to June. A Flower Mart is held on the first Friday and Saturday in May with rides, puppet shows, and other children's activities. In September, there is an open house, during which visitors can tour the bell tower.

Tours

Forty-five-minute guided tours (202/537-6207) of the Cathedral leave the west end of the nave between 10 and 11:45 am and between 12:45 and 3:15 pm Monday through Saturday and between 12:45 and 2:45 pm on Sunday. The Tuesday and Thursday afternoon tours are followed by a high tea, for which reservations are required and a fee is charged.

Washington National Cathedral. In 1791, Pierre L'Enfant envisioned "a great church for national purposes" in his plans for America's new and yet-to-be-developed capital, but a number of stumbling blocks stood in the way of its construction, including the War of 1812, the Civil War, World War I, the Great Depression, and World War II. Finally started in 1907, the building was finally completed with the placement of the final stone atop a pinnacle on the West front tower in 1990—83 years later.

English Gothic in its design, the cathedral was built in the shape of a cross atop Mount St Albans, the highest point in Washington, using construction techniques employed during the 14th century. Theodore Roosevelt laid the foundation stone using the same mallet that George Washington had used while setting the cornerstone of the US Capitol.

Once completed, the cathedral was the world's sixth largest church. The 57-acre grounds, or "close," now contain two gardens, a greenhouse, the Herb Cottage, and four schools, including the College of Preachers. Administered by the Episcopal church and officially known as the Cathedral Church of St Peter & St Paul, it is truly managed as "the nation's church." There is no local congregation. Such a diverse group of people as President Woodrow Wilson and his wife, Hellen Keller and her companion Anne Sullivan, Adm George Dewey, and two former Secretaries of State, Cordell Hull and Frank Kellogg, are buried here. The funeral services for both President Wilson and President Dwight D Eisenhower were held here, as were services celebrating the end of both World War I and World War II.

The Gloria in Excelsis central tower is 676 feet high. The exterior of the building is ornamented with exquisite stone carvings and gargoyles. Inside, the cathedral contains an abundance of art, architectural carvings, and statuary, including the figures of George Washington and Abraham Lincoln. The nave is 518 feet long and the vaulted ceiling above it is 102 feet high.

There are 200 stained glass windows, including the Space Window, which contains a fragment of moon rock and was dedicated to the Apollo 11 space mission. The Rose Window in the North Transept, best viewed around dusk, contains 10,000 individual pieces of stained glass. There are bays that honor George Washington and Woodrow Wilson, a War Memorial Chapel, and a Children's Chapel that has tiny child-size chairs and a pint-sized pipe organ.

Be sure to see the view of Washington from the Pilgrim Observatory Gallery, which contains no fewer than 70 windows. The gallery is open between 10 am and 4 pm from Monday through Saturday and between noon and 4 pm on Sunday.

South of the cathedral is the outdoor Bishop's Garden, which is modeled upon a medieval walled garden. The paths were made of stones taken from George Washington's own quarries. The garden contains numerous 12th- and 13th-century artifacts and is open daily during daylight hours.

The on-site Herb Cottage sells dried herbs, teas, gifts, and books, and is open from 9 am to 5 pm Monday through Saturday and from 10 am to 5 pm on Sunday. Growing herbs and plants can be purchased at the greenhouse on South Rd. The Herb Cottage, greenhouse, and Museum Shop (202/537-6267) are open daily except Christmas from 9:30 am to 5 pm.

Sidetrip—Adams-Morgan

Adjoining the upscale, embassy-studded neighborhoods of Embassy Row, DuPont Circle, and Kalorama as it does, is it any wonder that Adams-Morgan is one of the city's most colorful and multinational neighborhoods? Mexicans, Ethiopians, Brazilians, Italians, French, Cajuns, Caribbeans, Vietnamese, and representatives of nearly every other culture in the world live and mix freely here. Indeed, it was this feeling of multiculturalism and cooperation among numerous cultures that prompted the residents of the community to identify it in the 1950s as Adams-Morgan, a name formed by combining the name of the local all-white Adams school with that of the all-black Morgan school. Previously, the area had been known simply as Washington Heights.

Located along Columbia Rd between 18th St and Kalorama Park NW, Adams-Morgan is one of Washington's trendiest neighborhoods and one of the city's most popular centers for nightlife.

Strangely, Adams-Morgan often is overlooked by tourists. Perhaps because it contains no national monuments or Smithsonian museums. Yet a stroll through the area can produce countless hours of enjoyment, derived by examining the many colorful outdoor murals, the ethnic restaurants and groceries, the funky shops, the antique stores, the boutiques, the used book stores, and the lovely old Victorian townhouses. If you do not have the time to explore those exciting wonders in depth, at least schedule enough time to spend an evening in the area, where the dining and nightlife are unequaled in all of Washington.

Getting there
The nearest Metro station, Woodley Park/Zoo, is a 15-min walk away via the Duke Ellington Memorial Bridge on Calvert St on the West side of Rock Creek Park.

From DuPont Circle, Adams-Morgan is a 20-min walk—all uphill. Those who have the opportunity to drive should be forewarned that parking in the area is difficult. The L2 bus from McPherson Square runs up 18th St to Calvert St, but a taxi might be your best bet.

Seasonal highlights

In July, the community celebrates a colorful and exciting Latin American festival, and every September, a free neighborhood fair, Adams-Morgan Day (202/789-7000), is staged along 18th St NW and Florida Ave. The latter is extremely popular among the residents of Washington and includes crafts, music, and a seemingly-unending variety of foods from Central America, Africa, and various parts of Europe.

Adams-Morgan. This capital neighborhood centers on the intersection of Columbia Rd and 18th St NW and almost all of the points of interest can be found within three or four blocks of that intersection. *Start your exploration of Adams-Morgan at the corner of Columbia Rd and 18th St NW.* If you happen to be visiting on a Saturday, you will find a weekly market set up on the southwestern plaza.

Head north on 18th St to Ontario St. At the corner of 18th and Ontario overlooking Rock Creek Park is the **Ontario Building,,** built between 1903 and 1906. Often called the most glamorous of all Adams-Morgan buildings, the cupola-crowned building has been the residence of such famous individuals as Gen Douglas MacArthur, Adm Chester Nimitz, and journalist Bob Woodward, known for his coverage of the Watergate investigation during the Nixon administration.

Return to the south along 18th St. After you pass Columbia Rd on 18th St, the Adams-Morgan "restaurant row" begins—**Saigonnais** at #2307, **La Fourchette** at #2429, **Meskerem** at #2434, and **I Matti Trattoria** at #2436, among numerous others.

At Wyoming St, take a right. In 1909, 1831 Wyoming St was the residence of Adm Robert Perry, the explorer who first visited the North Pole. At 20th St, look for the **Altamont Building**, a lovely Italian Renaissance-style apartment building built in the early 1900s. Be sure to take a look at the ornate interior of the building.

At Connecticut St, turn left. On the corner of Connecticut St and T St stands the **Washington Hilton**, one of Washington's most illustrious hotels. This is where, while leaving the hotel in 1981, President Ronald Reagan was shot.

Returning to the north, take the right-hand fork onto Columbia Rd. At 2022 Columbia Rd, you will see the **Wyoming Building**, an apartment house built in the early 1900s. Examine the marble reception room, the mosaic floor, and the moulded ceilings. The Eisenhower family resided in this building from 1927 to 1935. Walking tours of the area begin outside the Wyoming Building every Sunday morning at 11 am ($5, 301/294-9514).

Take a short left turn at Kalorama Rd. The **Woburn Building** at 1910 Kalorama Rd is where President Lyndon Johnson lived during the early years of his marriage to Lady Bird.

Return to Columbia Rd and turn left. The **Norwood Building** at 1868 Columbia Rd is where stage and screen actress Tallulah Bankhead spent her teenage years. Bankhead's father was the Speaker of the House at that time.

Take another short left at Biltmore St. At 1940 Biltmore St stands the **Biltmore Building**, the former residence of Carl Bernstein. Bernstein was the Washington Post reporter who with Bob Woodward broke the story that became Watergate.

Retrace your steps to the intersection of Columbia Rd and 18th St NW where your walking tour began.

North by Northeast: Shaw & the National Arboretum

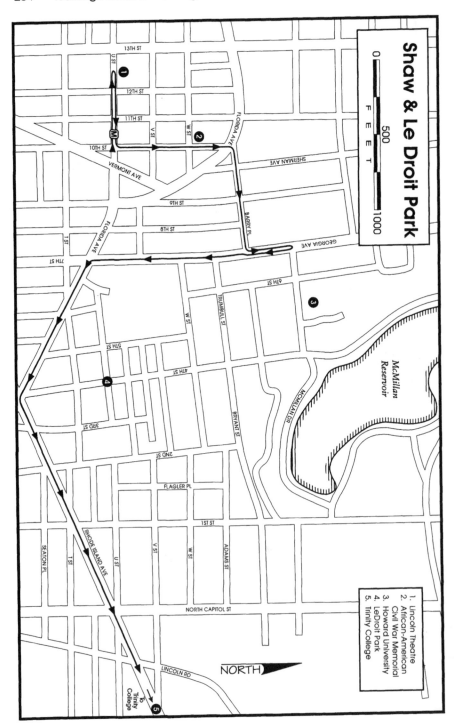

Shaw & Le Droit Park

FEET

0   500   1000

13TH ST

12TH ST

11TH ST

10TH ST

U ST

M

V ST

W ST

FLORIDA AVE

SHERMAN AVE

VERMONT AVE

9TH ST

8TH ST

BARRY PL

GEORGIA AVE

FLORIDA AVE

1ST ST

7TH ST

6TH ST

TRUMBULL ST

W ST

5TH ST

4TH ST

BRYANT ST

MCMILLAN DR

McMillan
Reservoir

3RD ST

2ND ST

FLAGLER PL

1ST ST

V ST

W ST

ADAMS ST

SEATON PL

1ST ST

RHODE ISLAND AVE

U ST

NORTH CAPITOL ST

LINCOLN RD

NORTH

To
Trinity
College

1. Lincoln Theatre
2. African-American
   Civil War Memorial
3. Howard University
4. LeDroit Park
5. Trinity College

Shaw

The area between Capitol St NE and 15th St North of M St was the business and retail center of Washington's African-American community prior to the end of segregation in the early 1950s. One of the key attractions was U St, famous throughout the country as "the Black Broadway." What Greenwich Village is to New York, the French Quarter is to New Orleans, or Gaslight Square is to St Louis, U Street once was to Shaw. A place where many of the nation's black entertainers performed, including native son Edward Kennedy "Duke" Ellington. Born in the Shaw region of Washington on April 29, 1899, Ellington spent the first 24 years of his life there. During his lifetime, Ellington made more than 10,000 recordings and wrote more than 2,500 pieces of music, including such favorites as *Satin Doll*, *Mood Indigo*, *I Got It Bad (and That Ain't Good)*, *Do Nothing 'Til You Hear From Me*, and *Don't Get Around Much Anymore*.

The U Street area, which extends along U Street from about 10th St to 15th St NW, was badly torn during the rioting and burnings that followed the assassination of Martin Luther King Jr in the 1950s. People moved away; buildings were deserted and left to decay. The area deteriorated so badly for the next several generations that it became one of the city's worst eye-sores. But today, there is a new interest in—and dedication to—the U Street area. An interesting Bohemian mix of cultures is once again trying to turn the street into one of the city's hippest neighborhoods. Old buildings are being torn down or renovated. New buildings are going up. At 1438 U Street, a former bank, later a Masonic lodge, has been converted into a fancy restaurant. Much of this work is being coordinated through the recently-formed Greater U Street Historic District. Importantly, "the New U" has another distinction: Its rebirth is being generated not by Government and not by Big Business, but by the will of the local peopl—a truly commendable feat.

An attempt to describe the shops and other attractions of the area would fall woefully short. People's interests vary so greatly that the things that would appeal to one group of tourists in an area such as this might go so far as to repulse another group. Not historical...not "cultural," in the classic sense of the word...U Street is simply one of the places in Washington where it's happening" today.

Indeed, the same thing can be said for much of the Shaw community, especially now that the city's new Convention Center is in the process of being built along N St between 7th St and 9th St NW. The facility will provide the neighborhood with a tremendous economic stimulus. And the colorful O Street Market also continues to remain high on the city's list of attractions.

Still, for the immediate future, Shaw will remain a region in transition. Drug trafficking continues to take place there, and it continues to be a place where it is unwise to stray far off the always-busy U Street, particularly after dark.

Getting there

Take the Metro Green Line and exit at the U Street-Cardozo station. The most convenient exits are on the southeast corner of 13th St and U St NW, which is elevator accessible. Another is on 10th St NW just South of U Street.

You also can take routes #90 or #92 on the U Street-Garfield Metrobus line or route #98 on the Adams-Morgan-U Street line. Routes #90, #91, #92, #93 and 9# all run along U Street, while routes #60 and #62 travel along Vermont Ave.

Seasonal highlights

One of the biggest cultural events in Washington each year is the award-winning Washington Theatre Festival, now entering its third decade. This festival annually develops over 70 new plays in workshops, readings, and the 10-Minute Play Competition. It is produced by the Source Theatre Co, a not-for-profit professional theatre located just two blocks south of U St on 14th St. The venues for the Theatre Festival, which takes place between mid-July and mid-August, are spread across the Washington landscape, including the Kennedy Center, the National Museum for Women in the Arts, and other theatres.

Exploring Shaw and Columbia Heights. *Begin your stroll at U St and 10th St NW.* Wander among the eclectic cafes, thrift shops, and nightspots that can be found there, and be sure to see what is happening in the historic (and restored) **Lincoln Theater** (202/328-6000) at 1215 U St, where such performers as Duke Ellington, Louis Armstrong, and Cab Calloway used to appear during the theatre's hey-day.

Nearby, on the corner of 10th St and W St NW, is the **African-American Civil War Memorial**, a tribute to the African-American soldiers who fought for the Union during the Civil War. The 9-foot sculpture contains bas reliefs bearing the names of 208,000 members of the US Colored Troops and their white officers who fought during that war.

East of Shaw is the community of Columbia Heights. **Howard University** extends from Georgia Ave on the west to the McMillan Reservoir on the east. Named for Gen Oliver Otis Howard, head of the post-Civil War Freedmen's Bureau, it is one of the most prestigious, historic Black universities in the country. The enrollment remains primarily black, although the university has always been open to students of any race, color or creed.

Financially supported by the federal government, yet privately controlled, Howard alumni include Supreme Court Justice Thurgood Marshall, Atlanta Mayor Andrew Young, US Sen Edward William Brooke of Massachusetts, sociologist E Franklin Frazier, playwright Imamu Baraka (LeRoi Jones), statesman Ralph Bunche, and the late Patricia Roberts Harris, Secretary of the US Department of Health & Human Resources. Bunche established the school's political science department.

Oliver Howard House, the only original house that remains on the campus, has been proclaimed a National Historic Landmark. The Gallery of Art in the College of Dine Art (202/806-7070), 2455 6th Ave NW, exhibits the African collection of Alain Locke in its east corridor. The Gallery is open from 9:30 am to 4:30 pm on weekdays and from 1 to 4 pm on Sundays.

Howard's Moorland Springarn Research Center, which contains the country's largest collection of materials documenting the history and culture of African-Americans, is open between 9 am and 4:45 pm from Monday through Thursday, until 4:30 pm on Friday, and until 5 pm on Saturday.

Exit the campus onto Georgia Ave and turn right (south). Walk to Florida Ave and turn left (east). Between 2nd St and 5th St NW is another historic area marked by 19th-century Romantic Revival-style houses. LeDroit Park was the home of African-American poet Paul Laurence Dunbar and author/educator Anna J Cooper. Griffith Stadium also was located in this area prior to the 1960s, when the Howard University Hospital was built. Current residents of the LeDroit Park area include Walter Washington, the city's first African-American mayor, and Jesse Jackson, political activist and sometime Presidential hopeful.

At Florida Ave and 4th St NW, Rhode Island Ave angles in from the northeast. Turn onto Rhode Island and travel four blocks. At 4th St NE, turn left (north). As you pass Franklin St, the campus of Trinity College will be on your left and Theological College on your right. The distance from LeDroit Park to Trinity College is about half a mile.

Founded in 1897, **Trinity College** (800/492-6882, www.trinitydc.edu), occupies a 26-acre campus at 125 Michigan Ave NE. The school's all-female student body, mostly black, includes some 1,100 students seeking undergraduate degrees and another 500 students enrolled in graduate programs.

Food & drink
In the U Street area, you might want to look into **Polly's Cafe** ($-$$, 202 /265-8385) at 1342 U St, **Coppi's** ($-$$, 202/319-7773) at 1414 U St, **U-topia** ($-$$, 202/483-7669) at 1418 U St, or **Julio's** ($-$$, 202/483-8500) at 1604 U St.

Nightlife
A number of exciting and unusual nightspots can be found along historic U Street in the Shaw neighborhood. These include **Black Cat** (202/667-7960), 1831 14th St NW, which caters to alternative music from country to surf to art-pop. Concerts are staged almost every night and there is a bar (the Red Room), but the menu is restricted to little more than burgers and vegetarian lasagna and the Black Cat *definitely is not the place to go* if you're looking to dance. The hours are 7 pm to 3 am on Friday and Saturday, and from 9 pm to 2 am the rest of the week.

Another popular hangout in the U Street area is **Nightclub 9:30** (202/393-0930), 815 V St NW, which has been a part of the Washington scene for more than 15 years. Tickets to their nightly shows can be purchased at their own box office between noon and 7 pm weekdays and from 6 to 11 pm on show days, including the weekends. Tickets also are available through TicketMaster (202/432-SEAT) and ProTix (703/218-6500).

We suggest that you inquire locally to determine the current hot spot along U Street at the time of your visit.

Sidetrip—The National Arboretum

South and east of Brookland, between Bladensburg Rd and the Anacostia River south of New York Ave, is the US National Arboretum. Established in 1927 the hilly 444-acre arboretum serves as a research and education facility for the US Department of Agriculture as well as a living museum, most popular from late March through October.

During spring, woodland flowers, magnolias, scilla, dogwoods, crabapples, peonies, and roses are the primary crowd-pleasers, while miniature daffodils adorn the Court of Honor and the slopes of Mount Hamilton are covered with azaleas. In summer, daylilies, crepe myrtles, and herbs take over, and waterlilies flourish on the Administration Building pond. By autumn, a change in color—beginning around late October—turns the tulip poplar and hickory a rich yellow, the black gum a bright red, and the sweet gum and dogwood a purplish red. The spider lilies and witch-hazels are in flower. Come winter, red holly berries provide much of the color until February or early March, when the camellias, Japanese apricots, witch-hazel, winter jasmine, and sweet box come into bloom. The **Court of Honor** displays new plants that have been developed for the nursery trade.

Information

US National Arboretum (202/245-2726, www.ars-grin.gov/ars/Beltsville/na/), 3501 New York Ave NE. Admission and parking are free. Open daily except Christmas from 8 am to 5 pm. **Arbor House** gift shop is open daily from March 1 to mid-December between 10 am and 3:30 pm. Parking lots are scattered throughout the grounds, allowing you to park, walk about, and then move on at your own pace.

Getting there

The nearest Metro station is the Stadium Armory stop on the Orange and Blue Lines. From there, transfer to the Metrobus B2 route, get off at R St, and walk 300 yards along R St to the entrance of the Arboretum.

If you drive you'll find plenty of parking at the arboretum.

First steps

Information centers are located opposite the Friendship Garden, near the New York Ave gate, and at the Administration Building. Pick up a map that will provide you with more details as to the various trails and some of the singular attractions to be found on the grounds, such as the Fern Valley Trail, where you can see a Franklin Tree, one of a species discovered in 1765 by a friend of Benjamin Franklin but now extinct in the wild.

Tours

Tram tours in the National Arboretum are conducted at 11 am and at 1, 2, 3 and 4 pm on Saturday and Sunday (same-day tickets cost $3 for adults and $2 for members, seniors, and children between the ages of 4 and 16).

The US National Arboretum. *Begin your w tour at the R St entrance. Once inside the gate and on the grounds, turn right onto Azalea Rd.* On your left, you will see the **Friendship Garden**, where perennials provide year-around beauty from the earliest spring bulbs to winter's ornamental grasses. The garden contains brick walkways, terraces, and a statue of Demeter, the Greek goddess of agriculture, as well as teak benches to rest on. On your right, opposite the Friendship Garden, is the **National Boxwood Collection**, the most complete living collection of boxwoods in the world. The collection covers five acres and contains over 100 specimens. Beyond that are the **Perennial Collections**, formal beds of peonies, irises, and daylilies which bloom from late April through July.

Follow Azalea Rd on a long loop past a grove of crabapple trees. As you round the next bend, the **Azalea Collections** will be on your left. Landscaped trails up **Mount Hamilton** are surrounded in late April and May by blooming azaleas. These are the most extensive plantings in America, numbering about 70,000 plants. In late April and May, the blooms surround the landscaped trails up Mount Hamilton, from which there is a marvelous view of the US Capitol.

At the first intersection (Eagle Nest Rd), take a right. On your left will be the **National Grove of State Trees**, where a collection of trees representing every state and the District of Columbia form a 30-acre living monument to the nation's forests.

Continue along Eagle Nest Rd to the next intersection and turn left. At the first opportunity (Crabtree Rd), turn right. On your right will be the **Youth Garden** and on your left the **Native Plant Collections**, ferns, wildflowers, shrubs, and trees representing the various natural habitats of the eastern United States.

Continue on Crabtree Rd until you cross a stream. On your left, you will see **Beech Spring Pond**.

Turn right onto Hickory Hill Rd. On your left will be a crabapple grove.

Follow Hickory Hill Rd past Holly Spring Rd. The **Asian Collections** will be on your right in a landscaped valley overlooking the Anacostia River. The collections feature rare plants from China, Japan, and Korea.

Continue on Hickory Hill Rd, staying to your right. You will pass two parking lots on your right and one on your left as you continue on. On the right will appear the **Dogwood Collection**, containing many varieties and species of dogwood. Once again, lovely vistas of the Anacostia River are at hand.

The name of the road you are on will change to Conifer Rd. Around the next big bend, on your left, will be the **Conifer Collections**. This collection of cone-bearing evergreens include the Gotelli Collection of Dwarf and Slow-Growing Conifers as well as the extensive Watnong Collection of Dwarf pines.

Take the first left (Holly Spring Rd), pass Hickory Lane, Meadow Rd, and one other side road. By the parking lot on your right will be the Arboretum's 10-acre **Holly and Magnolia Collections**, which display magnolia blossoms in spring and glossy green holly leaves and the colorful holly berries in winter.

Turn right on Hickory Hill Rd, go to the next intersection (Valley Rd), and turn right again. On the left, you will see **Beech Spring Pond**; on your right, a parking lot.

Beechwood Rd will soon appear on your left. Turn into it, cross a stream, and continue on to Ellipse Rd. Ahead of you will be the **Capitol Columns**, 22 sandstone Corinthian columns that once stood at the East portico of the US Capitol.

Now turn right onto Ellipse Rd and go to the next intersection (Meadow Rd). Across from the intersection will be the **National Bonsai & Penjing Museum**, a collection of artistically trained trees and related artifacts presented in four pavilions, each complemented by its own meditative garden. Included is a Japanese collection of 53 miniature trees, some over 300 years old, that was a gift from Japan at the time of the American Bicentennial. With the **American Bonsai Collection** of 56 North American plants, added in 1990, this constitutes the largest collection of bonsai in North America. Also displayed in the museum are 35 Chinese Penjing trees, given to the Arboretum in 1986. This museum is open daily from 10 am to 3:30 pm.

Turn left onto Meadow Rd. On your left, you will see the two and one-half-acre **National Herb Garden**, which holds 800 kinds of herbs from around the world in 10 theme gardens, as well as a cottage filled with 200 varieties of heritage roses and companion plants. Also on display are a formal 16th Century-style European knot garden, a garden of historic roses, and gardens of specialty herbs. On your right is the **Administration Building**, surrounded by a pond that contains aquatic plants and koi fish (Japanese carp) some 3 feet long and weighing 30 pounds. The Administration Building is open daily from 8 am to 4:30 pm on weekdays and from 9 am to 5 pm on most weekends. Behind the Administration Building is the Arboretum's extensive greenhouse complex.

The next right will take you back to the R St gate.

The Southwest Waterfront

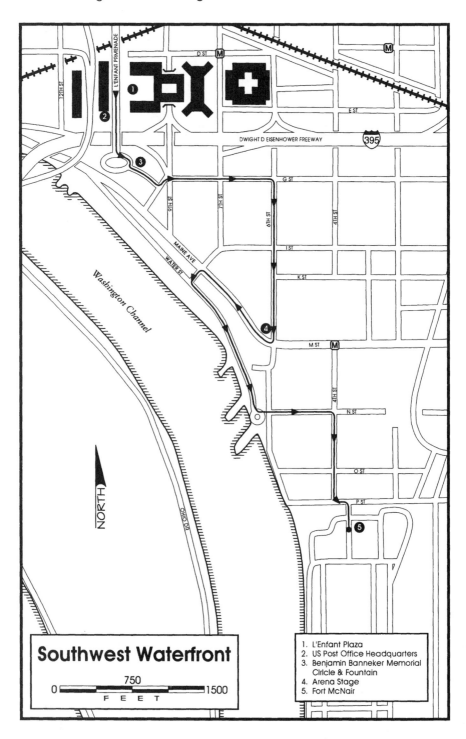

Southwest Waterfront

0 ⊢———750———⊣ 1500
F E E T

1. L'Enfant Plaza
2. US Post Office Headquarters
3. Benjamin Banneker Memorial
   Cllrcle & Fountain
4. Arena Stage
5. Fort McNair

The Southwest Waterfront

Most people are well acquainted with the close relationship between the nation's capital and the Potomac River that forms its western boundary. Few are even conscious of the other river in Washington—the historic Anacostia. Yet the banks of the Anacostia shelter a number of attractions that are of interest to many visitors, among them the colorful, yacht-filled waterfront, Arena Stage, Albert Einstein Planetarium, Fort Leslie J McNair, the Navy Memorial Museum, the Marine Corps Museum, Congressional Cemetery, the National Arboretum, the Smithsonian Institution's Anacostia Museum, and Kenilworth Aquatic Gardens.

South of theUS Capitol, there is a small neck of land separating The Mall and Washington's two rivers, the Potomac and the Anacostia. On this land are a number of interesting sites, foremost among them a couple of important and historic military facilities.

Information

US Post Office Headquarters (202/268-2020) is at 475 L'Enfant Plaza SW. The building is open to the public from 9 am to 5 pm Monday through Saturday.

Getting there

Two Metro stops are convenient to this area, L'Enfant Plaza and Waterfront. So is the Metrobus V5 Fairfax Village-L'Enfant Plaza Line.

Tours

Tours of the **Arena Stage** complex (Fichandler Stage, Kreeger Theater, and Old Vat Theater) are available by appointment.

The Southwest Waterfront. Bordered by D St SW, the 12th St Expressway, the 9th St Expressway, and the Southwest Freeway, **L'Enfant Plaza** was dedicated in 1968, a long-overdue tribute to Pierre L'Enfant, the man who laid out the capital.

Maj Pierre Charles L'Enfant, an arrogant, beak-nosed architect-engineer, first met George Washington at Valley Forge in 1777. He became an aide to Baron von Steuben, the Prussian drillmaster, and saw action in Savannah, where he was wounded and spent nearly two years as a prisoner of the British.

Following the Revolutionary War, L'Enfant renovated the New York City Hall in 1789 to serve as the Federal Hall for congress, at that point still lacking a capital for the newly-created nation. George Washington was inaugurated in that building. When congress finally agreed to seek, design, and eventually transport the government's offices to a new capital, L'Enfant volunteered to help design it. His offer was accepted 18 months later, and L'Enfant immediately set to work.

The job was not without its problems. Georgetown was already in existence and did not take kindly to being "absorbed" by the new District of Columbia. One wealthy resident has recently completed a new manor that unfortunately protruded into L'Enfant's projected New Jersey Ave. L'Enfant asked the owner to remove it, and when the request was refused, proceeded to have the manor demolished on his own order.

Uncompromising, condescending, and often abrasive, L'Enfant soon forced President Washington to remove him from his post, but not until he had laid most of the groundwork for creating the new capital. The only surviving copy of L'Enfant's plan is a large pencil sketch now displayed in the Library of Congress.

The rejected L'Enfant presented Congress with a $95,000 bill for the work he had put in. When Congress refused to pay it, L'Enfant sued. Years later, he was compelled to accept an offer of $2,500 to resolve the matter.

For several decades, L'Enfant wandered the city with his dog, dejected and lonely. James Monroe urged him to accept a professorship at West Point, but he would not. He died a pauper in 1825, but it wasn't until 1909 that his body was disinterred and his grave moved to a hillside in Arlington National Cemetery, where it overlooks the city that he was so instrumental in creating.

L'Enfant Plaza is Washington's only paved square. Surrounded by modern office buildings, it contains a central landscaped garden. Underground is a shopping mall, a movie theater, restaurants, and parking lots.

Beneath the popular Loew's L'Enfant Plaza hotel is the **L'Enfant Plaza Promenade**, a small underground shopping mall that is very popular with government employees and others working nearby. While it lacks the prestige shops of larger malls, it does offer a wide variety of the day-to-day necessities—among them, some fast food outlets, a post office, a drugstore, cleaners, and a copy center.

Indeed, the **US Post Office Headquarters** (202/268-2020) is at 475 L'Enfant Plaza SW. The building is open to the public from 9 am to 5 pm Monday through Saturday. On the ground floor, the building houses an interesting Hall of Stamps.

From the Post Office, head south on 10th St SW and cross the bridge over a network of I-385 interchanges. In a park between I-395 and Maine Ave is the **Benjamin Banneker Memorial Circle and Fountain.** Like L'Enfant, Banneker, who was an African-American mathematician, astronomer and "America's first black man of science," was a major contributor to the survey and design of the capital.

Walk east along G St to 6th St and turn south. At 1101 6th St SW is the **Arena Stage** (202/488-3300) and its three venues: the 818-seat, theater-in-the-round Fichandler Stage; the fan-shaped 514-seat Kreeger Theater; and the 180-seat Old Vat Theater.

Now nearing a half-century of use, the Arena Stage was founded by Zelda Fichandler. Today, the Fichandler and Kreeger theaters stage eight productions each year, while the Old Vat is used for new play readings and special productions. Past performers who have achieved national reputations include Ned Beatty, James Earl Jones, Robert Prosky, Jane Alexander, and George Grizzard. Tickets to new and classic plays average $23-$42, with discounts available for seniors, students, and the disabled. A limited number of half-priced tickets go on sale 90 minutes before the beginning of most performances (call HOTTIX).

Now walk southeast along Maine St past M St SW and begin to explore the waterfront along the Washington Channel with its fascinating array of boats, piers, and seafood markets. Then retrace your steps, this time walking along Water St, rather than Maine St (both streets are populated with excellent restaurants and bistros. Return to M St and head east to 4th St SW. Now turn right and head south.until you come to Fort McNair.

Occupying the tip of Buzzard Point where the Washington Channel of the Potomac River intersects with the Anacostia River, **Fort Leslie J McNair** is the third oldest Army installation in the United States in continuous use, following only West Point in New York and Carlisle Barracks in Pennsylvania. Well positioned to defend Washington, the fort sits on a site selected by Pierre L'Enfant himself as the location for a military garrison. Once known as Turkey Buzzard Point, the site later became known as Greenleaf Point. Dating from 1791, the fort originally occupied 28 acres and later expanded to 89 acres. Before the War of 1812 and extending to 1881, the fort was used as an arsenal. Today, it is an intelligence headquarters for national defense and the home of some top Army officials.

In 1948, the fort was renamed in honor of Lt Gen Lesley J McNair, commander of Army Ground Forces during World War II. McNair was killed in Normandy in 1944, the highest-ranking officer in the US Armed Forces to be killed by friendly fire.

Begin your tour at the fort's main gate. Notice that the gate posts actually are six coast-defense guns made in 1850 in Richmond, VA. The Tredegar Foundry in Richmond made weapons for the Confederacy during the Civil War.

Walk down Third Ave toward the flagpole. Surrounding the flagpole is a large collection of cannons. In its early days as an arsenal, the fort studied many kinds of cannons. Included among its present collection are two Spanish bronze cannons, one made between 1500 and 1558 for the King of Spain, and the other made in Seville in 1789 and captured from Mexico in 1846. Others around the flagpole and scattered throughout the grounds are from France, Great Britain, and the United States, each of which bears a plaque describing its history and significance.

At Third Ave and B St, turn right. The first building on your right is the **Inter-American Defense College**, opened in 1962. The college hosts students from the 22 nations belonging to the Inter-American Defense Board. Here, officers study solutions to various hemispheric defense problems.

Next to the college is **Walter Reed's Clinic**, which once housed a hospital in which Maj Walter Reed conducted research to determine the causes of such diseases as diphtheria, malaria, and abdominal typhus. Reed, of course, is best known for discovering the cause of yellow fever. While stationed here, Reed was struck with appendicitis and died of complications following surgery on November 23, 1902. The building is now used to house visiting officers.

In front of Reed's Clinic is Second Ave. Head down that street. On your left will be the **Parade Field**. On your right, **Generals' Row**, a line of red-brick houses designed in Colonial Revival style. Completed in 1905, these houses were the residences of some of the most powerful men in American military history at one time or another. They now house the Vice Chief of Staff of the Army, the US Army Surgeon General, the Army Inspector-General, and the Commanding General of the US Army Military District of Washington.

At the end of Generals' Row is the **Officers' Club**. Built in the Georgian Revival style in 1905, the building overlooks the Potomac, and its elegant ballroom has held many formal ceremonies over the decades.

Across Second Ave from the Officers' Club are some tennis courts. Beyond the tennis courts and on the edge of the Parade Field is the **Penitentiary**. Built in 1829, the building once constituted the East wing of America's first penitentiary. In 1865, it housed eight prisoners charged with conspiracy in the assassination of President Abraham Lincoln. Four of the eight were convicted and hanged where the tennis courts are now located. One, Mary Surratt, was the first American woman to be executed by federal order. Predictably, a number of interesting ghost stories have emerged over the years.

The building currently is used for officers' housing.

Return to Second Ave and turn left. You will be walking through the fort's golf course. Just past D St is the site of the old arsenal. During the War of 1812, a company of British soldiers tried to destroy the arsenal by blowing up the powder magazine, but before they arrived, some American soldiers hid the powder in a dry well nearby. As the story goes, the British used a lighted match to inspect the well, the powder exploded, and 30 British soldiers were killed. The surviving soldiers destroyed the arsenal buildings, but they were rebuilt after the war and were used extensively throughout the Civil War.

The imposing building ahead of you on D St is **Roosevelt Hall**, started in 1901 and later dedicated by President Theodore Roosevelt. The Spanish-American War in 1898 had underscored the need to provide additional training for America's senior military officers, and in 1903, the Army War College was established. It has occupied this building ever since.

During World War II, the Army War College was replaced by the Army-Navy Staff College, and in 1946, the National War College was formed. This was incorporated into the National Defense University in 1976.

Pass Roosevelt Hall on D St, walk to Fourth Ave, and turn left. On your right will be **Eisenhower Hall**. The building was dedicated in 1960 by President Dwight Eisenhower, himself a graduate of the Class of 1933, and houses the Industrial College of the Armed Forces, the nation's most advanced military school dedicated to the study of managing national resources to support national security strategy.

Continue along Fourth Ave to the next intersection and turn right. Ahead of you is the massive **George C Marshall Hall**, completed in 1991 and dedicated by President George Bush. The headquarters of the National Defense University, the building houses a library, the Institute of National Strategic Studies, and the Information Resources Management College, another NDU college. A fourth NDU college, the Armed Forces Staff College, is located in Norfolk, VA.

Return to Fourth Ave and turn right. Soon you will pass a sizeable picnic area. Beyond that, you will see **NCO (Non-Commissioned Officer) Row** on your right. Facing General's Row on the opposite side of the Parade Field, this row of houses was built from 1905 to 1906.

As you reach B St, you will see the headquarters of Company A, 3rd US Infantry (**The Old Guard**) across the street. Known as the Commander-in-Chief's Guard, the unit consists of three 40-man platoons which form a portion of the Presidential Honor Guard, which serves at the White House and at many official functions for the President. The Old Guard also performs in ceremonies at which it appears in period uniforms from the Revolutionary War.

Turn left onto B St and walk to the flagpole at the front and center of the Parade Field. Turn right on Third Ave and return to the Main Gate, where your tour began.

To the left of the Main Gate is the headquarters of the Military District of Washington, formed in 1971. The unit has three missions: (1) to respond to crises, disasters and other security requirements in the National Capital Region, (2) to provide support to Army and other Department of Defense organizations in the area, and (3) to conduct local and worldwide ceremonies on behalf of the nation's civilian and military leadership.

Lodging

Near the L'Enfant Plaza Metro station, the **Holiday Inn Capitol** ($$-$$$, 202/479-4000 or 800/HOLIDAY) at 550 C St SW is noteworthy for its restaurant, which specializes in such regional treats as Maryland crab cakes and Yankee pot roast.

Unquestionably one of the area's showplaces is the conveniently-located 370-room **Loew's L'Enfant Plaza Hotel** ($$$-$$$$, 202/484-1000 or 800 /23-LOEWS, www.loewshotels.com), at 480 L'Enfant Plaza SW. Unfortunately, its rooms not only are high-priced, but a $16-per-night parking fee is also assessed when a guest arrives by car.

A better bet might be the small **Channel Inn** ($$-$$$, 202/554-2400 or 800/368-5668) at 650 Water St SW. Washington's only pier-front hotel overlooks the boat-filled Washington Channel, where it occupies the top four floors of a 15-story office building, and each of its 100 rooms has a balcony. Other amenities include both indoor and outdoor swimming pools, complimentary garage parking, a fitness center, and a bathroom that contains both a telephone and a small TV. Its Engine Room lounge offers free hors d'oeuvres on weekdays and provides live jazz in the evening from Wednesday through Sunday.

Arts & culture

The **Arena Stage** complex hosts a four-part Saturday matinee series, and there is a Kids Play series ($80) that includes storytelling, behind-the-scenes demonstrations, and improvisations designed to amuse children during those Saturday matinees.

Food & drink

Travelers with children might enjoy **Bullfeathers** ($, 202/543-5005), 410 1st St SE, a kid-oriented eatery that is open from 11:15 am to 10:30 pm Monday through Thursday, 11:30 am to 1 am on Friday, from 10 am to 9 pm on Sa, and from 10:30 am to 3 pm for a Sunday brunch.

Vie de France ($$, 202/554-7870), 600 Maryland Ave SW, is located in the Capitol Gallery Building and has an office-building ambiance. It also has an attractive, skylit atrium cafe, a large outdoor patio with umbrella tables, and a charming garden room with French posters on the wall. Hours are 11 am to 8 pm on Monday and Tuesday and 11 am to 9 pm from Wednesday through Friday. The restaurant also operates the **Fast & Fresh** bakery next door.

On the banks of the Potomac River, **Phillips Flagship** ($$-$$$, 202/488-8515), 900 Water St SW, has large rooms and huge outdoor decks overlooking the Capitol Yacht Club marina. It features an all-you-can-eat buffet, an a la carte menu, and a sushi bar from Monday through Saturday. Outdoor seating is available in season and underground parking is available, but reservations are not accepted. **La Rivage** ($$, 202/488-8111), 1000 Water St SW, which also offers fine views of the marina and the downtown monuments, provides French cuisine at lunch on weekdays and at dinner daily. **Gangplank** ($$, 202/554-5000), 600 Water St SW, is open daily, has five dining areas, and serves lunch and dinner as well as a Sunday brunch, and **Hogate's** ($$$, 202/484-6300 or 800/424-9169), 800 Water St SW, has served the Washington area for more than 50 years.

Nightlife

Tunnicliff's Tavern (202/546-3663), 222 7th St SE, is open daily and serves American cuisine with Cajun accents. Live music is provided every Saturday night in a New Orleans ambiance.

DC's largest club, accommodating more than 1,500 people a night, is the **Capitol Ballroom** (202/554-1500), Half St and K St SE. Located near the Navy Yard, it occupies a converted boiler-company warehouse, which means that it is huge (there are half a dozen bars inside). Friday-night "Buzz Parties" feature six DJs playing techno, house, and jungle music from 10 pm to 6 am (once a month, they stay open until 9 am). On Saturdays, the music is alternative, industrial, progressive, and techno, and the rest of week there are live concerts featuring nationally-known acts. Customers must be 18 to get inside and 21 to buy a drink. A $7 cover is charged before 11 pm and a $9 cover after 11 pm; other nights, the cover ranges from $5 to $25, depending on the performer.

For a pleasant evening on the water, **Spirit Cruises** (202/554-8000), Pier #4, 6th St & Water St SW, operates cruises on the Potomac River during lunch and dinner that feature live entertainment and dancing. Similar cruises can be booked with **Odyssey Cruises** (202/488-6010), Gangplank Marina, 600 Water St SW.

Events

In September, the Benjamin Banneker NationTime Fest is held at the **L'Enfant Plaza Promenade**, 10th St and Independence Ave SW. The waterfront celebration includes children's activities, a festival, a fair, and a parade.

Alexandria

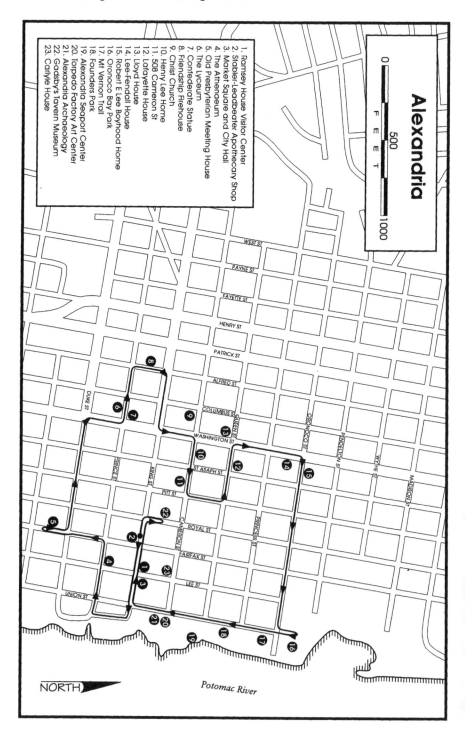

1. Ramsey House Visitor Center
2. Stabler-Leadbeater Apothecary Shop
3. Market Square and City Hall
4. The Athenaeum
5. Old Presbyterian Meeting House
6. The Lyceum
7. Confederate Statue
8. Friendship Firehouse
9. Christ Church
10. Henry Lee Home
11. 508 Cameron St
12. Lafayette House
13. Lloyd House
14. Lee-Fendall House
15. Robert E Lee Boyhood Home
16. Oronoco Bay Park
17. Mt Vernon Trail
18. Founders Park
19. Alexandria Seaport Center
20. Torpedo Factory Art Center
21. Alexandria Archaeology
22. Gadsby's Tavern Museum
23. Carlyle House

Alexandria

FEET

0   500   1000

NORTH

Potomac River

Alexandria

Where do Washington insiders go in the evenings, on weekends or on holidays? Quite often, they head for Alexandria, just eight miles south of the city on the western bank of the Potomac River.

In 1669, Scotsman John Alexander purchased the land of present-day Alexandria from an English ship captain for "six thousand pounds of Tobacco and Cask." In the fall of 1748, another group of Scots including merchants William Ramsay and John Carlyle petitioned the Virginia General Assembly to establish a town. Their petition was approved, and the following Spring the city fathers established the boundaries of the town and named it Alexandria, in honor of their predecessor, John Alexander.

The Scottish tobacco merchants who founded the city auctioned off a 60-acre tract of land, which they divided into half-acre lots. The surveyor who laid out the townsite had a young assistant—a 17-year-old boy named George Washington. The lots were auctioned off in Market Square, still the hub of Alexandria, and now constitute the heart of Old Town.

The town was incorporated 1749, a quarter-century before the American Revolution. Following the Revolution, while attempting to decide where the new nation's capital was to be located, the State of Virginia ceded Alexandria and a portion of Fairfax County to the District of Columbia (1789). By then, it had become an active port city of 300 homes. Formally accepted by Congress in 1801, Alexandria remained under the control of the federal government until it was retroceded to Virginia in 1847. Following the Civil War, Alexandria was made the capital of the Restored Government of Virginia, which represented a block of seven Virginia counties that had remained under Federal control during the war.

The Alexandria of today is distinguished by its waterfront location, its seemingly-limitless array of magnificent restaurants, and its colorful ambiance, including a number of quaint brick sidewalks, cobblestoned streets and alleys, and a smattering of gaslamp lighting. More than 2,000 18th- and 19th-century homes remain within the city's boundaries.

Information

The **Alexandria Convention & Visitors Association** (703/838-4200 or 800 /388-9119, www.FunSide.com) is located in the historic Ramsay House at 221 King St. It is open from 9 am to 5 pm daily, and offers a highly-interesting 13-minute video that summarizes the history of the city. Translations are available in 18 languages. Be sure to pick up a free walking tour brochure, bicycle trail map, Civil War walking tour, and parking map, plus any other literature that interests you. . While there, also consider purchasing a "block ticket" that enables you to tour five of the city's most popular historical properties: Gadsby's Tavern, Lee's Boyhood Home, Carlyle House, Stabler-Leadbeater Apothecary Shop, and Lee-Fendall House—for the reduced rate of $12, $5 for children 11-17.

Another source of information about the city is the **Alexandria Chamber of Commerce** (703/739-3810, http://ci.alexandria.va.us/oha) at 801 N Fairfax St, Suite 402.

Getting there

In Washington, it's George Washington Parkway; in Alexandria, it becomes Washington St. As you enter the town on Washington St, watch for King St. Turn left onto King St and drive a few blocks into the middle of Old Town.

If you are coming in on I-95, rather than the George Washington Parkway, take the Route 1 exit North onto Patrick St and turn right at King St. If you are riding the Metro, take either the Blue or Yellow line to the King St station.

If you are driving, stop at the Visitors Center on King St and ask for a free 24-hour parking pass that will enable you to park, free of charge, in any 2-hour metered space. Another program, "Park Alexandria" enables visitors to park in any of 14 garages scattered throughout Old Town and receive a $2 discount by having their parking ticket certified by a participating merchant

Alexandria's version of Washington's Metro bus system is called DASH (703/370-3274). The 85-cent fare requires exact change, but it includes a transfer good for a return trip for up to four hours. Tourist tokens for DASH can be purchased at the Visitor Center.

Seasonal highlights

Alexandria teems with special events of every ilk, which helps to explain why the town is perpetually packed with locals and tourists alike.

On the third Saturday, Sunday and Monday in February, it is time to celebrate **George Washington's birthday** (703/838-4200) with a parade through Old Town, banquets, balls, walking tours, and other special events.
St Patrick's Day (703/549-4535) is celebrated on the second Saturday in March with a parade along historic King St.

Then there is a **Christmas Tree Lighting** in Market Square on the Friday after Thanksgiving, accompanied by choir singing, puppet shows, dance performances, and an appearance by Santa Claus and his elves. The tree-lighting ceremony begins at 7 pm, and while the tree is lit thousands of tiny lights go on along King St as well.

On the first Saturday in December, Alexandria holds its annual **Scottish Christmas Walk** with heather, fresh wreaths, holly, kilted bagpipers, Highland dancers, a parade of Scottish clans with horses and dogs, caroling, fashion shows, children's' games, booths selling handicrafts, food, drinks, and antiques. An admission fee is charged for some events.

Tours

Doorways to Old Virginia (703/548-0100), a guided walking tour of Old Town, starts at the Ramsay House Visitor Center at 221 King St. Guides in 18th-century attire lead you through Alexandria's historic streets.

From mid-March to mid-November, one-hour **Old Town Ghost Tours**, also led by costumed guides, regale you with the legends, folklore, and ghost stories associated with Alexandria as they conduct you through a historic old cemetery. The tours leave the Visitor Center at 7:30 and 9 pm on Friday and Saturday and at 7:30 pm on Sunday. The fee is $5 for adults, $3 for children aged 7-17.

Also available are one-hour $5 Overview Tours offered by **Alexandria Tours** (703/329-1122) at 11 am from Monday through Saturday and at 2 pm on Sunday. The same company offers one-hour $5 Ghosts, Legends, and Folklore Tours that begin in Market Square at 7 pm on Friday and Saturday nights.

By appointment, **Old Town Experience** (703/836-0694) also provides a $5 tour.

In early April, a tour of Alexandria's kitchens is offered as well as the annual **Garden Week Tour**.

On the fourth Saturday in September, the Alexandria Hospital sponsors an annual **Tour of Homes**.

The October **Halloween Walking Tour** visits Alexandria graveyards while a lantern-carrying guide clad in 18th-century garb talks about ghosts, legends, myths and folklore.

During the second week in December, visitors to Alexandria can enjoy the **Old Town Christmas Candlelight Tour**, which visits decorated historic homes and an 18th-century tavern. Colonial dancing, string quartets, madrigal and opera singers, and refreshments are a part of the fun. Tickets, available at the Ramsay House Visitor Center, sell for $12, $5 for children up to 17.

Tours of the **Stabler-Leadbeater Apothecary Shop** are available on Sunday. A small admission fee is charged, and there is a gift shop.

Guided tours of **Christ Church** and the **Lloyd House** also are available.

Tours of the **Lee-Fendall House** start on the hour, with the last one starting at 3 pm. Wednesday mornings are reserved for school and other group tours.

Tours of the **Boyhood Home of Robert E Lee** are conducted from 10 am to 3:30 pm Monday through Saturday and 1 to 3:30 pm on Sunday. Admission is $3 for adults and $1 for children between 11 and 17. From December 15 to January 31, the house is open by appointment only. Special events held in the house include the celebration of both Henry's and Robert E Lee's birthdays on or about the third Sunday in January; a reenactment of the wedding of Mary Lee Fitzhugh and George

Washington Parke Custis, held in mid-July; and a celebration in recognition of the formal visit of Marquis de Lafayette, held in mid-October. The house also is a stop on Alexandria's Candlelight Tours during the second weekend in December.

From April 1 to September 30, **Gadsby's Tavern Museum** is open to the public from 10 am to 5 pm Tuesday through Saturday and from 1 to 5 pm on Sunday, with guided tours beginning at 15 minutes before the hour and 15 minutes past the hour, the last tour starting at 4:15. From October 1 to March 31, the museum's hours are 11 am to 4 pm Tuesday through Saturday and 1 to 4 pm on Sunday with tours conducted as before except that the last tour begins at 3:15. Admission is $3 for adults and $1 for children 11 to 17.

The two areas of greatest interest to students of Black history in Alexandria are widely separated and can be reached most easily by car or taxi. The **Black History Tour** (703/838-4356) has been designed for just that reason. Tours of the **Black History Resouce Center** are available, as are tours of the adjacent **Watson Reading Room.**

Historic tours of the **Fort Ward Museum and Historic Site** are conducted daily from 9 am to sunset. The grounds are the site of Civil War Reunion Day, a celebration held in mid-June, when soldiers drill, march, and talk about the Civil War. From June to mid-August, 7 pm concerts are staged on Thursday in the outdoor amphitheater (703/838-4686). Living history programs are offered in mid-August.

Guided tours of the **Masonic Memorial** Tower Rooms are offered on the half-hour in the mornings and on the hour in the afternoons. In late June, Commemoration Day is celebrated with a picnic dinner, a concert by the US Army Band, and fireworks.

Tours, programs, lectures, and trips related to a variety of subjects are provided for adults and children at **Green Spring Farm Park**. Classes are planned for children from 3 to 5 and from 6 to 9.

Old Town Alexandria. *Begin the tour at the historic Ramsay House, where the city Visitor Center is located.* William Ramsay, one of the founders of Alexandria and a friend of George Washington, was a Scottish merchant, one of the city's early postmasters, and its first Lord Mayor. His wife Anne was commended by Thomas Jefferson for having raised over $75,000 in support of the American Revolution. **Ramsay House**, with a gambrel roof and English garden, was built in 1724, making it Alexandria's oldest house. The house itself is believed to have been barged up-river from Dumfries, Virginia. The building later was used as a tavern, a grocery, and a cigar factory.

Walk across King St. At 105-107 S Fairfax St at the corner of King St is the **Stabler-Leadbeater Apothecary Shop** (703/836-3713), established in

1791. It was Alexandria's oldest mercantile establishment and served the community for 141 years until it was forced to close in 1933 due to the Depression. Past patrons included George and Martha Washington, George Mason, Henry Clay, John C Calhoun, Daniel Webster, and Robert E Lee, among others.

Edward Stabler, Quaker pharmacist, rented the three-story building in 1792. Today's pharmacy museum contains over 8,000 items dating from that period and into the 1930s, including some old scales stamped with the royal crown and equipment used for bloodletting, an early "cure" for many diseases. The collection of original handblown bottles, labeled with gold leaf, is the most valuable collection of antique medicine bottles in America. A clock on the rear wall, the porcelain-handled mahogany drawers, and two mortars and pestles date from 1790. Water-filled globes sat in the front window, where they served as a warning to illiterate residents that various illnesses had entered the area. The color of the water in the globes reflected the particular illness -- plague, cholera, yellow fever -- for the community to be concerned about.

Robert E Lee was in this store when JEB Stuart delivered an order from the War Department telling Lee to go to Harper's Ferry and put an end to the John Brown insurrection. During the War of 1812, the store was ransacked by British forces. Visiting hours are 10 am to 4 pm from Monday through Saturday and from 1 to 5 pm on Sunday.

Return to King St and take a right, heading south along Old Town's main street. In 1749, the planners of the city set aside two half-acre lots for a marketplace and a town hall -- the very place where today's **Market Square and City Hall** (703/838-4994) stand in the 100 block of King St. Between 5 and 9 am on Saturday, the **Farmers' Market** (703/838-4770) is held on the City Hall's South Plaza. It is the oldest Farmers' Market in the country, where George Washington became a trustee in 1766. Weekly, Washington sent wagons full of produce from his Mount Vernon estate to be sold there. The market is still a favorite among the locals, who love to shop here for fresh flowers, baked goods, produce, handicrafts, and much, much more.

Where King St reaches the Potomac River, take a right and enter the park. **Waterfront Park** (703/838-4844) is located where Prince St reaches the Potomac River.

A block south of King St, adjacent to the park, is Prince St. Head west along Prince. The first (100) block of Prince St is known as **Captain's Row**, named for sea captain John Harper, who had a number of the houses along here built for his many children. The street is cobblestoned, the sidewalk is fashioned of brick, and the homes are historic. It is said that much of the stone used on these streets and alleys was originally used as ballast aboard the sailing ships that once frequented the port of Alexandria, and were laid by Hessian mercenaries who had originally been employed by the British.

Captain's Row had an interesting beginning. When the city lots in Alexandria were auctioned off, Capt Harper and Col George Gilpin bought opposing lots on the waterfront. The property was then defined as running from the boundary marker to the water's edge. In the 1780s, the streets were graded and the excess dirt was dumped into a shallow crescent on the waterfront, thus filling it in and extending the property owned by Harper and Gilpin. Taking advantage of the situation, the two men subdivided their land and sold the extra parcels, which eventually came to be known as Captain's Row.

A number of the homes on Captain's Row were damaged or destroyed during the Great Fire of 1827, but all of the houses located there today are over 150 years old.

At 127 Prince St, look to the second floor for one of Alexandria's few remaining "busybodies," a peculiar arrangement of mirrors that allow the room's occupants to discreetly see people walking up and down the street. At 210 Prince St is the **Athenaeum** (703/548-0035), built to serve as a banking house in 1851. Now, the Greek Revival building houses the gallery of the Northern Virginia Fine Arts Association and exhibits a variety of contemporary art. The gallery is open Wednesday through Saturday from 11 am to 4 pm and Sunday from 1 to 4 pm. Admission is free.

The area between Fairfax St and Lee St on Prince St is known as **Gentry Row**, a snobbish tribute to the many leading citizens who lived in the three-story townhouses along here during the 18th and 19th centuries.

At Fairfax St, turn left and go south for two blocks. At 321 Fairfax St is the **Old Presbyterian Meeting House** (703/549-6670), originally built by Scottish pioneers in 1774. George Washington was buried from here in 1799, and the Meeting House bell tolled continuously for four days after his death. In the courtyard is the Tomb of the Unknown Soldier of the American Revolution, and markers denote the gravesites of John and Sara Carlyle, Dennis Ramsay, and Dr James Craik, who dressed Lafayette's wounds at Brandywine, ministered to the dying Braddock at Monongahela, and treated—some say killed—George Washington during his final days.

The brick church, which contains old-fashioned gate pews, was used as a meeting house as well as a church. The original building was gutted by a fire caused by lightning in 1835, but it was restored just a few years later. The original parsonage (manse) is still intact. The present bell, recast from the metal used in the original bell, was hung in a newly-constructed belfry in 1843, and a new organ was installed in 1849, but 40 years later (1889) the building was closed and sat virtually abandoned for the ensuing 60 years. In 1949, it was "reborn" as a Presbyterian USA church, open weekdays from 9 am to 3 pm. Admission is free.

Backtrack along Fairfax St to Duke St and turn left. At Washington St, turn right (North).

Alexandria's historical museum, **The Lyceum** (703/838-4994, http://ci.alexandria.va.us/oha) at 201 S Washington St, was built in 1839 as the community cultural center and library. Designed in a Doric temple style, the brick-and-stucco building was seized by the Union Army during the Civil War and used as a hospital. Later, it became a private residence, and was then subdivided into office space. In 1969, the City Council used its powers of eminent domain to preserve the building from being demolished in favor of a parking lot.

Visitors to the museum can see silver being made, a receipt for the sale of a slave ("female Monica, $20"), and a Confederate uniform and sword, among other historically interesting exhibits. The building contains the Coldsmith Gallery, a lecture hall, and a museum shop, plus a great deal of information relative to the State of Virginia. It is open daily from 10 am to 5 pm Monday through Saturday and from 1 to 5 pm on Sunday, excluding New Year's Day, Thanksgiving, and Christmas. Admission is free, as is the parking.

The **Confederate Statue** *Appomattox* stands at Prince St and S Washington St, honoring the nation's fallen Confederate soldiers. Dedicated in 1889, the bronze statue shows an unarmed soldier with his head bowed and clutching a rumpled hat, standing on a granite pedestal facing the battlefields to the south. The statue marks the spot on which some 700 Alexandrians, members of the 17th Virginia, left the city to fight for the Confederacy on May 24, 1861, the day Federal troops occupied the city.

Walk west along Prince St for two blocks to Alfred St. Then make a right.
At 107 S Alfred St is the **Friendship Firehouse Museum** (703/838-3891), a collection of early firefighting equipment. The Friendship Fire Company, the first volunteer fire company in Alexandria, was established in 1774,

and the current firehouse was built in 1855. Local tradition says George Washington was involved as a founding member, an active firefighter, and the man who purchased its first fire engine, but extensive research has produced no evidence in support of those claims. The old firehouse building was remodeled in 1871, then restored in 1992, and is open from 10 am to 4 pm on Friday and Saturday and from 1 to 4 pm on Sunday.

Walk on to King St, make a right, and go two blocks to Washington St. Turn left (north). At Cameron St and N Washington St is **Christ Church** (703/549-1450), the oldest church in Alexandria. Built between 1767 and 1773, it was first called the "Church in the Woods," and at the time, it was customary for parishioners to pay for the privilege of reserving a seat in the church. George Washington bought Pew 60 for 36 pounds 10 shillings. Robert E Lee, also a member of the congregation, was confirmed here in 1853. The pews of both Washington and Lee have been preserved.

George Washington went to live with his half-brother Lawrence and his wife Ann Fairfax of Belvoir in 1743. Lawrence owned Mount Vernon. As George grew into manhood, he served as a delegate to the First Continental Congress in Philadelphia, where he was appointed Commander-in-Chief of the Continental Army, and after the Revolutionary War, he resigned his commission to return to Mount Vernon. But he was then chosen to be a delegate to the Constitutional Convention in Philadelphia in 1787, where he was elected president. Following the convention, he became the first President of the United States and served two terms in that office.

It has become a tradition for US presidents to attend a service here on a Sunday close to Washington's birthday and to sit in his pew. On one such occasion, on New Year's Day 1942, Franklin Delano Roosevelt attended the services with Winston Churchill on the World Day of Prayer, shortly after Pearl Harbor.

The church has been in continuous use since 1773. It has a fine Palladian window, an interior balcony, and a wrought-brass and crystal chandelier brought from England. The windows contain handblown glass. A bell tower, church bell, and organ were added in the early 1800s, and the "wineglass" pulpit in 1891. The courtyard, which was Alexandria's first and only burial ground until 1805, contains the graves of Yankee seamen from 1771 as well as those of Confederate prisoners of war. Today an active Episcopal Parish, the building contains a number of interesting exhibits and a gift shop at the Columbus St entrance. It is open from 9 am to 4 pm Monday through Saturday and 2 to 4 pm on Sunday. *Turn the corner onto Cameron St.* At 611 Cameron St is the **Home of Gen Henry "Light Horse Harry" Lee**, now privately owned. Only marginally overshadowed by the Washingtons, the Lees were a fabulous and influential family. Richard Lee, born in Shropshire, England in 1613, emigrated to Virginia in 1639. He served as a court clerk in Jamestown, engaged in fur trading, and was appointed Colonial Secretary of State in 1649. Richard Henry Lee (1732-94) was a Virginia senator and a leader in the Continental Congress, as well as an influential force in the adoption of the Bill of Rights. Richard Henry Lee and Francis Lightfoot Lee (1734-97) were signers of the Declaration of Independence. Henry "Light Horse Harry" Lee (1756-1818) was a friend of George Washington and a Revolutionary War hero who served as Governor of Virginia and in Congress. It was he who wrote Alexandria's farewell to George Washington when Washington left to become the nation's first President. He also wrote the historic eulogy to George Washington that contains the well-known phrase "First in war, first in peace, and first in the hearts of his countrymen."

"Light Horse Harry" also was the father of Gen Robert E Lee (1807-70). Lincoln's choice to lead the Union Army, Lee chose instead to resign his Federal commission and join the Confederate Army. He assumed the rank of Major General in the Virginia military forces in 1861, and in February 1865 he was named general-in-chief of the Armies of the Confederate States, just two months before the surrender to Grant at Appomattox.

Seven years after moving into this house, "Light Horse Harry" Lee died, and his widow moved the family to 607 Oronoco St.

Go east on Cameron St for one block. At **508 Cameron St** is a replica of the townhouse in which George Washington lived when he was in Alexandria. The building occupies the same site as the original. In Washington's day, a considerable percentage of the population lived in the country and commuted into town only to obtain supplies. When individuals visited town often or for long periods of time—and could afford it—they would buy a place in town where they could stay on those occasions. This, of course, was their town-house, hence the origin of the term.

At the corner, take a left onto Pitt St and walk one block to Queen St. Turn left and walk one more block to St Asaph St. At 301 St Asaph St is the **Lafayette House**, the house loaned to Lafayette during his last visit to the United States in 1825. The house is privately owned.

Walk another block wast on Queen St to Washington St. In the middle of the block to your left is the late Georgian-style **Lloyd House** (703 /838-4577, www.alexandria.lib.va.us/lloyd.htm), 220 N Washington St, , built in 1797 by John Wise, a local tanner who also built Gadsby's Tavern. In the early 1800s, Charles Lee, US Attorney General under Washington and Adams, lived here. A later occupant was Jacob Hoffman, mayor of Alexandria, and in 1826, a Quaker schoolmaster named Benjamin Hallowell moved his school into the house. Hallowell tutored Robert E Lee.

In 1832, John Lloyd, a wealthy merchant, bought the house at auction. His wife, Anne Harriotte Lee, was a first cousin of Robert E Lee and entertained him here often. The house remained in the Lloyd family until 1918, when it was purchased by William Albert Smoot, a lumber dealer and also a mayor of Alexandria. Smoot's family owned the house until 1942.

Subsequently, the house served as a barracks for the WAVES, as a rooming house, and as an office for a geological firm. In 1956, when it became earmarked for demolition, the historic old building was saved by a geologist, Robert New. Threatened again with demolition in 1968, it was purchased by the Hoge Foundation, and is now used as a branch of the Alexandria Library. Inside is a sizeable Civil War collection, photos, maps, microforms, and manuscripts pertaining to Alexandria, the history of Virginia, and genealogy. On the second floor is the Virginia Research Collection, and behind the house are a brick patio and a large garden. The building is open Monday through Saturday from 9 am to 5 pm.

Walk north along Washington St for two blocks. At Oronoco St, turn right. "Light Horse Harry" Lee, Robert E Lee's father, sold the lot at 614 Oronoco St to Philip Fendall, an Alexandria lawyer, who built the wood-frame Early Victorian **Lee-Fendall House** (703/548-1789) in 1785. Fendall, himself a descendent of the Lee family, married Mary Lee, "Light Horse Harry's" sister, in the 1790s. The house was occupied by members of the Lee family (according to records, 37 different members of the family) between 1785 and 1903, a span of 118 years. Records also indicate that George Washington dined in this house on at least nine occasions.

During the Civil War, the house was seized and used as a Union hospital. The clapboard structure is furnished mostly with pieces donated by Lee descendents. It includes many family records, plus a collection of antique dolls and 19th- and 20th-century dolls' houses. A large Colonial garden with boxwood-lined paths contains roses and magnolia and chestnut trees. The house is open from 10 am to 4 pm Tuesday through Saturday and from 1 to 4 pm on Sunday, and an admission is charged.

Across the street at 607 Oronoco St is a Federal townhouse, The Boyhood Home of Robert E Lee (703/548-8454), the house where Lee lived for most of his boyhood years. Henry "Light Horse Harry" Lee and his wife Ann Hill Carter moved here in 1812 with their five children. Robert was just five at the time. George Washington had been an occasional guest of two earlier occupants of the house, John Potts, who built the home, and Col William Fitzhugh. In 1804, the Fitzhugh's daughter, Mary Lee, married Martha Washington's grandson, George Washington Parke Custis, in the drawing room of this house, which was made into a museum in 1967.

Robert E Lee, who had entered West Point, married Mary Anna Randolph Custis, great-granddaughter of Martha Washington in 1831. He then served in the Mexican War on the staff of Gen Winfield Scott and with the Confederate forces during the Civil War. At the conclusion of the Civil War in 1865, he became president of Washington and Lee University in Lexington, Virginia, and died there in 1870. The house is open from 10 am to 4 pm Monday through Saturday and from 1 to 4 pm on Sunday.

Follow Oronoco St East for five blocks to the Potomac River. Oronoco Bay Park occupies the riverfront between Pendleton St and Madison St. Passing through the park on its 18.5-mile journey from Mount Vernon to Theodore Roosevelt Island is the Mount Vernon Trail, popular among walkers, joggers, and bicycle riders of all ages. Get a map at the Visitor Center. Sights along the route include the Dyke Marsh wildlife habitat to the North, which contains 250 species of birds, and Jones Point Park to the South, which features a colorful 19th-century lighthouse. If you left your bike at home, you can rent one at Big Wheel Bikes (703/739-2300), 2 Prince St.

Following the river's edge through the park will take you to Pendleton St. Make a left-right jog onto Union St and continue heading south. Founders Park, the next riverfront park, is between Cameron St and Oronoco St. Just south of the park is Alexandria Seaport Foundation's Seaport Center, a floating museum that houses a working museum and a library, conducts a boat-building program, and harbors a marine sciences laboratory. Visitors also can rent small sailing and rowing craft at a boat livery located here.

At 105 N Union St, paralleling the waterfront, is the Torpedo Factory Art Center (703/838-4565, http://torpedofactory.org). Built in 1918, the plant was used to manufacture torpedos during two World Wars. The block-long, three-story structure now serves as a working studio for more than 150 artists. You can buy a lovely painting or sculpture and meet the artist who has created it, all at the same place. Open daily from 10 am to 5 pm, the building houses 83 artists' studios, five co-op galleries, and an Art League school. In Studio 327 is the **Alexandria Archaeology Museum** (703/838-4399), which conducts hands-on programs devoted to the study, preservation, and interpretation of sites within the city. Items dating from 3000 BC can be examined there, and there is a library which is open from 10 am to 3 pm Tuesday through Friday, from 10 am to 3 pm on Saturday, and from 1 to 5 pm on Sunday.

As Union St meets King St, take a right and walk three blocks past Old Town's restaurants, ice cream parlors, gift shops, and boutiques until you reach Royal St. Turn right (North). **Gadsby's Tavern** (703/548-1288) at 138 N Royal St is undeniably one of Alexandria's most colorful establishments. Actually consisting of two buildings, a Georgian tavern dating from 1770 and the City Tavern and Hotel dating from 1792, the establishment is named for John Gadsby, who operated the tavern from 1796 to 1808. Serving as both a tavern and a hotel, the 18th-century hostelry was the setting for local society balls during the 1700s. It was a political, business, and social meeting place of the early patriots. George Washington, who had a kitchenless townhouse nearby, ate here often, and in 1754, set up an office here for the purpose of enrolling volunteers in his first command. The building became a military headquarters during the French and Indian War. On November 5, 1798, Washington reviewed the Alexandria Independent Blues, a company of militia volunteers, from the steps of this tavern.

Receptions for several presidents were held here. George and Martha Washington often danced in the tavern's second-floor ballroom, and twice attended the annual Birthnight Ball that was held in his honor and is now reenacted each year. John Adams, John Quincy Adams, Thomas Jefferson, James Madison, the Marquis de Lafayette, John Paul Jones, and Baron de Kalb are among the famous patriots who also were entertained here.

In the 18th century, one did not rent a hotel room, but instead rented bed (or floor) space in a room to be shared with others. Since this hotel often served as a gathering place for political meetings, it is easy to understand the origin of the phrase "politics makes strange bedfellows." In 1929, the building was purchased by American Legion Post 24 to save it from demolition. In 1972, the buildings were given to the city, restored, and reopened in time for the 1976 Bicentennial.

Blackbeard, the pirate, was beheaded after he was killed by Governor

Spottswood's troops in 1718, and his skull was displayed as a warning to other pirates, but according to local legend, Blackbeard's comrades soon stole the skull and made it into a silver drinking cup with the inscription "Deth to Spotswoode" engraved on the rim. Decades later, the skull was displayed at Gadsby's Tavern. Since then, it is said, Blackbeard's ghost has returned to the tavern each Halloween to search for the missing skull and to enjoy an evening in Old Town. (Guides from Doorways to Old Virginia conduct a tour between 6:30 and 9:30 pm on Halloween, introducing visitors to Blackbeard and members of his pirate crew while touring Gadsby's, the Stabler-Leadbeater Apothecary Museum, and the Carlyle House. The festivities include music, swordplay, and a scavenger hunt for Blackbeard's skull.)

Blackbeard's ghost is not the only eerie visitor to the tavern. In July 1816, a handsome Englishman and his wife docked at the port of Alexandria. The woman was very ill, and was taken to rooms above Gadsby's Tavern, where she was tended by a doctor. Witnesses were asked to promise that they would never divulge the woman's name. When the young woman died a few days later, she was buried in St Paul's Cemetery, where her tabletop tombstone reads simply: "In memory of the female stranger, died Oct. 14, 1816, age 23 years 8 months." Soon after the woman's death, the widower disappeared without paying his bills, and was never seen in town again. Some say they have seen the young woman, still walking the halls of Gadsby's Tavern. Owned and operated by the City of Alexandria, **Gadsby's Tavern Museum** (703/838-4242, www.ct.alexandria.va.us/oha/gadsbystavern.html) at 134 N Royal St, contains a number of interesting exhibits.

Return to King St, turn left, and walk one block to Fairfax St, then turn left. **Carlyle House** (703/549-2997), 121 N Fairfax St, was the residence of one of Alexandria's founders, Scottish merchant John Carlyle. Carlyle was married to Sarah Fairfax of Belvoir, a niece of Thomas Lord Fairfax of England, who owned over six million acres of land in northern Virginia in the Colonial days. One of the city's grandest houses, the stone Scottish/English-style manor house was built in 1753. It has a beautiful Palladian window on the stairway and hand-hewn beams secured with hand-wrought nails. It has been restored with period furnishings, pointed cedars define the main entrance walk, and the gardens are listed among *The Restored Historic Gardens of Virginia*, a publication produced by The Garden Club of Virginia.

In 1755, British Maj Gen Edward Braddock used this house for his headquarters and discussed strategy for conducting the French and Indian

War with five British Colonial governors, whom he asked to tax the colonists in order to finance the campaign. The Colonial legislatures' refusal to be taxed was one of the first instances of a serious rift between America and Great Britain.

Carlyle owned three working plantations, where he raised wheat and corn and bred racehorses. A friend of George Washington, Carlyle helped him to mill his wheat and ship it to England. When he was in town, Washington visited Carlyle's house almost every Sunday after church.

Carlyle House is open from 10 am to 4:30 pm Tuesday through Saturday and from noon to 4:30 pm on Sunday. Tours are given every half hour, beginning in the servant's hall, where you will hear a recorded "conversation" between mannequin slaves Charles and Penny. Admission is $3 for adults and $1 for children ages 11 through 17.

You are now back to the Visitor Center where you began your foot tour of Alexandria.

Lodging

Those who enjoy the additional elbow-room and hominess afforded by suite-style inns will find a considerable number of them available in Alexandria. **Doubletree Guest Suites** ($$$-$$$$, 703/370-9600 or 800/222-8733) at 100 S Reynolds St, offers suites with fully-equipped kitchens, a complimentary continental breakfast, and an Olympic-size pool. **Embassy Suites Alexandria** ($$$-$$$$, 703/684-5900 or 800/EMBASSY) at 1900 Diagonal Rd, provides two-room suites across the street from the Metro station, also accompanied by a complimentary breakfast plus a manager's reception in the evening. **Executive Club Suites** ($$$-$$$$, 703/739-2582 or 800/535-2582) at 610 Bashford Ln, furnishes full kitchens, a complimentary breakfast, and an evening reception, while **Sheraton Suites** ($$$-$$$$, 703 /836-4700 or 800/325-3535) at 801 N Saint Asaph St, can offer 247 two-room suites in a historic Old Town setting, plus an afternoon reception, an indoor pool, a health club, a complimentary shuttle throughout the area, and the excellent Fin & Hoof Restaurant.

For more of the Colonial feeling, try the **Morrison House** (703/838-8000 or 800/367-0800, www.morrisonhouse.com) at 116 S Alfred St. Done in the style of an 18th-century manor house, the building contains only 45 rooms, which includes three suites. The rooms are decorated with mahogany four-poster beds, fireplaces, and Italian marble baths. A complimentary continental breakfast can be followed later in the day with dinner in the award-winning Elysium Restaurant.

Other familiar favorites include **Best Western Old Colony Inn**, ($$-$$$, 703/739-2222 or 800/528-1234), 625 First St; **Holiday Inn Select—Old Town** ($$$-$$$$, 703/549-6080 or 800/368-5047), 480 King St, the only hotel in the heart of the historic district; **Ramada Plaza Old Town** ($$$-$$$$, 703/683-6000 or

800/2-RAMADA), 901 Fairfax St, a high-rise affording lovely views of the Potomac River waterfront.

Arts & culture

On most Sunday afternoons at 4, concerts are held at **The Lyceum** in Alexandria..

On January 17, Alexandria celebrates the **birthday of Henry "Light Horse Harry" Lee** at the Lee-Fendall House and the birthday of his son, Robert E Lee, at The Boyhood Home of Robert E Lee. Refreshments, period music, and house tours are a part of the festivities, and admission is free.

In May, a jazz festival is held in Alexandria's Oronoco Bay Park on **Memorial Day.**

Twice-a-month outdoor concerts are hosted in Alexandria's **Waterfront Park** on Fridays during the Summer and on Mondays from mid-June to early August. Visitors sit on the grass and enjoy the music.

In mid-September, the **Caravan Stage Barge** puts in at Jones Park. A replica of a Thames River Sailing Barge, the ship becomes a stage and the crew becomes the actors. Performances begin at dark.

Food & drink

Colorful dining establishments abound in Alexandria. It is almost sinful to dine at the same place twice.

Gadsby's Tavern ($$, 703/548-1288), 138 N Royal St, is far more than a stop on the walking tour. It's a must-see for dinner as well. Inside the historic old building are three elegant Colonial dining rooms where visitors dine by candlelight off pewter plates. Servers are dressed in authentic Colonial attire, and entertainment is a part of the experience. On Sunday and Monday evenings and at brunch on Sunday, strolling violinist Jim Diehl slowly wends his way between the tables. Tuesday through Saturday, an "18th-century gentleman," John Douglas Hall, visits each table, entertaining diners with "current events" of an era 200 years ago, occasionally pausing to play a tune on his lute. Outdoor dining in a flagstoned courtyard edged with flower beds is available during the Summer, and menu items include such unusual delights as thick slices of toast dipped in a batter of rum and spices, and served with sausage, hash browns, and hot cinnamon syrup. Or perhaps you would like to try the cheese pye, English trifle, creamy buttermilk-custard pye, Scottish apple gingerbread, or bourbon apple pye. Beverages also reflect the tavern's Colonial heritage, and include scuppernong (a white aromatic table wine made from a cultivated muscadine grape that bears a yellowish-green, plum-flavored fruit called scuppernong) or Wench's Punch. The tavern is open for lunch from 11:30 am to 3 pm Monday through Saturday, for Sunday brunch from 11 am to 3 pm, and for dinner from 5:30 to 10 pm nightly.

Some of the flavor of the pre-Revolutionary period can be enjoyed at **The Tea Cosy** (703/836-8181), 119 S Royal, a true British tearoom that serves assorted tea sandwiches and oven-fresh scones, meat pies and shepherd pies. A magazine rack is loaded with current British periodicals and newspapers, and there is a small store in the back. The tearoom is open from 10 am to 6 pm Saturday through Thursday and from 10 am to 7 pm on Friday.

Another interesting place to dine is **The Seaport Inn** (703/549-2341), 6 King St, Old Town Alexandria's first restaurant. The waterfront building, a former warehouse, was purchased by Col John Fitzgerald, who was George Washington's military aide at Valley Forge. Fitzgerald later served as Harbormaster and as mayor of Alexandria. The original beams and oyster mortar walls are still visible in the restaurant's four banquet rooms, which afford both riverview and fireside dining. A Sunday brunch is served, and live entertainment is provided in the inn's George Washington Tavern Room.

Setting the historic atmosphere aside, excellent French and Basque cuisine can be found at **La Bergerie** (703/683-1007), 218 N Lee St, www.LaBergerie.com, and choice Italian dining is available at **Villa D'Este** ($$, 703/549-9477), 818 N St Asaph St.

Nightlife

Mysteries, musicals, dramas, and comedies are offered by the **West End Dinner Theatre** (703/370-2500 or 800/368-3799, www.wedt.com), 4615 Duke St. Tiered seating is offered for good viewing, there is an Art Deco lounge, and free parking is provided. Performances are provided at dinner from 8 to 11 pm from Tuesday through Sunday and lunch on Wednesdays and Sundays. Alexandria also features a traditional comedy club, the **Headliners & Comedy Club** (703/379-HAHA) at 2460 Eisenhower Ave.

For theatrical entertainment apart from dinner, check what's playing at **MetroStage** (703/548-9044), 3200 Mount Vernon Ave, and **Little Theatre of Alexandria** (703/683-5778), 600 Wolfe St.

The riverboat **Dandy** (703/683-6076, www.dandydinnerboat.com), Zero Prince St on the waterfront, , offers gourmet dining, dancing, and magnificent waterfront views during a three-hour dinner-dance, available year-around, day or night, rain or shine. Lunch cruises and Sunday champagne brunch cruises also are available.

Music aficionados might try **The Birchmere** (703/549-7500), 3701 Mount Vernon Ave, for country, folk and blues; **Casablanca & Rick's Cafe** (703 /549-6464), 1504 King St, for belly dancing and flamenco dancing on weekends; **Fin & Hoof** (703/549-6622), 801 N St Asaph St, for jazz piano Wednesday through Saturday and Sunday during brunch; **Las Tapas** (703/836-4000), 710 King St, for flamenco dancing on weekends; or **Trattoria Da Franco** (703/548-9338), 305 S Washington St, for nightly piano music at 7:30 pm.

Alexandria's sports bars include **Armands/Penalty Box** (703/683-0313), 111 King St; **Barcelona Soccer Lounge** (703/548-1670), 815 King St; and **Joe Theismann's Restaurant** (703/739-0777), 1800 Diagonal Rd.

Union Street Public House ($$, 703/548-1785) at 121 S Union St in Old Town features 11 draft beers in an old-fashioned saloon atmosphere. It is open daily for brunch, lunch, and dinner.

Events

In May, the **Old Town Arts & Crafts Fair** (703/836-2176) is scheduled.

One weekend in June is set aside for the **Red Cross Waterfront Festival** (703/549-8300) in Oronoco Bay Park. "Tall ships" sail into port, there is a blessing of the fleet, and river cruises, races, arts and crafts exhibits, food, a variety of music, and fireworks are featured.

In late June, an **18th-Century Fair** is held on Cameron St in front of Gadsby's and in Market Square on King St. Festivities include games, artisans, entertainment, and demonstrations.

On the fourth weekend in July, the **Virginia Scottish Games** (703/838-5005) consume two days with a Celtic festival that includes Highland dancing, bagpipe music, the US National Highland Heptathlon, a fiddling competition, an antique car show, displays, food, and a grand parade of the Scottish clans. An admission fee is charged, and tickets may be acquired at the gate or at the Visitor Center.

In August, a Firehouse Festival at the **Friendship Firehouse Museum** allows kids to play with dalmatians, get balloons and firehats, and eat birthday cake.

On the second Saturday in August, a Civil War Living History program is presented at **Fort Ward**. Authentically equipped and dressed military units demonstrate camp life during the Civil War days. An admission free is charged.

Each September, **Oronoco Bay Park** is the site of the Hard Times Chili Cook-Off, which features live bands, food, and games.

The American Horticultural Society offers free classes, lectures, and picnic facilities at **River Farm**.

Falls Church

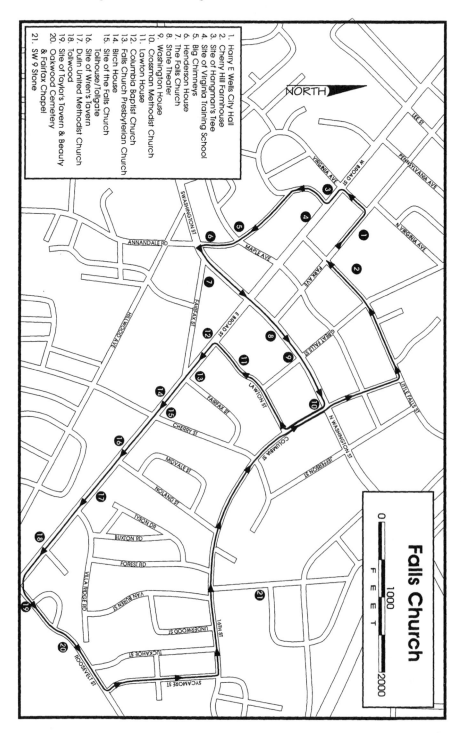

1. Harry E Wells City Hall
2. Cherry Hill Farmhouse
3. Site of Hangman's Tree
4. Site of Virginia Training School
5. Big Chimneys
6. Henderson House
7. The Falls Church
8. State Theater
9. Washington House
10. Crossman Methodist Church
11. Lawton House
12. Columbia Baptist Church
13. Falls Church Presbyterian Church
14. Birch House
15. Site of the Falls Church
16. Tollhouse/Tollgate
17. Site of Wren's Tavern
18. Dulin United Methodist Church
19. Tollwood
19. Site of Taylor's Tavern & Beauty
20. Oakwood Cemetery
    & Fairfax Chapel
21. SW 9 Stone

NORTH

Falls Church

FEET

0   1000   2000

Falls Church

A church that grew into a community. The history of the Falls Church area dates from the late 1600s, when an early Colonial settlement was shared with the local Native Americans residing beside an old Indian trail. The trail led north to the falls on the Potomac River, so when a church was built there in 1734, it was only reasonable that it should be called The Falls Church. In time, the church attracted some prominent citizens from the surrounding region, including George Washington and George Mason, and slowly, a town began to grow around the church.

Lee Highway eventually replaced the old Indian trail, and another road, the Leesburg Pike, was developed, the two roads intersecting close to the church. This provided the community with another reason for continued growth. In 1875, the area became a township; in 1948, Falls Church became an independent city.

Falls Church is a quiet residential town of about 11,000 population, enjoyed by the residents for its 10 city parks, 10 tennis courts, bike trail, hiking trail, summertime farmers' market, and annual Arts-in-the-Park festival. Falls Church is situated almost due west of Washington in an area bounded by Arlington County on the east, Alexandria on the south, Tysons Corner on the north, and the Capital Beltway on the west. The town has repeatedly earned the Tree City USA award from the National Arbor Day Foundation, and in 1962 was proclaimed an All-American City.

Information
Greater Falls Church Chamber of Commerce (703/532-1050), 417 W Broad St, PO Box 491, Falls Church, VA 22040. Falls Church Public Information Office (703/241-5003)

Getting there
I-66 runs along the town's northern boundary, providing easy access to downtown Washington, DC. There are two Metro stations, East Falls Church and West Falls Church, and Metrorail also links the community to Washington's midtown Union Station, where there is AMTRAK access to the entire eastern seaboard.

First steps
The city maintains "Walking Tour Information Boards" at several places around town—S Washington St and Annandale Rd, the W&OD Trail Bridge at Route 7, and adjacent to the City Library at Park St and N Virginia Ave. Maps and literature about public facilities, restaurants, and merchants are all free for the taking.

Falls Church. *Start your tour of Falls Church at the intersection of Park Ave and Little Falls St.* Before you at 300 Park Ave is the **Harry E Wells City Hall**, named for the man who served as the town's City Manager from 1964 to 1983. The cornerstone for the City Hall was laid in 1957 on a 14.6-acre site that once was a part of the Cherry Hill farm. The adjacent Community Center was built in 1968, and in 1982 the historic **Gage House**, an original occupant of the Cherry Hill farm, was renovated for use as a Senior Center.

The **Cherry Hill Farmhouse** at 312 Park Ave was built in 1845, and an adjacent timber-frame home was built about 1856. The property was then owned by the Riley family, which had moved to Falls Church in 1873. Joseph S Riley was the uncle of poet James Whitcomb Riley, and his nephew paid many visits to the farm. Both the farmhouse and the barn are listed on the National Register of Historic Places.

Cross Park Ave, pass the library, and follow Virginia Ave to Broad St and turn left. Near this corner was the **Hangman's Tree**, a towering oak that once draped across Leesburg Pike, now known as Broad St. According to local legend, Confederate Col John Mosby ordered his men to hang Union soldiers from this tree during the Civil War, although no evidence has ever been produced to substantiate such a claim. The tree had to be removed in 1968.

Continue along Broad St to the 300 block. In 1899, Ms Mattie A Gundry opened the **Virginia Training School** for mentally retarded children in the former Duryee house at 309 W Broad St. The school was the only one of its kind in the South and it became the second largest in the United States. Gundry retired in 1946 and the building was torn down in 1947.

Take the next right, walk one short block to Annandale, and turn left one block to Maple. **Big Chimneys**, a big log structure with two huge chimneys once stood at this intersection. Since the datestone on one of the chimneys read 1699, the date commonly associated with the founding of the town, it was believed to have been the first permanent structure in Falls Church. the building was torn down in 1908.

Near here were two of the "rolling roads"—originally Indian foot trails—used by Colonial settlers. They derived their name from the fact that, in the 1740s, large cylindrical casks (hogsheads) of tobacco were literally *rolled* along the roads to market.

Turn right on Maple. The **Henderson House** at 307 S Maple Ave was built in 1914 by Edwin Bancroft Henderson and his wife Mary Ellen. In 1904, Dr Henderson became the first black American in the United States to be certified as a physical training instructor, and from 1926 to 1954, he served the schools in Washington in that capacity. Henderson and his wife formed the local chapter of the NAACP, and in 1955 Dr Henderson served as resident of the Virginia State NAACP. He also wrote *The Negro in Sports* in 1939, won numerous honors and awards, and was inducted into the Negro Sports Hall of Fame in 1972. Mary Ellen Henderson became principal of an elementary school in the area.

Return to Annandale Rd, turn right, and go to Washington St. The Falls Church (703/532-7600) for which the city is named stands on the northeast corner. The first church on this site, part of the official Church of England, was built in 1733 and was officially known as the New Church in Truro Parish. In 1745, the wooden structure became the Upper Church, and sometime around 1757, The Falls Church. A two-story hip-roofed Georgian-style brick church was designed and built next door to the original church by James Wren between 1767 and 1769. During the Civil War, the church was used as a recruiting station, as a hospital, and later as a stable. The chancel was enlarged in 1959 and a major addition was completed in 1992. The church of the 1760s is still in use. The church is open from 9 am to 4 pm on weekdays and from 9 am to 1 pm on weekends.

In 1880, the city's first Town Hall was built across the street in the 100 block of S Washington St. A simple frame building, it had a bell that signalled both council meetings and fire alarms. Later, the building was used as a police station until it was torn down in 1953.

Continue North along Washington St. The State Theater at 220 N Washington St opened in 1935 and was the first movie theater in Virginia to open for Sunday performances. The theater operated continuously until 1989.

Washington House at 222 N Washington St was built in 1879 to serve as the First Congregational Church. A wooden Gothic-style building with a steepled bell tower, the building later served as a library, the town hall, a school, a polling place, a police station, a drug store, and a recreation center. In 1961, it was purchased by the Woman's Club of Falls Church.

Continue along Washington St to Columbia St. **Crossman Methodist Church**, at the intersection of Washington St and Columbia St, was the *second* church established in Falls Church. The original wooden structure was built on land donated by Isaac Crossman about 1875 and it had a prominent steeple. That building was demolished in 1963 and replaced by the current building in 1957.

Turn right on Columbia St and right again at the next intersection

(Lawton St). When it was built in 1854, the hipped-roof, clapboard-over-frame **Lawton House** at 203 Lawton St was called Home Hill. As the fortunes of North and South shifted back and forth during the Civil War, the home was used by both sides during the conflict. In 1889, Gen Henry Ware Lawton bought the house, but Lawton was killed during the Spanish-American War. Since 1900, the house has been renovated several times and the grounds have been landscaped extensively.

Continue on Lawton to Broad St. The **Columbia Baptist Church** was built at the intersection of Lawton St and Broad St in 1857. During the Civil War, the pastor was shot as a Union spy. A two-story clapboard-over-timber building with a tall steeple, the church has been used as a Union hospital, as a center for community programs from 1865 to 1879, as the site of the first Town Council meetings in 1875, and by the Jefferson Institute from 1875 to 1882.

Continue East along Broad St to Fairfax St. A Presbyterian congregation was formed in Falls Church in 1848, but it met in private homes until 1856, the year in which Dr Simon J Groot built a hall at Broad St and Fairfax St. Groot Hall subsequently became a Presbyterian Sunday School building, a town hall, a community gathering place, a Union Army hospital, and a private school. The Presbyterian congregation bought the hall in 1866, tore it down in 1925, and built the present steepled Gothic-style **Falls Church Presbyterian Church** in 1884. It was the first stone building in Falls Church. At least half of the 1884 structure still stands today as a part of the remodeled church.

The oldest portion of the **Birch House** at 312 E Broad St was built around 1840. In 1852, Joseph Edward Birch, a farmer and blacksmith, bought the house and 12 acres of land for the grand sum of $483.75. In the 1870s, the Birch family made major changes to the house, where they lived until 1968. By the early 1970s, the house was empty and subject to vandalism, so the house and 2.5 acres of the property were purchased by Historic Falls Church, Inc. They, in turn, sold part of the land to a townhouse developer in 1976, and the developer has subsequently restored the house.

Continue walking east along Broad St to N Cherry St. Roads were vital to the agricultural economy of the area in the late 18th and early 19th centuries. The Alexandria-Leesburg Turnpike was chartered in 1813, but not completed until after 1838, when it was used to carry much of the freight between the port and the inland markets. It continued to perform that role until the coming of the railroads in the 1850s. The **Falls Church Tollhouse and Tollgate** stood at the intersection of Broad St and Cherry

St, collecting tolls until 1872, when Fairfax County purchased the turnpike for $300. The tollhouse land was sold in 1879.

In 1882, this same intersection became the home of **Jefferson Institute**, the first public school in Falls Church. The Institute erected a two-story brick building featuring a prominent belfry and containing six classrooms. Prior to that time, the Institute had held classes in the Columbia Baptist Church. In the early years, three teachers administered to as many as 193 students in seven grades in this school, which remained active until 1956. After that, the city used the building for offices and recreational activities until it was demolished in 1958.

Continue walking east along Broad St. Its precise location is not known today, but in the early 1800s **Wren's Tavern** faced south onto the original Alexandria-Leesburg road, located about halfway between today's Broad St and Hillwood Ave. A well-known wayside stop, the tavern was named for its owner, James Wren, who also was the architect of the Falls Church. The tavern was visited by Thomas Jefferson as he rode to his presidential inauguration in 1801, and President James Madison is said to have stopped here as he fled Washington during the War of 1812. Mordecai Booth said that he stayed here while transporting gunpowder from the US Navy Magazine to Dulany's farm about a mile from The Falls church.

Dulin United Methodist Church at 513 E Broad St was one of two Methodist churches that were established in Falls Church after the Civil War. Dulin Chapel, built in 1869 on land donated by William Dulin, belonged to the Southern Methodist Church. the original Gothic Revival-style chapel now forms the rear and right-hand portions of the sanctuary and vestibule. Stained glass windows, a tower, and the present entrance were added in 1892. A Sunday School addition was built in 1926, and the entire exterior of the church has been stuccoed.

Tollwood, at 708 E Broad St, was built on a large farm in 1870, and at one time the brick residence was accompanied by a windmill and a large red barn. Yale Rice, a descendent of Elihu Yale, bought the farm in 1890. From 1938 to 1943, the farm was owned by Dr and Mrs Milton Eisenhower, and for a brief time during the early days of World War II, his brother, Gen Dwight D Eisenhower, stayed there. In 1943, Dr Howard Berger bought the house and named it Tollwood.

Walk an additional block to Roosevelt St. Here, on the southeast corner, stood **Taylor's Tavern and Battery**, an 1860s two-story frame building with verandas that faced onto Leesburg Pike. The tavern flourished during the mid-19th century. During the Civil War, Union troops occupied the tavern and surrounding high ground, and in October 1861 constructed a cannon battery that formed part of a protective ring around the nation's capital.

Turn left off Broad St onto Roosevelt St. Circuit-riding ministers introduced Methodism to this area in the late 1700s, and the Fairfax Circuit was established in 1776. Itinerant preachers held meetings in private homes until 1779, after which a series of three structures were erected on the site of the present **Oakwood Cemetery and Fairfax Chapel.** Union soldiers tore down the chapel in 1862 to make room for camp structures. In 1885, the cemetery was deeded to a private corporation and is still in use.

Follow Roosevelt St North and turn left into Sycamore St. Follow Sycamore to 16th St and turn left again. Then turn into the first street on your right. In 1790, after much debate, Congress chose a spot along the Potomac River to be the site of the nation's new capital. During the two years that followed, Maj Andrew Ellicott used sandstone markers to establish the boundary of that 100-sq mi district. Each of Ellicott's markers was one foot square, and they were positioned along the boundary line at one-mile intervals. Two of those original sandstone markers are on the Falls Church boundary line, including the **SW 9 Stone** found here on your right. In 1916, the Daughters of the American Revolution erected protective fences around the stones, and they were rededicated in 1989. The Afro-American Bicentennial Corporation chose this site as a National Historic Landmark to commemorate the life and contributions of Benjamin Bannecker, a free black farmer, mathematician, inventor, astronomer, writer, surveyor, scientist, and humanitarian who was a member of the original surveying team.

Return to 16th St and turn right (west). The road will gradually bend to your right and merge into Columbia St. Follow Columbia to Little Falls St and turn left. Two blocks more and you will be back at City Hall where you began.

Lodging

Smaller than many of the nearby communities, Falls Church may lack some of the variety of the larger towns, but it lacks none of their ambiance. **Comfort Inn/Washington Gateway** ($$, 703/534-9100), 6100 Arlington Rd, is new and comfortable. It is three stories high and contains 111 rooms. By contrast, **Doubletree Hotel at Tyson's Corner** ($$-$$$, 703/893-1340), 7801 Leesburg Pk, is 10 stories tall and has 405 rooms, a heated indoor pool, a restaurant and lounge, and a gift shop, while **Falls Church Motel** ($$-$$$, 703/533-8600 or 800 /831-1883), 7155 Lee Hwy, sits on a secluded, wooded lot, and offers a large swimming pool, and restaurants.

Food & drink

Conveying the atmosphere of Colonial Williamsburg, the **Sir Walter Raleigh Inn** (703/560-6768), 9120 Gatehouse Rd, is open from 11:30 am to 2 pm and from 5 to 9 pm Monday through Thursday, to 10 pm on Friday and Saturday, and from 4 to 8:30 pm on Sunday.

Haandi (703/533-3501), 1222 W Broad St in Falls Plaza, specializes in Indian cuisine amid an atmosphere of calming soft pastels and crystal chandeliers. It is open from 11:30 am to 2:30 pm and from 5 to 10 pm Sunday through Thursday and to 10:30 pm on Friday and Saturday.

Events

Every Saturday throughout the summer, the Falls Church Farmers' Market is held in front of the City Hall between 8 am and noon.

Index